De expugnatione Lyxbonensi
The Conquest of Lisbon

RECORDS OF WESTERN CIVILIZATION

Corpus Christi College, Cambridge, MS. No. 470, fol. 125r—the first page
of the De expugnatione Lyxbonensi.

De expugnatione Lyxbonensi

THE CONQUEST OF LISBON

EDITED FROM THE UNIQUE MANUSCRIPT IN
CORPUS CHRISTI COLLEGE, CAMBRIDGE,
WITH A TRANSLATION INTO ENGLISH BY

Charles Wendell David

PROFESSOR OF EUROPEAN HISTORY
IN BRYN MAWR COLLEGE

WITH A FOREWORD AND BIBLIOGRAPHY BY
JONATHAN PHILLIPS
ROYAL HOLLOWAY, UNIVERSITY OF LONDON

Non est vero crudelitas, pro Deo pietas
—ST. JEROME, QUOTED BY PETER,
BISHOP OF OPORTO

COLUMBIA UNIVERSITY PRESS

NEW YORK

Columbia University Press
Publishers Since 1893
New York   Chichester, West Sussex

Copyright © 1936, 2001 Columbia University Press

Library of Congress Cataloging-in-Publication Data

De expugnatione Lyxbonensi. English & Latin.
    De expugnatione Lyxbonensi = The conquest of Lisbon / edited from the
unique manuscript in Corpus Christi College, Cambridge, with a translation
into English, by Charles Wendell David ; with a foreword and bibliography
by Jonathan Philipps.
        p. cm. — (Records of Western civilization)
    English and Latin.
    Attributed to Osbernus and Raol.
    Originally published: New York : Columbia University Press, 1936, in series:
Records of civilization—sources and studies ; no. 24. With new foreword and
bibliography.
    Includes bibliographical references and index.
    ISBN 0–231–12122–9 (alk. paper)—ISBN 0–231–12123–7 (pbk. : alk. paper)
    1. Lisbon (Portugal)—History—Siege, 1147—Sources.   2. Crusades—
Second, 1147–1139—Sources.   I. Title: Conquest of Lisbon.   II. David,
Charles Wendell, 1885–   III. Phillips, Jonathan (Jonathan P.)   IV. Osbernus,
12th cent.   V. Raol, 12th cent.   VI. Corpus Christi College (University of
Cambridge). Library. Manuscript. 470, fol. 125–146.   VII. Title.   VIII. Series.

D162.E96 2000
946.9'42502—dc21

00–060327

Casebound editions of Columbia University Press books
are printed on permanent and durable acid-free paper.
Printed in the United States of America
c 10 9 8 7 6 5 4 3 2 1
p 10 9 8 7 6 5 4 3 2 1

TO

H. L. G.

THIS ATTEMPT TO GIVE CURRENCY
TO A REMARKABLE RECORD OF LIFE
IN THE TWELFTH CENTURY
IS DEDICATED

Contents

MAPS AND ILLUSTRATIONS

Foreword

De expugnatione Lyxbonensi—The Conquest of Lisbon

JONATHAN PHILLIPS

ROYAL HOLLOWAY, UNIVERSITY OF LONDON[1]

IT IS sixty-four years since Charles Wendell David first published his introduction and text of *De expugnatione Lyxbonensi*.[2] This remarkable work—an eye-witness account of the capture of Lisbon (October 1147) by the combined forces of King Afonso Henriques of Portugal (1128–85) and a fleet of crusaders from the Anglo-Norman realm, Flanders and the Rhineland—is one of the richest and most exciting sources to survive from this period. It provides a vivid description of a key event in the history of the Iberian peninsula and outlines one of the few successes of the Second Crusade (1145–49). But *De expugnatione* is far more than a narrative: it contains a wealth of information on ideas of crusading and holy war, military organization and siege techniques, and Muslim views of Christianity. It also reveals the tensions in trying to balance the spiritual motives of a crusader army against its needs and desires for secular rewards.

David wrote a lengthy and comprehensive introduction to his work that covered the following points: the Anglo-Norman aristocracy in the early history of the crusades, early crusading enterprises of the maritime populations of England and the Low Countries, and a discussion of the manuscript and the author of the text. Except for the section concerning the identity of the author, the majority of this work remains as scholarly and accurate as when it was first published; and therefore it has been reprinted here, following this foreword. The concerns of this present writer are: first, to locate the conquest of Lisbon within the history of the crusades; second, to place it in the context of the Second Crusade; third, to provide material that was unavailable to David—principally in

establishing the identity of the author; and last, to examine why *De expugnatione* was written and to consider how the author constructed his work.

Pope Urban II launched the First Crusade with a sermon at the Council of Clermont, in November 1095. In his speech he appealed for a holy war to liberate the oppressed Christians of the East and to regain Christ's patrimony. Contemporary churchmen had developed a doctrine, based largely upon the writings of Saint Augustine, that, in certain circumstances, violence and the use of force were justified. Such situations included acts of self-defence and the recovery of that which had been wrongfully taken—both scenarios fitted the call made by Urban. A holy war also required legitimate authority, provided here by the pope in his capacity as God's representative on earth. Within the framework of holy war, the crusaders had to procede with right intention, that is, with pure motives; to use reasonable, but not excessive, force; and to engage in war when it was "the only practicable means of achieving the justifiable purpose for which it was fought."[3] In return for performing this act—which the Church regarded as a most arduous form of penance—the crusaders would be rewarded with the remission of all the sins they had confessed. The violent lifestyle of the medieval knight was regarded as a certain path to the fires of hell, but the crusade offered a way to avoid this fate.[4] A contemporary author, Guibert of Nogent, wrote of "a new way to attain salvation," because the crusade enabled knights to perform acts of spiritual merit while continuing to fight.[5] The response to Urban's speech at Clermont and his subsequent preaching tour through France was enormous. His appeal had been directed at the knights of France, but people from all areas of Christian Europe and all levels of society flocked to take the cross.[6] Alongside the wish for salvation, some also saw the expedition as an opportunity to secure land and money, although, in fact, relatively few of the First Crusaders settled in the Levant and there is practically no evidence that any returned home

wealthy. A series of armies set out for the Levant in 1096, and after a journey of extraordinary hardships, they captured Jerusalem in July 1099 to establish a Catholic presence in the Holy Land that lasted until 1291.

During the fifty years prior to the First Crusade, the papacy did much to encourage the spiritual cleansing of the Church and society at large. Christian Europe was a society of intense religiosity, which manifested itself in a variety of ways—for example, through the increasing popularity of pilgrimage and the rise in donations to, and establishment of, monastic houses.[7] Alongside this climate of moral reform was an escalation in the ongoing conflict with the Islamic world. Between 1060 and 1091 the Normans drove the Muslims from Sicily, and in the decades prior to the First Crusade, the Christians of the Iberian peninsula fought the forces of Islam with growing vigour.[8] The Muslims had conquered Iberia in the eighth century, and by the turn of the millennium they continued to hold the majority of the peninsula, with Christian territories forming a strip of landholdings across the north. In the course of the eleventh century these nascent kingdoms grew in strength and started to exert pressure on Muslim lands to the south. In 1085 King Alfonso VI of Leon-Castile (1065–1109) captured the important city of Toledo, marking a significant advance for the Christians.[9]

When Pope Urban II called the First Crusade in 1095, he created a dilemma for the knights of the *Reconquista*, because the emotive pull of the Holy Land and the unprecedented spiritual rewards offered for the crusade to the East meant that many who fought against Islam in Spain wanted to take the cross for the Levant. Urban tried (not entirely successfully) to encourage these knights to remain in the peninsula and wrote, "It is no virtue to rescue Christians from Muslims in one place, only to expose them to the tyranny and oppression of the Muslims in another." As a war of Christian liberation, therefore, the *Reconquista* in Spain had a fundamental link with the Jerusalem crusade from the start of the movement.[10] In the decades after the First Crusade, the papacy used the crusade to further Christian progress in Iberia. We know of papal appeals authorizing crusades in this region in 1114, 1116, 1117–18, and 1123. Other ties between the Holy Land and Spain also

emerged: Marcus Bull has shown how a number of knights from southern France fought both in the *Reconquista* and in the Levant, and he observed that there were many ties between the crusading nobility of France and the leading families of the peninsula.[11] Similar connections continued through to the time of the Second Crusade, most pertinently here in the case of King Afonso Henriques of Portugal, the nephew of Duke Odo I of Burgundy who had taken part in the 1101 crusade. Afonso himself forged links with a crusading family when, in 1146, he married Mathilda the daughter of Amadeus III of Savoy, who himself took the cross for the Levant in 1147–48.[12]

The shared conflict with Islam also saw the development of a series of connections between the religious institutions of Iberia and the Latin East. For example, in 1120, in the aftermath of the heavy Frankish defeat at the Battle of the Field of Blood (1119) in northern Syria, Patriarch Warmund of Jerusalem sent an appeal for help to Archbishop Diego of Compostela and urged him to send men, money, and supplies to the Holy Land as soon as possible. Thus, two of the major centers of pilgrimage in the twelfth-century worked together to support the crusade. The same letter also acknowledged a recent gift to the Church of the Holy Sepulchre from the clergy of Compostela.[13] Other ties existed between the two theaters of war. The most high-profile of these concerned the Military Orders—the Templars and the Hospitallers—warrior-monks sworn to help pilgrims and to protect their fellow Christians from the infidel. The Templars were founded in Jerusalem in 1120, and in 1128 they received papal approval as a religious order and were granted a formal rule, or way of life. Their first master, Hugh of Payns, traveled to western Europe (1127–29) to seek recruits and donations for his bretheren. The response to his tour was impressive, and the Templars rapidly became an important institution in the struggle against Islam. Afonso Henriques of Portugal was one individual who responded to Hugh's efforts, and, in a document dated 1128, he described himself as a brother (*confrater*) of the Order, which shows his interest in the warrior-monks from their earliest appearance in the West.[14] The Hospital of Saint John had been founded in Jerusalem as a medical institution to care for sick pilgrims

prior to the First Crusade. In the aftermath of the Frankish conquest, however, the Hospital grew substantially as grateful and pious travelers from all over western Europe granted it land and rights from their homelands. By the 1130s the Hospitallers became militarized and joined the Templars in the defence of the Latin East.[15]

Connections between the Military Orders and the *Reconquista* would emerge with startling clarity upon the death of King Alfonso I of Aragon (1104–34), an enthusiastic proponent of the *Reconquista*. He died childless, and his will provided that his entire kingdom should be divided between the Templars, the Hospitallers, and the Canons of the Church of the Holy Sepulchre. To ignore any local claimants and to entrust his lands to institutions based in Jerusalem was a remarkable move. Alfonso's nobles eventually frustrated his wishes, but his aim shows the powerful appeal of the warrior-monks and demostrates how the Christians of Spain and the Latin East shared in the struggle against Islam.[16] A document from 1125 drew an even closer connection between the two areas. Archbishop Diego of Compostela summoned a crusade in Spain with this appeal:

> Just as the knights of Christ and the faithful sons of the Holy Church opened the way to Jerusalem with much labour and spilling of blood, so we should become knights of Christ and, after defeating his wicked enemies the Muslims, open the way to the same Sepulchre of the Lord through Spain which is closer and less laborious.[17]

There is no evidence that the Lisbon crusaders of 1147 were aware of this text, but it shows how fighting in the peninsula could be a part of the journey to the earthly Jerusalem, and perhaps, in an allegorical sense, to the heavenly one as well.

THE CONQUEST OF LISBON IN THE CONTEXT OF THE SECOND CRUSADE

In December 1144 the Muslims of northern Syria captured the Frankish city of Edessa. Messengers from Antioch and Jerusalem appealed to the pope and the kings of France and Germany, and

in December 1145 Pope Eugenius III issued the bull *Quantum praedecessores* to elicit support for a new crusade to defend the Latin
East.[18] King Louis VII of France (1137–80)—a man of great personal piety—was keen to respond and, with the endorsement of
Eugenius's bull and the preaching of Abbot Bernard of Clairvaux
(the greatest churchman of the age), the enterprise began to gather
momentum. The king and many of his nobles took the cross at an
assembly at Vézelay, in central France, on Easter Sunday 1146.[19]
Thousands of people (from all levels of society) joined the crusade
in France, and in the autumn of that year Bernard began a preaching tour of the Low Countries and the Rhineland.[20] As the abbot
recruited men from imperial territories in northern Europe, in October 1146 Pope Eugenius issued the bull *Divina dispensatione I* to
encourage the people of Italy (also part of the German Empire at
this time) to join the crusade.[21] By Christmas 1146, after the internal
security of his lands was assured, King Conrad III of Germany took
the cross to lead a large force to the East.[22] No kings of such standing had been on crusade before, yet in 1146 the two leading secular
rulers of the West had commited themselves to the cause of the
Holy Land.

    Louis and Conrad set out for the Levant in the summer of
1147. They marched across Europe and through the Byzantine
Empire to Constantinople. The Greek emperor Manuel Comnenus
feared the crusaders' ambitions—first, with regard to the safety of
his own city and, second, their potential to interfere with his hard-
won overlordship of the Frankish principality of Antioch in northern Syria. Poor relations with the Greeks caused the crusaders to
struggle for supplies as they crossed Asia Minor and may have led
the Byzantines to look sympathetically on Seljuk Turkish attempts
to confront the Christian armies. Both the French and German
armies were defeated by the Turks in separate battles. In the summer of 1148 the survivors gathered in the Latin East where, in con-
junction with troops from the kingdom of Jerusalem, they decided
to attack the key Muslim city of Damascus, but after a siege lasting
only five days, the Christian armies were forced to withdraw.[23] The
shock of this defeat was profound. The might of Latin Christendom had been humbled and an explanation had to be sought. The

crusaders blamed their failure on the greed and treachery of the
Latin settlers, the settlers pointed at the crusaders' own ambitions,
while the base conduct of the Greeks, the Templars, and the prince
of Antioch was also put forward to explain the reverse. Practical
explanations centred upon poor leadership and the presence of too
many noncombatants. Finally, the motives and intentions of the
crusaders were criticized, with some accusing them of seeking honors and money.[24] Bernard of Clairvaux faced particular hostility because his preaching had aroused such high hopes. His letter to the
English, written in 1146, stated, "God is good, and were he intent
on your punishment he would not have asked of you this present
service." How could Bernard explain what had happened? The abbot's response identified the wrong intention of the crusaders and
argued that their sins had brought down God's judgement upon
them.[25] For whatever reason, it was the failure of the main armies
at Damascus, coupled with the unsuccessful diversion of a group of
German nobles to fight against the pagans of northern Europe, that
caused the Second Crusade to be branded a disaster.[26] Yet there
were also some successes, most notably in the Iberian peninsula.

As noted earlier, there was a tradition of crusading in Spain,
and because of this it was perhaps logical that the scope of the
Second Crusade extended to embrace military campaigns in Iberia.
In late summer of 1147 King Alfonso VII of Leon-Castile (1126–57)
and a fleet from Genoa captured Almeria in southern Spain
(although the Muslims were to regain the city ten years later).[27]
Eugenius III indicated papal enthusiasm for the venture by his comment that Alfonso's efforts against the Saracens had God's support.[28] In the following year, the Genoese, Count Raymond Ber-
engar of Barcelona, knights from southern France, and some
veterans from the Lisbon campaign en route home from the Holy
Land captured (and retained) Tortosa on the north-eastern coast of
Spain to extend the Christian hold on the region.[29] Finally, as
Simon Barton has recently demonstrated, Alfonso VII's unsuccesful
campaign at Jaen in 1148 was also part of the Second Crusade and,
again, received papal endorsement.[30] If, as some twelfth-century
writers did, one takes an overview of the Second Crusade, it is
possible to see it as a three-pronged offensive against the enemies

of Christianity that encompassed the Holy Land, the Baltic, and the Iberian peninsula.[31] Helmold of Bosau, who wrote in northern Germany in the late 1160s, encapsulated this view: "The initiators of the expedition, however, deemed it advisable to design one part of the army for eastern regions, another for Spain, and a third against the Slavs."[32]

What part did the Lisbon campaign play in the Second Crusade? It has long been held that the involvement of the northern European fleet at the siege was a chance event. It is said that the crusaders were sailing to the Holy Land when they were hailed en route and persuaded to join Afonso of Portugal in his attack on the city.[33] While it is true that no papal bull mentioning Afonso's campaign survives, there is a considerable body of evidence to suggest that there was a strong element of forward planning and coordination between the northern Europeans and the king.[34] The key to this lies in a previously undated letter from Saint Bernard to Afonso Henriques. Harold Livermore has connected this to the events of 1146–47, and he has convincingly shown it to be a response to an appeal for the endorsement of a crusade:[35]

> I have received the letter of Your Highness with great pleasure in Him who sent deliverance to Jacob. What I have done in the matter will be evident from the outcome, as you will see for yourself. You will see with what promptitude I have complied with your request and the exigencies of the matter. Pedro, the brother of Your Highness, and a prince worthy of all honour, has acquainted me with your wishes. After having travelled through all Gaul in arms, he is campaigning in Lorraine, and will soon be fighting in the hosts of the Lord. My son Roland will bring you documents which set forth the liberality of the Holy See.[36]

Bernard's message suggests that the king (through an envoy of royal status) had asked for his approval to attack the Muslims and noted that the abbot had replied both rapidly and affirmatively to this request through the papal documents borne by his representative. This letter shows that the authorities were aware of Afonso's plans and offered him support. Once the crusade to the Holy Land was called, Afonso may well have anticipated that a contingent of north

Europeans would sail around the Iberian peninsula to the East. As David noted in his introduction, there was a tradition of naval traffic between the regions, and in earlier decades a series of maritime expeditions had passed from the North Sea to take part in crusading activity in the Levant. An Anglo-Norman contingent had joined Afonso in an attack on Lisbon in 1140 or 1142 (the evidence for the exact date of this event is confused), and from his actions in 1146–47 it is apparent that the king believed he needed outside assistance to capture the city were he to try again.[37]

There is other material to support the idea of coordination between Afonso and the crusaders. First, on Bernard's preaching tour of the Low Countries and the Rhineland he covered areas that would contribute substantially to the fleet that sailed to the Levant. It can be proven that during his visit to Flanders he met Christian of Gistel, the leader of the Flemish contingent at Lisbon, and this may have provided an opportunity for the abbot to raise the prospect of campaigning in Portugal.[38] Afonso himself seems to have made preparations to anticipate the crusaders' arrival. In mid-March 1147, before the northern European fleet set out, he besieged the town of Santarem—an essential precursor to the capture of Lisbon, as the king himself noted in a contemporary privilege granted to the Templars.[39] Afonso was certainly aware of the expedition's departure from Dartmouth in southern England in May 1147 because he dispatched Bishop Peter of Oporto to meet the crusaders when they reached northern Spain. *De expugnatione* noted that "the bishop knew in advance" of the crusaders' coming.[40] Another contemporary source described the bishop as "waiting for our arrival."[41] Peter greeted the crusaders and opened detailed discussions on Afonso's behalf to establish the precise terms on which the northern Europeans would fight at Lisbon and to convince the crusaders that their endeavours were spiritually meritorious as well as financially rewarding.[42] While religious motivation was of central importance to the crusaders' efforts, it should not be forgotten that their expectations of earthly rewards had to be satisfied as well. This desire revealed itself on numerous occasions, and *De expugnatione* is a rich source to study the conflicting needs of secular and spiritual motivations amongst crusaders.[43] Once a deal with Afonso was finalized,

the siege began and after seventeen weeks reached a successful conclusion on October 24, 1147. Most of the crusaders wintered at Lisbon before they carried on to the Latin East to complete their vows and join up with the main armies.[44] It should be noted that had the northern Europeans not fought at Lisbon but sailed directly to the Levant, they would have arrived in the Holy Land nine months before the forces marching overland. This would have entailed a lengthy and expensive period of waiting, but if they intended to fight en route, then an early departure date was logical.

In short, it seems likely that Afonso seized the opportunity to use the Second Crusade to enlarge his own lands and to further the Christian cause in his area. Portugal itself was a fledgling political entity (Afonso had first styled himself *rex* as recently as 1139) that had emerged from the dynastic instabilities of the northern Spanish kingdoms, and the capture of such an important city as Lisbon would add considerable gloss to its new status.[45] As we have seen, Afonso himself had connections with the Templars, and he was also a strong supporter of the Cistercians and other monastic orders. In other words, his personal piety and his political needs coalesced in the prospect of conquering the city and returning it to Christianity. This in turn matched the aspirations of the Church leaders of the Second Crusade who, as noted above, intended to expand Christendom on a number of fronts. Saint Bernard endorsed Afonso's idea, and on his tour of northern Europe in the autumn of 1146, the abbot raised the possibility of fighting at Lisbon en route to the Holy Land. Once the crusaders had concluded an agreement with the king, their combined forces secured the Conquest of Lisbon—one of the few permanent successes of the Second Crusade.

THE AUTHOR

The identity of the author of the letter known to us as *De expugnatione Lyxbonensi* has been the subject of considerable scholarly controversy over the decades.[46] The text begins "To Osbert of Bawdsey, R., greeting."[47] Osbert of Bawdsey was a cleric connected to the Glanvills, prominent landowners in East Anglia whose family

member, Hervey, led the Anglo-Norman contingent on the crusade. In 1990, Livermore convincingly identified the author as Raol, an Anglo-French priest.[48] Raol was a close associate of Hervey de Glanvill and a figure of some considerable standing in his own right. He carried a piece of the True Cross, he gave the address to the crusaders before the final assault on the city, and he had substantial financial resources. Raol constructed a chapel and a cemetery for the English dead and gave both of these, along with a gift of 200 silver marks, to the Augustinian monastery of Santa Cruz at Coimbra prior to his departure for the Holy Land. He was also involved in negotiations concerning the terms of agreement with Afonso when the crusaders reached northern Spain.

The text itself is a narrative of the campaign from the departure of the fleet from Dartmouth (May 1147) to the capture of Lisbon (October 1147). Raol was a participant in the events that he described, and much of his writing has a sense of real involvement, which, combined with the letter format of the text, indicates that some form of communication was sent back from Lisbon to Osbert of Bawdsey in East Anglia in late autumn of 1147, or the early spring of 1148, before the crusaders continued on to the Holy Land. The factual accuracy of the piece can be corroborated by the other key source for these events, the so-called Lisbon letter. Susan Edgington has recently edited this text (which is also in the form of a contemporary letter, although rather more succinct than *De expugnatione*), which was dispatched from Portugal to the Rhineland and the Low Countries to inform people of the progress of the crusade.[49]

David's edition of *De expugnatione* is based upon the sole surviving exemplar of the work, and its handwriting has been dated to the 1160s or 1170s. As the reader will realize, however, closer analysis shows that it is far more than a simple report. As we saw earlier, a crusade required just cause, legitimate authority, and right intention. All of these factors were considered in *De expugnatione*, with special emphasis on right intention. Raol's work is a sophisticated exposition on the correct moral framework for a crusade to take place. The basic narrative is interspersed with a series of speeches made by key players in the story, namely: the bishop of

Oporto, King Afonso Henriques of Portugal, Hervey de Glanvill, a Muslim elder, and a crusader preacher (who was probably Raol himself). It was a common rhetorical device in medieval literature to place speeches in the mouths of characters in order for them to convey the author's message. It appears likely that Raol followed this practice and, as will become plain, altered and augmented the speeches noted above to reflect his own agenda.[50] There are occasions when certain phrases recur in speeches made by different people, such as when both Hervey de Glanvill and a Muslim elder describe the fear of exchanging "certainties for uncertainties."[51] Similarly, the idea of substituting "vices for virtues" appears in three separate places.[52] Such "coincidences" are one sign that the speeches were manipulated, but it must be indicated that they were not entirely at odds with their settings. For example, when Hervey de Glanvill tries to convince a group of Anglo-Normans not to leave the expedition, his message begins with a sophisticated theological passage concerning right intention yet concludes with a more straightforward and practical appeal for the men to stay.[53] Perhaps Hervey felt such a mix of arguments appropriate for his audience of truculent adventurers, but in the circumstances of a turbulent public meeting, one imagines the finer points of his address may have been missed. It is likely, therefore, that Raol presents the reader with a conflation of his own ideas and Hervey's speech. Intriguingly, a marginal note in the same hand as the rest of the text comments that the words of Hervey's speech were not exactly those he uttered.[54] Because Osbert of Bawdsey was the recipient of *De expugnatione*, it is likely that Hervey may have seen or heard the work, and Raol covered his manipulation of the text by acknowledging this to his reader.

To demonstrate the idea of right intention, a number of themes become plain. The need to avoid the sins of greed and envy runs through the entire work. Such ideas appear in all the main speeches as well as in the narrative.[55] Similarly, the notion of unity—a vital element in the crusaders' success—is consistently expressed. The need for "this unanimous association,"[56] in both a practical and a moral sense, was emphasized at the start of the campaign, when the entire force swore to abide by a series of strict regulations imposed to ensure good order and right intention.[57]

References to unity pervade the text, arising whenever tensions between the various contingents threatened the crusaders' military strength and moral force.[58] Failing this, divisiveness could open the way for the sins of greed, pride, and envy to enter the army and detract from the right intention needed to preserve God's favor, which would ensure and ultimately explain their victory. In demonstrating these points, Raol also revealed his strong allegiance to the Anglo-Normans and highlighted their powerful sense of group identity as distinct from the Flemings and the Rhinelanders. His frequent antipathy toward the latter groups was based on their alleged greed and duplicity (in other words, wrong intention), which might have provoked a split in the crusaders' unity. Raol's hostility might also have reflected regional rivalries from northern Europe. Conflicts of this sort were commonplace amongst crusading forces; similar tensions had often broken out during the First Crusade, and the sworn association of the Lisbon crusaders was clearly designed to try to prevent such episodes repeating themselves.[59]

Raol was able to sustain his theme of right intention by deploying a number of sources from biblical and patristic texts. There is much to suggest that he was a well-educated individual, although little credit for this has been given to him in the past.[60] David noted that the author had a working knowledge of the Bible and Solinus (a classical writer whose observations on the flora and fauna of Portugal were used in the text) but ascribed little other learning to him.[61] In contrast, Ernst-Dieter Hehl's work has demonstrated the considerable range of canon law deployed in the bishop of Oporto's speech.[62] To justify the crusaders fighting at Lisbon, Bishop Peter employed Saint Jerome's widely used lines concerning the need to perform good works on the path to Heaven. He argued that because the campaign was part of a penitential act (a crusade) and strove to reclaim Christian lands, the expedition to Lisbon could be seen as a good work on the way to a heavenly and an earthly Jerusalem.[63] Livermore suggests that some in England may have viewed the planned stop in Lisbon as a diversion from the true purpose of the crusade, but through this speech, and by the ultimate success of the campaign, such a notion was rejected.[64]

The ideas of Saint Augustine are found widely in *De expugnatione* and were used to underpin the ideas of legitimate au-

thority, just cause, and right intention. Many of these principles
were codified in the canon law collections of Ivo of Chartres (1094)
and Gratian (*c.*1140) with which Raol was evidently familiar.[65] To
justify regaining Christian lands, the bishop of Oporto cited Gratian's *Causa* 23, which concerned the defence of one's patrimony
against barbarians, warding off enemies at home, and resisting
thieves and robbers (as the Muslims were characterized).[66] Numerous precedents for righteous violence from Ivo of Chartres and Gratian were also put forward in this speech.[67] Further examination of
De expugnatione reveals the continued use of these sources (and
others), suggesting that, at the very least, Raol shared the bishop
of Oporto's learning. In his closing comments Raol himself—again
following Gratian and fitting in with the canonical requirements of
a holy war—advised that the crusaders' behaviour should be mod-
erate, and he counseled that humility in victory and guarding
against glorifying in their success would ensure God's favour.[68] Earlier, in his speech before the final assault on the city, he repeated
the argument used by Bishop Peter that the Muslims were thieves
and robbers and could therefore be attacked legitimately.[69]

In the preaching of the Second Crusade, it is likely that
Pope Eugenius III's bull *Quantum Praedecessores* and the letters of
Saint Bernard of Clairvaux circulated widely in Europe. In light of
their prominence, it is not surprising that the ideas of these two
men influenced Raol. Hehl has noted how Saint Bernard's emphasis
on the opportunity for rebirth afforded by the Second Crusade was
echoed in the bishop of Oporto's outline of the penitential aspect
of the expedition. This was demonstrated by the crusaders' sacrifices
in exchanging "all their honours and dignities for a blessed pilgrimage in order to obtain from God an eternal reward."[70] Raol himself
repeated the idea of rebirth in his closing speech when he described
"the beginning of your [the crusaders'] conversion" and observed
how through the crusade the participants "had been cleansed by the
baptism of new repentance."[71] A further parallel between Bernard's
writings and the text of *De expugnatione* can be seen in the abbot's
description of the crusade as "a cause in which to conquer is glorious
and for which to die is gain," set against Raol's "to live is glory and
to die is gain."[72] A strong resonance of Eugenius III's *Quantum*

praedecessores can also be discerned in Hervey de Glanvill's speech. The bull emphasized the deeds of the previous generation of crusaders, and Hervey mirrored the phrase, "For the glorious deeds of the ancients kept in memory by posterity are the marks of affection and honour. If you show yourself worthy emulators of the ancients, honour and glory will be yours, but if unworthy, then disgraceful reproaches."[73]

A knowledge of First Crusade writers was also part of Raol's repertoire. For example, Guibert of Nogent seems to have influenced the words used by the bishop of Oporto in praise for the crusaders' sacrifices in taking the cross and leaving their wives, children, and friends to follow Christ.[74]

Alongside a recognition of Raol's learning and determination to show the crusaders' right intention, it is possible to glean much else of value from *De expugatione*. Raol's writing illuminates contemporary Muslim views of the Christian faith.[75] Kedar has commented on the accuracy of the Muslim elder's criticisms of Christianity, namely an attack on Christ's humanity and the veneration of the son of a poor woman.[76] This suggests that Raol was interested in preserving Muslim perceptions of Christianity, in part reflecting a contemporary trend to learn more about Islam (Abbot Peter the Venerable of Cluny had the Koran translated into Latin c.1140)[77] and in part to allow the author to refute their criticism of the faith.[78] *De expugnatione* is also a rich source for the military historian. The detailed descriptions of siege engines, tunnelling, supplies and logistics, and the processes of parley and surrender are all of interest. Recent studies by Randall Rogers, and especially Matthew Bennett, draw out these points very clearly, and the reader is directed to these works.[79]

In conclusion, *De expugnatione* is an eye-witness account of the capture of Lisbon with, embroidered on top of it, a work on right intention for crusaders probably composed at some point between the end of the siege and the date of the extant manuscript. Raol explained the crusaders' success through God's grace, which was won through their right intention and based upon unity, faith, and humility. His only comment to foreshadow the crusaders' victory noted the last of these ideas: "For God had foreordained es-

pecially in these times that vengeance should be wrought upon the enemies of the cross through the most insignificant of men."[80] The achievement of these "insignificant" men was noted by contemporaries, some of whom drew stark contrasts between the capture of Lisbon and the failure of the armies of King Louis and King Conrad at Damascus. Henry of Huntingdon wrote:

> In the same year [1148] the armies of the emperor of Germany[81] and the French king, which marched out with great pride under illustrious commanders, came to nothing because God despised them. . . . Meanwhile, a naval force that was made up of ordinary, rather than powerful, men, and was not supported by any great leader, except Almighty God, prospered a great deal better because they set out in humility. Truly, "God resists the proud but gives grace to the humble." For the armies of the French king and the emperor had been more splendid and larger than that which earlier had conquered Jerusalem, and yet were crushed by very much smaller forces and were destroyed like a spider's web. But no host had been able to withstand the poor men of whom I spoke above, and the large forces who attacked them were reduced to weakness.[82]

The idea that the crusaders' humility lay behind their success shows how such a notion was accepted as a valid explanation for their triumph and matched one of the key themes of *De expugnatione* itself. Aside from its immediate function as a narrative of the conquest of Lisbon, those later crusaders, or potential crusaders, who came to hear or read Raol's work would have had little doubt about how to achieve victory in their endeavours. However, in light of the unique nature of the manuscript of *De expugnatione*, it appears that the text was little circulated. We know that Hervey de Glanvill's brother Roger, Roger's son Ranulf, and Ranulf's nephew Hubert Walter all took part in the Third Crusade, so these individuals at least probably had some familiarity with Raol's work.[83] In any case, his advice, both practical and theoretical, outlined something that few crusade writers (other than those of the First Crusade) had an opportunity to do—to describe a success.

Notes

1. I would like to thank Ann Miller of Columbia University Press for offering me the opportunity to write about this wonderful text. My appreciation also to Dr. Tessa Webber for dating the manuscript, Dr. Thomas Asbridge for his helpful comments, and my heartfelt thanks to Juliette Constantinou for her support and advice.

2. Charles Wendell David, *De expugnatione Lyxbonensi* (New York: Columbia University Press, 1936) [henceforth *DeL*]. The surviving manuscript has no title, but Stubbs, who edited the work in the nineteenth century, gave it the name David adopted, and since then it has fallen into common use.

3. Jonathan Riley-Smith, *What Were the Crusades?*, second edition (London: Macmillan, 1992), 1–12.

4. Jonathan Riley-Smith, *The First Crusade and the Idea of Crusading* (London: Athlone, 1986), 13–30.

5. Guibert of Nogent, "Dei gesta per Francos," ed. Robert Huygens, *Corpus Christianorum Continuatio Medievalis*, vol. 127A (Turnhout: Brepols, 1996), 87. Translated as: *The Deeds of God Through the Franks*, trans. Robert Levine (Woodbridge: Boydell, 1997), 28.

6. Jonathan Riley-Smith, *The First Crusaders, 1095–1131* (Cambridge: Cambridge University Press, 1999).

7. Riley-Smith, *First Crusade and the Idea of Crusading*, 4–12; Marcus Bull, "The Roots of Lay Enthusiasm for the First Crusade," *History* 78 (1993): 365–70.

8. Donald Matthew, *The Norman Kingdom of Sicily* (Cambridge: Cambridge University Press, 1992), 19–32; Bernard Reilly, *The Contest of Christian and Muslim Spain, 1031–1157* (Oxford: Blackwell, 1992), 1–98; Hugh Kennedy, *Muslim Spain and Portugal: A Political History of al-Andalus* (London: Longman, 1996), 149–71.

9. Reilly, *Contest of Christian and Muslim Spain*, 79–86.

10. Jonathan Riley-Smith, *The Crusades: A Short History* (London: Athlone, 1987), 6–8.

11. Marcus Bull, *Knightly Piety and the Lay Response to the First Crusade: The Limousin and Gascony, c.970–c.1130* (Oxford: Clarendon Press, 1993), 70–114.

12. Odo of Deuil, *De profectione ludovici VII in orientem (The Journey of Louis VII to the Orient)*, ed. and trans. Virginia Berry (New York: Columbia University Press, 1948), 79; Harold Livermore, *A New History of Portugal*, second edition (Cambridge: Cambridge University Press, 1976), 54.

13. Jonathan Phillips, *Defenders of the Holy Land: Relations Between the Latin East and the West, 1119–1187* (Oxford: Clarendon Press, 1996), 14–17.

14. Malcolm Barber, *The New Knighthood: A History of the Order of the Temple* (Cambridge: Cambridge University Press, 1994), 1–15, 32–34.

15. Riley-Smith, *Crusades: Short History*, 57–61.

16. Barber, *New Knighthood*, 27–31.

17. Jonathan Riley-Smith, "The Venetian Crusade of 1122–24," in Gabriella Airaldi and Benjamin Kedar, eds. *I comuni italiani nel regno crociato di Gerusalemme: Atti del colloquio* (The Italian Communes in the Crusading Kingdom of Jerusalem) (Genoa: Universita di Genova, Instituto di Medievistica, 1986), 347.

18. "Der text der kreuzzugsbulle Eugens III," in Paul Rassow, ed., *Neues Archiv der Gesellschaft für ältere deustsche Geschichtskunde* 45 (1924): 302–5. For a translation, see: Louise and Jonathan Riley-Smith, eds., *The Crusades, Idea and Reality: 1095–1274* (London: Arnold, 1981), 57–9.

19. Phillips, *Defenders of the Holy Land*, 73–82.

20. Jonathan Phillips, "Saint Bernard of Clairvaux, the Low Countries and the Lisbon Letter of the Second Crusade," *Journal of Ecclesiastical History* 48 (1997): 485–97.

21. Rudolf Hiestand, *Papsturkunden für Kirchen im Heiligen Lande* (Göttingen: Vardenhoeck and Ruprecht, 1985), 193–95.

22. Jonathan Phillips, "Papacy, Empire and the Second Crusade," in Martin Hoch and Jonathan Phillips, eds., *The Second Crusade: Scope and Consequences* (Manchester: Manchester University Press, 2001).

23. Phillips, *Defenders of the Holy Land*, 83–99.

24. Ibid., 108–12.

25. Bernard of Clairvaux, "De consideratione ad Eugenium papam," in Jean Leclercq and Henri Rochais, eds., *Opera*, 8 vols. (Rome: Editiones Cisterciences, 1957–77), 3:410–13.

26. For details of the crusade against the pagans, see: Eric Christiansen, *The Northern Crusades*, second edition, (London: Penguin, 1997), 50–59 ("No medieval enterprise started with more splendid hopes," yet the crusade's end was "ignominious" and "brought to nothing."); Steven Runciman, *History of the Crusades*, 3 vols. (Cambridge: Cambridge University Press, 1951–54), 2: 288.

27. Stephen Epstein, *Genoa and the Genoese, 958–1528* (Chapel Hill: University of North Carolina Press, 1996), 49–52.

28. Eugenius III, "Epistolae et privilegia," in Jean Migne, ed., *Patrologia Latina*, 217 vols. (Paris: Garnier Fratres, 1844–64), 180:1203–4.

29. John Williams, "The Making of a Crusade: The Genoese Anti-Muslim Attacks in Spain, 1146–48," *Journal of Medieval History* 23 (1997): 29–53; Nikolas Jaspert, "*Capta est Dertosa, clavis Christianorum: Tortosa and the Crusades*," in Martin Hoch and Jonathan Phillips, eds., *The Second Crusade: Scope and Consequences* (Manchester: Manchester University Press, 2001).

30. Simon Barton, "A Forgotten Crusade: Alfonso VII of León-Castile and the Campaign for Jaén (1148)," in: *Historical Research* 73 (forthcoming, 2000).

31. The evidence for this idea is gathered in: Giles Constable, "The Second Crusade as Seen by Contemporaries," *Traditio* 9 (1953): 213–79.

32. By "the Slavs," the author meant the pagan tribes of northern Europe. Helmold of Bosau, *The Chronicle of the Slavs*, trans. Francis Tschan (New York: Columbia University Press, 1935), 172.

33. Joseph O'Callaghan, *A History of Medieval Spain* (Ithaca: Cornell University Press, 1975), 230; Christopher Tyerman, *England and the Crusades, 1095–1588* (Chicago: Chicago University Press, 1988), 33.

34. Phillips, "Saint Bernard of Clairvaux, the Low Countries and the Lisbon Letter of the Second Crusade," 485–97.

35. Harold Livermore, "The 'Conquest of Lisbon' and Its Author," *Portuguese Studies* 6 (1990): 116.

36. Bernard of Clairvaux, "Epistolae," in Jean Leclercq and Henri Rochais, eds., *Opera*, 8 vols. (Rome: Editiones Cistercienses, 1955–77), 8:228. Translated in: *The Letters of Saint Bernard of Clairvaux*, trans. Bruno Scott James, second edition, (Stroud: Alan Sutton, 1998), 469.

37. David, *DeL*, 12–26.

38. Thérèse de Hemptinne and Adriaan Verhulst, *De oorkonden der graven van Vlaanderen (Juli 1128–September 1191)* (Brussels: Académie royale de Belgique, 1988), 152.

39. Phillips, "Saint Bernard of Clairvaux, the Low Countries and the Lisbon Letter of the Second Crusade," 494; Barber, *New Knighthood*, 33.

40. David, *DeL*, 69 (see also 85, 99).

41. Susan Edgington, "The Lisbon Letter of the Second Crusade," *Historical Research* 69 (1996): 336–39. For a translation, see: Susan Edgington, "Albert of Aachen, Saint Bernard and the Second Crusade," in Martin Hoch and Jonathan Phillips, eds., *The Second Crusade: Scope and Consequences* (Manchester: Manchester University Press, 2001).

42. David, *DeL*, 111–13.

43. Ibid., 99–115, 119–23, 167–77.

44. Giles Constable, "A Note on the Route of the Anglo-Flemish Crusaders of 1147," *Speculum* 28 (1953) 525–26.

45. Livermore, *New History of Portugal*, 52–53.

46. David, *DeL*, 4046; Livermore, " 'Conquest of Lisbon,' " 1–3.

47. David, *DeL*, 53.

48. Livermore, " 'Conquest of Lisbon,' " passim.

49. See note 42.

50. Jonathan Phillips, "Ideas of Crusade and Holy War in *De expugnatione Lyxbonensi* (The Conquest of Lisbon)," in Robert Swanson, ed., *Holy Land, Holy Lands, and Christian History*. Studies in Church History. Vol. 36 (Woodbridge: Boydell, 2000). 123–41.

51. David, *DeL*, 109, 121.

52. Ibid., 77, 121, 169.

53. Ibid., 101–11.

54. Ibid., 104.

55. For the main speeches, see: Ibid., 75, 107, 121, 147. For the narrative, see: 167–77.

56. Ibid., 71.

57. Ibid., 57.

58. Ibid., 75, 79, 99, 105–11, 167, 171–77.

59. Likewise, in 1147, as the armies of King Louis and King Conrad marched across the Byzantine Empire, contact between the two groups sparked tension. Odo of Deuil (Louis's chaplain) wrote that the Germans "were unbearable" and often criticised their boorish behaviour and lack of discipline. Odo of Deuil, *De profectione ludovici VII in orientem* (The Journey of Louis VII to the Orient), 45.

60. Constable wrote that Raol "showed the attitudes of a simple crusader." Constable, "Second Crusade as Seen by Contemporaries," 221.

61. David, *DeL*, 40, 45.

62. Ernst-Dieter Hehl, *Kirche und Krieg im 12. Jahrhundert: Studien zu kanonischem Recht und politischer Wirklichkeit* (Stuttgart: Hiersemann, 1980), 259–61.

63. David, *DeL*, 77–83.

64. Livermore, " 'Conquest of Lisbon,' " 16.

65. For a detailed discussion of these authorities and holy war, see: Frederick Russell, *The Just War in the Middle Ages* (Cambridge: Cambridge University Press, 1975).

66. David, *DeL*, 79–81.

67. Ibid., 81–83.

68. Ibid., 183.

69. Ibid., 155.

70. Ibid., 71; Hehl, *Kirche und Krieg*, 141.

71. David, *DeL*, 153–55.

72. Bernard of Clairvaux, "Epistolae," 315; David, *DeL*, 157.

73. For *Quantum Praedecessores*, see note 18; David, *DeL*, 105–7.

74. Guibert of Nogent, "Gesta Dei per Francos," 125. For a translation, see: Guibert of Nogent, *The Deeds of God Through the Franks*, 28–29.

75. Ibid., 121–23, 131–33.

76. Benjamin Kedar, *Crusade and Mission: European Approaches Toward the Muslims* (Princeton: Princeton University Press, 1984), 89 n. 130, 85–96.

77. James Kritzeck, *Peter the Venerable and Islam* (Princeton: Princeton University Press, 1964).

78. David, *DeL*, 151.

79. Randall Rogers, *Latin Siege Warfare in the Twelfth Century*, (Oxford: Clarendon Press, 1992), 18289, 192; Matthew Bennett, "Military Aspects of the Capture of Lisbon, 1147," in Martin Hoch and Jonathan Phillips, eds., *The Second Crusade: Scope and Consequences* (Manchester: Manchester University Press, 2001).

80. David, *DeL*, 133.

81. Henry is in error here—King Conrad III was never crowned emperor.

82. Henry, Archdeacon of Huntingdon, *Historia Anglorum*, ed. and trans. Diana Greenway (Oxford: Oxford University Press, 1996), 752–53.

83. Richard Mortimer, "The Family of Rannulf de Glanville," *Bulletin of the Institute of Historical Research* 54 (1981): 1–10.

Preface

IT IS not easy to understand why the remarkable historical memoir which goes under the name *De expugnatione Lyxbonensi* should hitherto have attracted so little attention and remained so little known as appears to be the case. The episode with which it deals—the Christian conquest of Lisbon from the Moors in 1147—was not only the sole important success achieved by the Second Crusade; it was an event of the utmost importance in the early development of the Portuguese monarchy; and, since it was the first notable success in a series of similar enterprises by northern crusaders, it laid the foundation for an intercourse and coöperation between England and the Low Countries, on the one hand, and Portugal, on the other, which were destined to have a far-reaching effect on the maritime and commercial development of both regions. Moreover, the period in question is one for which there is a general dearth of important contemporary histories. William Stubbs once remarked of the middle years of the twelfth century that they are "more scantily illustrated by contemporary historians" than any other period in the history of England after the ninth century; and R. L. Poole has recently observed that, Otto of Freising notwithstanding, the situation is but little better with respect to the Continent;[1] and all students of the Second Crusade are aware how unsatisfactory are the accounts of it which we possess when placed in comparison with the great histories which the First Crusade inspired. It would seem, therefore, that so detailed, dependable, and informative a narrative as the *De expugnatione Lyxbonensi* should be regarded as doubly precious.

Moreover, the conquest of Lisbon was, as Henry of Huntingdon well expressed it, the achievement of "lesser folk who

---

[1] See John of Salisbury, *Historia pontificalis* (ed. R. L. Poole, Oxford, 1927), Preface, p. vii.

were dependent upon no great leader except omnipotent God."[1] The modern world feels an immense interest in these obscure "lesser folk" who were so largely overlooked and ignored by most writers of the Middle Ages, and in the pages of the *De expugnatione Lyxbonensi* they live once more before us. For the author of this work was himself one of them. He shared their interests and emotions. And being an enthusiastic and active participant in the stirring events which he records, as well as an alert observer with an instinctive understanding of all things human, he has succeeded to an extraordinary degree in recreating and preserving in rude, but for the most part simple and direct, language the atmosphere of a crusade.

The *De expugnatione Lyxbonensi* has long been available in print, having been published in Portugal in 1861 under the editorship of Alexandre Herculano and in England in 1864 under that of William Stubbs. Both were scholars who stood in the very front rank of the historical profession in their respective countries; and it is unpleasant to have to say that at this point their work was unsatisfactory, particularly in view of the fact that the present editor has so often profited from it, as will be evident to all users of the present volume. But editorial standards have been greatly advanced in the last seventy-five years, and it also seems apparent that neither Stubbs nor Herculano gave his best efforts to this work. In any case the texts which they produced are inaccurate and unsatisfactory, and their treatment of editorial problems is very inadequate. Thus this remarkable source has remained unattractive and difficult to use.

I cannot claim to have solved all the problems with which I have been confronted in the course of the present undertaking. But I have done my utmost to produce an accurate text and to provide such information as is necessary for its convenient and intelligent use. Those who enjoy great familiarity with the Bible and with the writings of the church fathers will doubtless discover some passages derived therefrom which I have failed to note; but I hope that, building

---

[1] See below, pp. 12–13.

upon the excellent work which was begun by Stubbs, I have succeeded in indicating all the more important derivations from these sources.

In adding a translation into English I have been influenced by the belief that the history of the Lisbon crusade can never again be told with such vividness and directness as in this original narrative and that this is a record of sufficient interest to deserve a wider circle of readers than would be willing or able to use it in the Latin text. Endeavoring to make the translation as readable as possible, I have not hesitated to make slight departures from strict grammatical construction when the rudeness of the Latin seemed to require it. It would doubtless be objectionable to mar the English version through a slavish adherence to literalness, but there is surely no occasion to try to improve upon the original. If I have to any degree succeeded in letting the author's personality stand forth as it is revealed in his own at times curious text, I shall be more than content. Quotations from the Bible, which are often fragmentary and sometimes inaccurate, I have generally rendered in the language which has been made familiar by the King James Version in so far as the words used by the author would permit.

To Corpus Christi College, Cambridge, and to the librarian of that institution, Sir Edwyn Hoskyns, who so generously placed his treasures before me under ideal conditions for so long a time as I required, I acknowledge a very particular debt of gratitude. I am also deeply grateful to the American Council of Learned Societies for the generous assistance which enabled me not only to work in European libraries but to travel over the route of the Lisbon crusade in Portugal and Spain and make some study of important features of local topography. To the libraries of Harvard University and of Bryn Mawr College I am also under a heavy obligation. Only those who have worked in those two institutions, so different in resources but so much alike in the spirit which animates their expert and efficient staffs, can appreciate the good fortune of scholars who are privileged to use them. Space forbids

an enumeration of all the individuals who have placed me in their debt in the course of this work, but there are some whose assistance has meant too much to be covered by any general expression of gratitude. Professor Charles H. Haskins of Harvard University, notwithstanding his failing health and retirement, has been an inspiration and a help from the beginning. It is a source of profound regret that the untimely death of Professor Dana C. Munro of Princeton University has prevented me from thanking him as I should for many helpful criticisms and for reading my manuscript and urging its publication. Two accomplished Latinists, Professor Dino Bigongiari of Columbia University and Dr. T. R. S. Broughton of Bryn Mawr College, have saved me from many a pitfall. I am also much indebted to Professor Henry T. Cadbury, now of Harvard University, and to Professor Georgiana Goddard King and Dr. Stephen J. Herben of Bryn Mawr College. Professor King has not only put her extraordinary knowledge of mediaeval Spain at my disposal but has had the patience to read the whole of my manuscript and criticize it in detail. The skillful pen of my wife has been mainly responsible for the map and plan. To Professor Austin P. Evans, editor of the *Records of Civilization*, and to the authorities of the Columbia University Press I am obligated for the efficiency and care with which this volume has been handled in the printing. Finally I express my thanks to Mr. Howard L. Goodhart, whose generosity has terminated a long delay in its publication.

For the information of American scholars who may be interested in the manuscript of the *De expugnatione Lyxbonensi*, it should be noted that the photostatic copy which I have used is to be placed in the Library of Congress, in accordance with the recently devised plan whereby that institution has been made a national repository for such reproductions of foreign manuscript material.

C. W. DAVID

BRYN MAWR COLLEGE
JANUARY, 1936

Abbreviations

HC . . . *Recueil des historiens des croisades*, publié par les soins de l'Académie des inscriptions et belles-lettres, 16 vols., Paris, 1841–1906.

HF . . . *Recueil des historiens des Gaules et de la France*, ed. Martin Bouquet and others, 24 vols. in 25, Paris, 1738–1904.

Itinerarium *Itinerarium peregrinorum et gesta regis Ricardi*, in *Chronicles and Memorials of the Reign of Richard I*, ed. William Stubbs, 2 vols., London, 1864–65, Vol. I.

MGH . . *Monumenta Germaniae historica*, ed. G. H. Pertz and others, Hanover, etc., 1826– .

Migne . . *Patrologiae cursus completus*, ed. J. P. Migne, Series Latina, 221 vols., Paris, 1844–64.

PMH . . *Portugaliae monumenta historica*, [ed. Alexandre Herculano] for the Academia das sciencias de Lisboa, Lisbon, 1856–91 (incomplete).

De expugnatione Lyxbonensi
The Conquest of Lisbon

MAP ILLUSTRATING THE LISBON CRUSADE

Introduction

THE ANGLO–NORMAN ARISTOCRACY IN THE EARLY HISTORY
OF THE CRUSADES

TO THE student who views the crusading movement broadly from its inception until the conclusion of the Second Crusade,[1] it must seem a very remarkable fact that this vast enterprise, which in one way or another came to embrace practically all the peoples of western christendom, should have been so largely dominated by France,[2] and that England, whose connections with the continent through Normandy and through the church were for the most part close, should appear to have played so small a part in it. It can hardly seem surprising that to the Muslims everywhere, whether in Portugal or Spain or Syria, the crusaders were known as Franks, if one pauses to consider that most of the early histories of the crusades were the work of French writers, that all the evidence goes to show that from no other region of Europe was there so great an outpouring of the population on crusade, and that in no other part of Europe did events in the Kingdom of Jerusalem claim such a continuous interest or arouse such an immediate response in time of need.

If one makes allowance for the changing conditions of the ages, it would be difficult to name any other event in the whole history of France which produced a more immediate or striking impression on contemporary French historiography than

[1] The subsequent period would doubtless repay investigation, but since my present purpose is to do no more than provide the necessary background for an understanding of the full significance of the *De expugnatione Lyxbonensi* (1147), I have made no attempt to extend the present inquiry beyond the middle of the twelfth century.

[2] I do not, of course, intend to imply that there was a French nation in any modern sense during the crusading epoch. I use the word loosely, as was occasionally done by writers of the twelfth century, to designate approximately the regions which have come to be embraced in modern France.

did the First Crusade. In an age when historical memoirs and monographs were far from common, writers in France or originating in France—several of them actual participants in the crusade—began almost at once to record its history; and within a few years we have an imposing list of works bearing such titles as *Historia Hierosolymitana, Historia Francorum qui ceperunt Ierusalem,* and *Gesta Dei per Francos.*[1] The continuing interest in the movement in France is well illustrated by the fact that Ordericus Vitalis, writing about 1130 or 1135, thought it necessary to insert in his vast *Historia ecclesiastica* a whole book which is practically a monograph on the First Crusade, and that he devoted a considerable portion of another book to a detailed account of the far less glorious events which followed the first great victory. At a still later period the tragic fiasco of the Second Crusade produced the unique record of Odo of Deuil, the secretary and chaplain of King Louis VII, who followed his master on the expedition.

Apart from the *De expugnatione Lyxbonensi,* which is concerned with an enterprise of the humbler population which the articulate and ruling classes considered hardly worthy of their attention, one looks in vain for anything in England which is to be compared with the imposing array of works produced in France. The Anglo-Saxon chronicler declares that the preaching of Pope Urban caused "a great excitement through all this nation," and he adds a few lines concerning the early stages of the crusading movement and then turns to other things. Florence of Worcester and Simeon of Durham insert a few scattered notices concerning the First Crusade in the course of their annals. Henry of Huntingdon gives it a dozen brief pages. But William of Malmesbury is the only writer in England who feels called upon to deal with it in any fullness; and he is embarrassed for want of information and complains a little mournfully, and in mixed metaphor, that "the fame of Asiatic affairs illumines with but a faint murmur

---

[1] On the literature of the crusades for the period under consideration, see Auguste Molinier, *Les Sources de l'histoire de France* (Paris, 1901–6), II, 266–304; L. J. Paetow, *A Guide to the Study of Medieval History* (rev. ed., New York, 1931), pp. 228–38.

the dark places beyond the British Ocean."[1] The mission of Hugh de Payns, master of the Templars, to England and Scotland in 1128 in search of recruits for the Holy Land caused a considerable stir and received some attention from the chroniclers and local annalists; and the Second Crusade is treated in a paragraph or two by Henry of Huntingdon and in the anonymous *Gesta Stephani regis Anglorum*. Altogether, it must be acknowledged that these meagre and scattered notices make but a poor showing.

It is unfortunately impossible to compile any statistics with respect to the numbers of those who took the cross in different countries; but some impression of the appeal which the crusades made to the more important members of society in a given land may perhaps be gained from the number of individual crusaders who can be identified by name. It is difficult, of course, to compile extensive lists of early crusaders from any country; but it is surely significant that while two score or more crusaders can be named who marched with Robert Curthose in the north French contingent on the First Crusade,[2] a diligent search has revealed the names of only two from England who joined the company, namely, the Norman William de Percy, benefactor of Whitby Abbey, and Arnulf of Hesdin, a Fleming.[3] The situation is much the same in England with respect to the Second Crusade.[4] I have discovered only Count Waleran of Meulan,[5] William of Warenne, earl of

---

[1] *Gesta regum* (ed. William Stubbs, London, 1887–89), II, 431: "trans oceanum Britannicum abditos vix tenui murmure rerum Asianarum fama illustrat."

[2] See the list of fifty-two names in my *Robert Curthose, Duke of Normandy* (Cambridge, Mass., 1920), pp. 221–29. This list includes the names of the two known crusaders from England as well as a number of doubtful cases.

[3] *Ibid.*, pp. 94–95, 222, 229. Edgar Aetheling and Robert, son of Godwin, evidently went on crusade at a somewhat later date. In any case, they belonged to the conquered rather than to the ruling race. On them see below, p. 24 and notes 1 and 3.

[4] It is unfortunately impossible to cite any dependable list of known crusaders from France on the Second Crusade, but were such a list to be compiled, it would doubtless extend to a considerable length.

[5] Robert of Torigny, *Chronique* (ed. Léopold Delisle, Rouen, 1872–73), I, 241; *Chronicon Valassense* (ed. F. Somménil, Rouen, 1868), pp. 8–9. One almost hesitates to reckon him a member of the English nobility, since at his father's death in 1118 he received the continental fiefs, while the English went to his twin brother, Robert de Beaumont,

Surrey,[1] and Roger of Mowbray,[2] of whom it may be said with certainty that they joined the expedition of the king of France; but to these must probably be added Philip, a son of Earl Robert of Gloucester,[3] and William of Dover, one of Earl Robert's knights,[4] and perhaps also Roger de Clinton, bishop of Coventry.[5] Between the First and the Second Crusades there is record of some individuals who took the cross in England, but the number is small indeed. In 1102 Ivo of

earl of Leicester, and since throughout his life he appears not to have used an English title in any known document. But he was often in England and played an ambitious rôle there during the early years of Stephen's reign, having been betrothed to the king's two-year-old daughter in 1136 and having received an important grant in the city of Worcester, perhaps as her marriage portion. He deserted the cause of Stephen for that of the Empress Matilda and her husband in 1141; but the importance of his position in Worcestershire both before and after this date is certain; and it now seems to have been demonstrated, particularly from a study of his seals, that he held the title of earl of Worcester, both under the king and under the empress, for a number of years, perhaps having received the grant of the earldom from Stephen in 1138. G. H. White, "King Stephen's Earldoms," in Royal Historical Society, *Transactions*, 4th ser., XIII (1930), 51, 55–72. On his whole career see now G. H. White, "The Career of Waleran, Count of Meulan and Earl of Worcester," *ibid.*, XVII (1934), 19–48.

[1] John of Hexham, *Historia*, in Simeon of Durham, *Opera omnia* (ed. Thomas Arnold, London, 1882–85), II, 319; Robert of Torigny, *Chronique*, I, 241. His death in the disaster which overtook the French forces beyond Laodicea-ad-Lycum (modern Denizli) in Asia Minor is reported by Louis VII in a letter to Abbot Suger of Saint-Denis (*HF*, XV, 496) and by Odo of Deuil (*De Ludovici VII profectione in Orientem*, in Migne, CLXXXV, 1237). It is dated 13 January, 1148, in the Lewes cartulary, according to J. H. Round, *Ancient Charters* (London, 1888), p. 50.

[2] John of Hexham, *loc. cit.*

[3] *Gesta Stephani regis Anglorum*, in *Chronicles of the Reigns of Stephen, Henry II, and Richard I* (ed. R. Howlett, London, 1884–89), III, 121–22.

[4] *Ibid.*, 113–14.

[5] He died and was buried at Antioch. William Dugdale, *Monasticon Anglicanum* (new ed., London, 1817–30), VI, 1242. The date of his death is given as 16 April, 1148, on what authority I have failed to discover. See Ordericus Vitalis, *Historia ecclesiastica* (ed. Auguste Le Prévost, Paris, 1838–55), IV, 428, note 1; William Stubbs, *Registrum sacrum Anglicanum* (2d ed., Oxford, 1897), p. 44.

The name of Walter Fitz Gilbert (de Clare), brother of the first earl of Pembroke, should possibly be added, though there is no certainty as to the date of his pilgrimage. See R. Howlett, in *Chronicles of the Reigns of Stephen, Henry II, and Richard I*, III, p. xxxviii.

Odo of Deuil (*De Ludovici VII profectione in Orientem*, in Migne, CLXXXV, 1210) mentions a body of Normans and English under Arnulf, bishop of Lisieux, which joined the forces of Louis VII after he had crossed the Rhine, but we hear no more of this contingent, and it is evident that it can have been of no great importance.

Grandmesnil, a Norman, who had been on the First Crusade and had caused a public scandal by his flight from Antioch, and who, on his return to the West, had been so rash as to engage in private war in England, was brought to justice before the court of King Henry I. Being covered with shame because of his record of cowardice and despairing of ever regaining the king's friendship, he found it advisable to pledge his lands for a loan to Count Robert of Meulan and go a second time on crusade. Departing with his wife, who is said to have been a daughter of Gilbert of Ghent, the restorer of Bardney Abbey, he died somewhere on the way.[1] It is recorded that Robert de Baskervill returned from Jerusalem to Gloucester in 1109;[2] and from beyond the Welsh border it is reported that Morgan, son of Cadwgan, who had slain his brother, went to Jerusalem *propter fratricidium* in 1128 and died in Cyprus on the way home.[3] At about the same time, or shortly afterwards, the prominent and wealthy Londoner, Roger "nepos Huberti," father of the better-known Gervase de Cornhill, set out for Jerusalem; and it is probable that he also did not live to return.[4]

To judge from the statements of the chroniclers, one might suppose that the rising military order of the Templars made a strong appeal to the generous impulses of the propertied classes of England.[5] The mission of Hugh de Payns, master

---

[1] David, *Robert Curthose*, pp. 108, 139.

[2] *Historia et cartularium monasterii S. Petri Gloucestriae* (ed. W. H. Hart, London, 1863–67), I, 81.

[3] *Annales Cambriae* (ed. John Williams ab Ithel, London, 1860), p. 38. A Iohannes Anglicus and a Guillelmus Anglicus are to be met with in documents of the Kingdom of Jerusalem, of the years 1144 and 1146; but it would be rash to conclude from their names alone that they were crusaders from England. Reinhold Röhricht, *Regesta regni Hierosolymitani* (Innsbruck, 1893), Nos. 226, 229, 242.

[4] For all that is known about him, see J. H. Round, *Geoffrey de Mandeville* (London, 1892), pp. 305–306, 308–309; idem, *The Commune of London* (Westminster, 1899), p. 107. He was dead and his son had succeeded to his estate in 1130. Round has shown that he was joint sheriff of London in 1125.

[5] *Annales de Waverleia*, in *Annales monastici* (ed. H. R. Luard, London, 1864–69), II, 221; Henry of Huntingdon, *Historia Anglorum* (ed. Thomas Arnold, London, 1879), p. 250; *Two of the Saxon Chronicles Parallel* (ed. Charles Plummer, Oxford, 1892–99), I, 259.

of the Templars, in 1128 is thus described in the *Anglo-Saxon Chronicle:*

In the same year Hugh of the Temple came from Jerusalem to the king in Normandy; and the king received him with much honor and gave him much treasure in gold and silver. And afterwards he sent him to England, and there he was received by all good men, and all gave him treasures; and in Scotland also. And they sent in all a great sum of gold and silver by him to Jerusalem. And he invited the people out to Jerusalem; and there went with him and after him so great a number as never before since the first expedition in the days of Pope Urban. Yet it availed little: he said that there was a furious war between the Christians and the heathens, and when they came there it was nothing but lying. Thus were all these people miserably betrayed.[1]

This passage seems impressive; yet we know of no individual crusader from England who followed Hugh de Payns back to Jerusalem;[2] and in the final observation of the chronicler we may detect a note of realism, not to say of cynicism, which suggests but scant enthusiasm for the crusades or for the Templars in England. But the best test of the English attitude towards the Templars is doubtless to be found in the surviving charters of donations which were made in their favor. Hugh de Payns may have gathered "a great sum of gold and silver" during his sojourn in England and Scotland, but there appears to be no record of grants of land or endowments to the Templars before the close of Henry I's reign. They fared considerably better during the reign of Stephen, when enthusiasm for the endowment of religious houses was at its height among the English nobility[3] and when the king and queen led the way in conferring favors upon them.[4] But there was no St. Bernard

---

[1] *Ibid.* The translation is that of J. A. Giles, with slight modifications.

[2] It is possible that Morgan, son of Cadwgan, and Roger "nepos Huberti," who have just been referred to, were of his company, but direct evidence on the point is lacking.

[3] "Denique multo plura sub brevitate temporis, quo Stephanus regnavit, vel potius nomen regis obtinuit, quam centum retro annis servorum et ancillarum Dei monasteria initium in Anglia sumpsisse noscuntur." William of Newburgh, *Historia rerum Anglicarum*, in *Chronicles of the Reigns of Stephen, Henry II, and Richard I*, I, 53.

[4] Clarence Perkins, "The Knights Templars in the British Isles," in *English Historical Review*, XXV (1910), 213; *Cartulaire général de l'Ordre du Temple, 1119-1150*

to be their advocate in England as he was in France; and while we have some two score charters in their favor down to about 1150, these make but an unimpressive array when placed in comparison with the approximately three hundred charters on their behalf which have survived from the same period in France.[1]

It seems clear, therefore, that so far as the upper or ruling classes were concerned—the classes whose interests are naturally reflected by the chroniclers and in the charters of the period—the crusades aroused an interest and called forth a support in England which compare but poorly with the enthusiasm, generosity, and ambition which they awakened in France. A partial explanation of this English lukewarmness is perhaps to be found in the attitude of certain of the English kings. We know what considerable efforts were made by Pope Urban, through his agent, the abbot of Saint-Bénigne of Dijon, to conclude a treaty of peace between England and Normandy in 1096, so that Robert Curthose might be free to lead a Norman contingent on the First Crusade.[2] There is no evidence that any parallel effort was made to promote the crusade in England, and it does not seem a very rash conjecture that it was recognized that such an attempt would meet with small success. We do not know that William Rufus was actively opposed to the preaching of the crusades in England, but such was almost certainly the attitude of Henry I, at least during the early years of his reign. In 1106 Bohemond, prince of Antioch, visited France and other regions of the North for the purpose of recruiting an army for a crusade against the eastern emperor. Before leaving Italy on his north-

---

(ed. Marquis d'Albon, Paris, 1913), Nos. 114, 124, 178, 179, 208, 247, 248, 250, 255, 256, 271, 272, 273, 377, 449, 450, 482, 483; *Records of the Templars in England in the Twelfth Century* (ed. Beatrice A. Lees, London, 1935), pp. 145–46, 148–51, 156, 176–80, 188–89, 201, 211–13, 215–16, 219–22.

[1] *Cartulaire général de l'Ordre du Temple, passim.* The best account of the early history of the Templars in England is now to be found in the introduction to the recent edition of *Records of the Templars in England in the Twelfth Century* by Beatrice A. Lees, especially pp. xxxviii ff. Miss Lees finds "about sixty charters, royal and private, issued during Stephen's reign in favor of the English Templars."

[2] David, *Robert Curthose*, pp. 90–91.

ward journey, he sent representatives to Henry I in England, who explained the nature of the enterprise and besought an invitation to the English royal court; but the king, fearing that Bohemond might draw away his choice fighting forces, sent word that he ought not to risk the dangers of a winter crossing of the English Channel, particularly in view of the fact that the king himself would be in Normandy before Easter and would meet him there.[1] We know of no knights from England who joined the forces of Bohemond against the Greek emperor; but we learn significantly of a Norman, Robert of Montfort, who was put on trial before the Norman *curia* in 1107 for breaking the peace and who, being granted permission to go to Jerusalem, went to join the forces of Bohemond in Apulia.[2] The case is strikingly like that of Ivo of Grandmesnil, above mentioned. King Henry was willing enough to see rebels and peace-breakers depart on crusade, but not his loyal vassals. Later in his reign, when he felt absolutely secure in his rule of both Normandy and England, his attitude may well have undergone some change, for, as has been seen, he lent his countenance to the mission of Hugh de Payns, master of the Templars.

Of the attitude of King Stephen towards the crusades nothing certain is known; but that it was not unfavorable would seem to be a fair inference from his generosity towards the Templars. Nevertheless, there was evidently no great outpouring of the English nobility on the Second Crusade,[3] and it is a fact of some interest that some, at least, who went had fought on the losing side against the king in the civil war.[4]

But the royal attitude alone, whatever it was, can hardly

---

[1] Ordericus Vitalis, *Historia ecclesiastica*, IV, 211; cf. R. B. Yewdale, *Bohemond I, Prince of Antioch* [Princeton, N.J., 1924], pp. 105–12.

[2] Ordericus Vitalis, *Historia ecclesiastica*, IV, 239.

[3] The statement of the writer of the *Gesta Stephani regis Anglorum* (*Chronicles of the Reigns of Stephen, Henry II, and Richard I*, III, 122) might lead to a different conclusion were it not so highly rhetorical and were it not for the meagreness of the evidence concerning individual crusaders, which has been pointed out above.

[4] Philip, son of Earl Robert of Gloucester, and William of Dover. See above, p. 6, notes 3, 4.

have been the controlling factor in determining the interest of the English upper classes in the crusades. Some deeper and more fundamental explanation is required, and I venture to suggest that the Anglo-Norman aristocracy were not greatly drawn towards the Holy Land primarily because, for this class, England itself was so great a land of opportunity. Less a land of adventure than the Iberian Peninsula or the Orient, it was perhaps the greatest land of opportunity anywhere in the world in the epoch with which we are here concerned. A recently conquered country with a government which, for the most part, was strong and efficient and stable, there was no place else where an ambitious and talented man might hope to win wealth and honor and a successful career so readily, provided he enjoyed the favor of the king. Under Stephen there was, to be sure, a period of royal weakness and great disorder; but the powerful and the ambitious were often able to turn the civil war to their own advantage by playing off one side against the other. Even the church, from which the Anglo-Saxon prelates had been removed to make way for the Norman, the Italian, and the French, offered opportunities for the ambitious and the able which were hardly to be matched elsewhere. It was only when a career in England had made shipwreck that an ambitious man was likely to turn his attention towards the East. The case of Ivo of Grandmesnil in 1102 may well be regarded as typical. That of Arnulf of Hesdin was evidently much like it. Notwithstanding the fact that he had been falsely accused of complicity in the conspiracy of Robert of Mowbray and had won his case in trial by battle, he still withdrew from England, *tanto dolore et ira commotus*, and joined the First Crusade.[1] And a much more prominent member of that expedition was the Breton, Ralph de Gael, the one-time earl of Norfolk, who, having been driven from England by the Conqueror, found an English career closed to him.[2] Analogous cases are to be met with in Normandy under Henry I; that of Robert of Montfort in 1107 has already been noted;[3] likewise in 1128, upon the death of William Clito,

---

[1] David, *Robert Curthose*, p. 222. [2] *Ibid.*, p. 226. [3] Above, p. 10.

son of Robert Curthose and potential claimant to the English throne, some of his late supporters made their peace with King Henry, if they could, but others, we are told, took the cross and went to Jerusalem.[1] In such cases the crusades offered a tempting avenue of escape from a difficult situation; but for the successful members of the upper classes, the evidence seems to indicate that England was hardly a land from which one would be inclined through personal interest to depart.

EARLY CRUSADING ENTERPRISES OF THE MARITIME POPULATIONS OF ENGLAND AND THE LOW COUNTRIES

Whatever be the truth about the crusading interest of the English ruling classes, there was a humbler element in the population for whom England under the rule of the Norman monarchy may not have seemed such a land of opportunity, and it is not necessary to explain in terms of religious zeal alone the apparent enthusiasm with which the middle and lower classes turned to the crusades. For it is evident that by the beginning of the crusading epoch considerable numbers of this population had developed a way of life upon the sea (whether commercial or piratical) which led them to see in the crusades opportunities for gain which were singularly appealing. It is for the light which it sheds on this seafaring population—which is so largely overlooked in other sources of the period—that the De expugnatione Lyxbonensi will be seen to possess perhaps its greatest interest.

The hardy maritime crusaders of the Lisbon expedition are, to be sure, not wholly ignored by other writers of the time. Odo of Deuil refers to them as the maritimi and notes the beginning of their enterprise;[2] Henry of Huntingdon knows

[1] Ordericus Vitalis, Historia ecclesiastica, IV, 483. According to the chronicle of Hyde Abbey (Liber monasterii de Hyda, ed. Edward Edwards, London, 1866, pp. 320–21), in 1120, when the fortunes of William Clito were at a low ebb, he sent messengers to King Henry and besought him to release his father from captivity, and promised, if his request were granted, to depart with him for Jerusalem and never again to appear this side the Julian Alps. Compare David, Robert Curthose, p. 184.

[2] "Interea fama volat, Angliam transfretat, et aliarum recessus penetrat insularum. Parent naves maritimi cum rege navigio processuri." De Ludovici VII profectione in Orientem, in Migne, CLXXXV, 1208.

them as "the lesser folk who were dependent on no great leader except omnipotent God," and he is unstinting in his praise of their achievement, contrasting their brilliant success with the disastrous failure of the Second Crusade at Damascus.[1] But it is only from the *De expugnatione Lyxbonensi* that one can gain a clear view of this enterprise and of the status and interests of the people who were engaged in it. Here we are confronted with a very considerable body of active, adventurous men. It is made up of both English and Norman elements, but the nobility has practically no part in it. (No one except Saher of Archelle is ever referred to as a lord.)[2] It is recruited primarily from the eastern and southern counties, and especially from the seaports all the way from the harbors of East Anglia to Bristol. These men are not only accustomed to the sea, but they are accustomed to acting together in an organized way. Before they set out from England they form a sworn association and establish drastic regulations for the maintenance of discipline. They choose their own judges (*iudices et coniurati*), one of whose functions is evidently the equitable distribution of the profits or spoils of their enterprise. They recognize leadership where there is talent, but major decisions respecting plans and agreements are arrived at in public assembly and debate. They treat the king of Portugal with democratic nonchalance and haggle over the terms on which they will serve him in his struggle with the Moors. Whatever the religious motives of their enterprise, it is expected to be profitable. The chances of profit in this plan or in that are made the subject of earnest debate, and no fine

[1] "Interea quidam exercitus navalis virorum non potentium, nec alicui magno duci innixi nisi Deo omnipotenti, quia humiliter profecti sunt, optime profecerunt. Civitatem namque in Hispania, quae vocatur Ulixisbona . . . et regiones adiacentes a multis pauci Deo cooperante bellis obtinuerunt. Vere Deus superbis resistit, humilibus autem dat gratiam. Exercitus namque regis Francorum et imperatoris splendidior et maior fuerat quam ille qui prius Iherosolimam conquisierat, et a paucissimis contriti sunt, et quasi telae aranearum disterminati sunt et demoliti. His autem pauperibus de quibus praedixi nulla multitudo resistere poterat, sed quando eis plures insurgebant, debiliores efficiebantur. Pars autem eorum maxima venerat ex Anglia." *Historia Anglorum*, p. 281.

[2] Though his part in the enterprise was evidently secondary to that of Hervey de Glanvill, he is repeatedly called *dominus*.

distinction is drawn between the profits of piracy and the rewards of more legitimate enterprise.

Moreover, these men are able to deal—though, to be sure, with some difficulty—in organized coöperation with other men of their own kind from beyond the Straits of Dover and the North Sea, and it would seem not unlikely that the combined forces from the territory of Boulogne, from Flanders, and from the region of Cologne in 1147 actually outnumbered the English contingent.[1]

How far back such coöperation between the maritime populations of England and the Low Countries may go, it seems impossible to say. The surviving evidence indicates that a seafaring and commercial life had been developed in Flanders and Frisia and Lower Lotharingia much earlier than in England, and it is not unlikely that the English learned it from the merchants of these regions. The commercial activities of these merchants in London can be traced in a well-known list of market tolls of the reign of Aethelred the Redeless, probably dating from between the years 991 and 1002; and it may be noted that already the subjects of the emperor who came in their ships (*homines imperatoris qui veniebant in navibus suis*) enjoyed a privileged position.[2] Much more extensive regulations concerning the activities of these men of the emperor, who are identified with the merchants of Lower Lotharingia,[3] are believed to date from before the reign of Henry II, perhaps from about the year 1130.[4] Information concerning the Flem-

[1] Henry of Huntingdon, in the passage quoted above (p. 13, note 1) claims numerical superiority for the English; but the fact that the continentals were given a preponderance of the select troops that were sent into the city in advance to occupy the strategic positions at the time of the surrender of Lisbon would seem to indicate that the English were in the minority. See below, pp. 172–75. Continental writers not unnaturally assign to the English a secondary rôle on this occasion.

[2] *The Laws of the Kings of England from Edmund to Henry I* (ed. A. J. Robertson, Cambridge, 1925), pp. 72–73, 322–23; Felix Liebermann, *Die Gesetze der Angelsachsen* (Halle, 1898–1916), I, 232–34; III, 161–63.

[3] Mary Bateson, "A London Municipal Collection of the Reign of John," in *English Historical Review*, XVII (1902), 495–502. On the dating of the manuscript see *ibid.*, pp. 482–83, and XXVIII (1913), 734.

[4] *Ibid.*, XVII (1902), 483, 495; cf. Konstantin Höhlbaum, in *Hansisches Urkundenbuch*, III (1882–86), 388–90. Attention may also be drawn to the well-known description

ings is less satisfactory, for they do not figure in these commercial regulations of the first half of the twelfth century. But they are mentioned in connection with the market tolls of Aethelred's reign; and the Flemish Hanse of London, the main purpose of which was the exploitation of trade by Flemish merchants in England, is revealed as an organization already in full vigor in a well-known Latin text which dates from but little after 1187.[1] The English, therefore, had long had an opportunity to make the acquaintance of these aliens from beyond the sea and to learn to imitate their ways; and it need occasion no surprise to find Flemings and men of the Empire (*a Romani imperii partibus*)[2] joining forces with the maritime population of eastern and southern England in the naval crusade of 1147, from which commercial[3] or piratical as well as spiritual benefits were expected to be realized.

For the maritime enterprises of these populations were by no means confined to the narrow seas. Long before this the way from the North Sea and the English Channel through the Straits of Gibraltar into the Mediterranean had been made familiar by the Vikings;[4] and the oldest extant mediaeval portolano, apparently dating from the eleventh century, has come down to us, not, as one might expect, from the Mediterranean basin, but from the North; and it gives the sailing

---

of London at about the same period by William of Malmesbury (*Gesta pontificum*, ed. N. E. S. A. Hamilton, London, 1870, p. 140): "constipata negotiatorum ex omni terra et maxime ex Germania venientium commertiis."

[1] L. A. Warnkoenig, *Flandrische Staats- und Rechtsgeschichte* (Tübingen, 1835–42), I, Appendix, No. 39. For other editions, for corrections, and for the dating of the text, and on the Flemish Hanse of London in general, see Henri Pirenne, "La Hanse flamande de Londres," in Académie Royale de Belgique, *Bulletin*, 3d ser., XXXVII (1899), 65–108.

[2] Below, pp. 52, 54.

[3] Note especially the provision of the convention between the crusaders and the king of Portugal on p. 112 below: "Naves insuper et res eorum vel heredum eorum qui ad urbis Lyxbonensis obsidionem una mecum fuere ab omni consuetudine mercatoria, que vulgo pedatica dicitur, a modo et in perpetuum per totam terram meam firmiter et bona fide concedo."

[4] T. D. Kendrick, *A History of the Vikings* (New York, 1930), chap. vii; Paul Riant, *Les Expéditions et pèlerinages des Scandinaves en Terre-Sainte au temps des croisades* (Paris, 1865), *passim*; R. Dozy, *Recherches sur l'histoire et la littérature de l'Espagne pendant le moyen âge* (3d ed., Paris and Leyden, 1881), II, 250–371.

course from Denmark and Flanders to Acre in Syria.[1] Over this course the mariners of the Low Countries and of England inevitably learned to sail and it is apparent that they were making the journey with considerable frequency during the early period of the crusades.

The *De expugnatione Lyxbonensi* would be a far less interesting record than it actually is if it were necessary to regard the Lisbon crusade of 1147 as an isolated enterprise. But it was clearly unique only in its extraordinary success. According to the *Chronica Gothorum*, in the year 1140 a fleet of almost seventy vessels from parts of the Gauls (*de partibus Galliarum*),[2] loaded with armed men who had taken vows to go to Jerusalem, entered the mouth of the Douro in Portugal. Received with joy by the king, Affonso Henriques, they entered into a compact with him for a joint attack upon the Moors in the great stronghold of Lisbon. As the fleet sailed for the mouth of the Tagus, the king marched overland with his army and in due course the city was invested. But its conquest proved impossible, and after the suburbs had been invaded and the surrounding country devastated, the king withdrew to his own country while the crusaders proceeded on their way towards Jerusalem.[3] This reads like a rehearsal of the expedition of 1147, and it may well be true, as has generally been assumed,[4] that this episode is to be identified with a vain attack upon Lisbon which is repeatedly referred to in the *De expugnatione Lyxbonensi* as having taken place five years before the successful siege of 1147, or in 1142. But the identification is not necessary or certain. What is clear, apart from the *Chronica Gothorum*, is that there had been an unsuccessful coöperative attack upon Lisbon, apparently in 1142, in which a considerable body of the crusaders of 1147—presumably men from Southampton and Hastings, and perhaps also from Bristol—

---

[1] Adam of Bremen, *Gesta Hammaburgensis ecclesiae pontificum* (ed. J. M. Lappenberg, 2d ed., Hanover, 1876), pp. 154–55 (scholia 96); also in Konrad Kretschmer, *Die italienischen Portolane des Mittelalters* (Berlin, 1909), p. 235; cf. *ibid.*, pp. 195–99.

[2] The phrase is exactly the same as that which is applied in the *Chronica Gothorum* to the crusading fleet of 1147. *PMH, Scriptores*, I, 15.

[3] *PMH, Scriptores*, I, 13–14.   [4] See below, pp. 96–97, note 3.

had taken part, and that the experience of these men on that occasion, and especially the king's dealings with them, had left them with little enthusiasm for undertaking a new siege in 1147.[1] But the *De expugnatione Lyxbonensi* seems to contain references to still other unsuccessful attacks upon Lisbon in which northern crusaders had taken part. In the exchange of declarations preliminary to the siege of 1147, the Moorish elder, addressing the archbishop of Braga, is made to say, "How many times now within our memory have you come hither with pilgrims and barbarians to subdue us and drive us hence!" And the bishop of Oporto, in closing the exchange, freely acknowledges the truth of the implication.[2] Whether these speeches be genuine, or the literary devices of the author of the *De expugnatione Lyxbonensi*, makes little difference. The inference is clear that the attack of 1147 was but one of a series of such undertakings.

Nor did such enterprises cease with 1147. Lisbon once in Christian hands became a base from which further operations could be conducted by the rising power of Portugal with the assistance of crusaders from the North. Already in 1150 Gilbert of Hastings, the new bishop of Lisbon, is reported to have been back in England, preaching a fresh crusade and seeking recruits for an attack upon Seville.[3] Our concern, however, is not with these later operations,[4] but with the earlier maritime enterprises of the English and of their neighbors across the North Sea, which in large part form the necessary background for a full understanding of the great achievement of 1147 and which, though the evidence is fragmentary and often unsatisfactory, may be traced back to the First Crusade and perhaps even beyond it.

[1] Below, pp. 102–111; cf. pp. 164, 165.

[2] Below, pp. 120, 121, 124, 125.

[3] See below, pp. 178–79, note 3. A. Herculano (*Historia de Portugal*, 8th ed., by D. Lopes and P. de Azevedo, Paris and Lisbon, n.d., III, 65) believed that some of Bishop Gilbert's recruits may have assisted the king of Portugal in an unsuccessful attack on Alcácer do Sal. Compare *Chronica Gothorum*, in *PMH, Scriptores*, I, 15.

[4] On these Friedrich Kurth, *Der Anteil niederdeutscher Kreuzfahrer an den Kämpfen der Portugiesen gegen die Mauren*, in Institut für österreichische Geschichtsforschung, *Mitteilungen*, Ergänzungsband VIII (1909), 159 ff., may be consulted with profit.

Attention may first be directed to a curious passage in the *Historia Compostelana*—a very respectable source for the matter in question—which relates to events of the year 1112.[1] The death of Alfonso VI of Castile without male issue had created a grave succession problem, and the country was rent by civil war as a result of the bitter struggle between his daughter, Urraca, and Alfonso I of Aragon, her husband.[2] Though Diego Gelmírez, the celebrated bishop of Santiago de Compostela, was a staunch and vigorous upholder of her authority in Galicia, he had met with only partial success in suppressing a rising against her; and two incorrigible rebels, Pelayo Godesteiz and Rabinat Núñez, had set him at defiance and were holding out against him in two strongholds in western Galicia, one of which seems to have been Puente Sampayo on the upper end of Vigo Bay.[3] Urged on by a letter from Queen Urraca, who was away campaigning against her husband, the bishop ordered a siege of the latter stronghold by land and sea. This he was able to undertake because he had at his disposal not only a considerable land force but also a small navy, which it appears that, through an arrangement with the seafaring inhabitants of Padron and other nearby ports, he had taken the initiative in creating.[4] But the rebels also were not without naval resources, for just at this time there had arrived most opportunely on the coast of Galicia a force of English pirates, who were bound for Jerusalem, but who were not averse to turning their hands to some profitable

[1] In Enrique Flórez, *España sagrada* (Madrid, 1747–1879), XX, 130–36. For the more significant parts of the text see below, p. 19, note 4. For the date see Antonio López Ferreiro, *Historia de la santa A. M. Iglesia de Santiago de Compostela* (Santiago, 1898–1909), III, 384.

[2] For a fuller account see López Ferreiro, *op. cit.*, III, chaps. xiii–xv.

[3] "Castellum Sancti Pelagii de Luto et Daravum." *Historia Compostelana*, in Flórez, *España sagrada*, XX, 132. López Ferreiro, *op. cit.*, III, 382, has made a tentative identification of the castles with Puente Sampayo and with Darbo on Vigo Bay near Cangas.

[4] *Historia Compostelana*, in Flórez, *España sagrada*, XX, 133–35. The bishop is reputed to have been the earliest organizer of Spanish naval power on the Atlantic. Compare C. Fernández Duro, *La Marina de Castilla desde su origen* (Madrid, 1894), pp. 20–23; *Enciclopedia universal ilustrada Europeo-Americana* (Barcelona: J. Espasa, etc. [1912–30]), XXV, 1182.

enterprise in the course of their journey.[1] Taking these pirates into their employ, the rebels put themselves in a position to practice depredations along the coast and even for some distance inland, and the pillagings and atrocities which followed this arrangement are likened in the *Historia Compostelana* to the inhumanities of the Almoravides.[2] At the very moment that the Gallegan naval forces, acting on the bishop's orders, were making their way up Vigo Bay to blockade the rebel stronghold, the pirates were engaged in loading their vessels with the plunder of a church which they had just destroyed; and as soon as the bishop's marines sighted them a great way off, we are told that they recognized that they would without any doubt be English pirates. In the fight which ensued the Gallegan forces gained a decisive victory. The enemy ships were boarded, and three of them were captured.[3] Some members of the crews were slain, but others were taken alive and bound with their hands behind their backs. And then the victors, laden with spoils, continued their way to the siege and landed with their captives. The bishop, it appears, was entitled to one-fifth of the booty which his naval forces had taken, but when he beheld the English captives weeping and wailing, he was moved with compassion, and, giving up his right to share in the rest of the spoils, he asked that the captives be surrendered to him; when his request had been granted, he set them at liberty—but only after he had bound them with an oath never again to be disturbers of Christians or to practice such iniquities against Christians as those in which they had recently been engaged.[4]

[1] "Ces soi-disant croisés, ces sacrilèges qui pillaient les églises, venaient sans doute des Orcades, où l'on n'était encore chrétien que de nom," says Dozy, *Recherches sur l'histoire et la littérature de l'Espagne*, II, 328, but there is no need for any such assumption.

[2] The author calls them *Moabites*. For the meaning of this word in the sources of the period see below, pp. 68–69, note 1.

[3] Only one of the captured vessels is said to have been English, the other two having been supplied by the rebel leaders. See the text in note 4, below.

[4] *Historia Compostelana, loc. cit.*, XX, 133–35: "Eodem tempore Pelagius Godesteides et Rabinatus Nunides piratas pretio conductos sibi in auxilium assumpserant, qui ab Angliae partibus venientes causa adeundi Hierosolyman Hesperiam attigerant, et

With the bishop's decisive victory over the rebels, which followed the signal success of his naval forces, we are not here concerned; nor are we able to say whether the English captives, having regained their liberty, were able to continue on their way to Jerusalem. What concerns us here to note is that

---

hac de causa eos sibi assumpserant, ut, illorum auxilio muniti, ipsi adiacentes partes depraedando et depopulando inquietarent, et Anglici piratae, utpote gens nullius pietatis melle condita, et remota et mari finitima pesundarent et atrocitatis suae rabiem exercerent, quod haud aliter accidit. Equidem Anglici ex improviso cursu velifero maris confinia invadentes, hos trucidabant illos denudantes omnibus bonis suis privabant, alios, acsi essent Moabitae, captos et catenatos ad redemptionem cogebant; quin etiam nimia pecuniae cupiditate obcaecati, proh nefas, ecclesias violabant, tantique sacrilegii rei quaecumque necessaria ibi inventa et etiam homines inde abstrahebant. Sed beati Iacobi intercessio a nefanda gente provinciam suam pesundari et depopulari haud impune permisit, tantumque nefas non inultum remanere voluit.

"Interea dum Irienses nautae virique qui de Santa Maria de Lanchata venerant ut ad supradictam obsidionem tenderent, forte praedicti praedones solito more ad praedam venerant et, destructa quadam ecclesia, spolia ad classem comportabant. Quos ubi Irienses ceterique in quadam a se remota parte litoris viderunt, proculdubio Anglicos piratas fore arbitrati sunt. Post haec arma capiebant, scuta, gladios, tela aptabant, et ad bella alacriter properabant, nec tamen a remigis officio cessabant. Anglici quoque eadem faciebant, sed, empediente reatu, aut ad armandum aut ad remigandum vix illis tempus sufficiebat. Quid plura? Bellum utrinque exoritur. Tela ad instar grandinis mittuntur, et maxime lapidibus quos ad hoc in carinis ferebant bellum geritur. Denique Irienses et homines de Santa Maria de Lanchata, auxiliante beato Iacobo, acrius in hostes insurgunt et celeri saltu hostium naves conscendunt. Igitur hos telis transverberant, hos lapidibus obruunt, illos iunctis manibus post terga vivere permittunt; et ingredientes Anglicorum piratarum biremem et alias duas naves quas Pelegius Godesteides et Rabinatus Nunides Anglicis in auxilium dederant, incoeptum iter peragunt, tantoque triumpho laetantes, captivos secum ducunt et ad supradictam obsidionem tendunt; quae postquam ad aures domini sui, scilicet ecclesiae beati Iacobi venerabilis episcopi, uti gesta fuerant, pervenerunt, magno gavisus gaudio, omnipotenti Deo summas grates tradidit, qui provinciam apostoli sui Iacobi a malignis praedonibus defendere et protegere dignatus est. Cum autem praedicti victores se litori applicuissent, episcopus videns Anglicos captos flentes et eiulantes, paterna pietate compunctus, misericordia motus est. . . . Tunc alloquutus est nautas suos, ita dicens: 'Fratres, scitis quintam partem omnium quae in hac victoria, Deo iuvante, adepti estis ad me iure pertinere, quae, quamquam plura et pretiosa sint, nihil tamen a vobis accipere volo; sed tantummodo captivos in portionem meam mihi date.' Hoc autem dicebat volens illos a vinculis solvere et a captivitatis iugo eruere. Acceptis itaque in portionem captivis, ipse episcopus eos iuramento astrinxit ne amplius Christianorum inquietatores essent aut tale quid quod superius dictum est in Christianos facere praesumerent, sicque solvens eos a vinculis liberos abire permisit." Compare López Ferreiro, *op. cit.*, III, 379–86; Dozy, *op. cit.*, II, 326–28; Alberto Sampaio, "As Póvoas marítimas do norte de Portugal," in *Portugalia*, II (1905–8), 397–98.

the text which we have paraphrased carries the clear implication that depredations of English pirates on the coast of Galicia were no extraordinary occurrence in 1112—the bishop's marines knew at the very first sight of the plunderers that they had to do with English pirates—and that, although these pirates are described as men without piety (*gens nullius pietatis melle condita*), they were none the less crusaders on their way to Jerusalem. They had turned aside to accept service under Christians against Christians in a civil strife, but otherwise their conduct was much like that of the crusaders of 1140(?), who, according to the *Chronica Gothorum*, proceeded on their way towards Jerusalem after the failure of their attack upon Lisbon,[1] and that of the crusaders of 1147, who, after their great victory, are said to have passed the winter in Lisbon until the Calends of the following February and then to have continued their voyage and fulfilled their vows at the Sepulchre.[2]

For the next information which enables us to connect crusaders from England and from neighboring lands beyond the North Sea with Galicia and with the eastern Mediterranean, we are unfortunately mainly dependent on the somewhat uncertain authority of Albert of Aix. According to this writer, in July, 1102, a naval force of two hundred vessels arrived at Jaffa and rendered invaluable services both by land and sea to the hard-pressed Baldwin, king of Jerusalem, in his struggle with the Saracens. We have the names of the leaders of this expedition, which are as follows: Bernard Witarzh of the land of Galicia, Harding of England, Otto of *Roges*, and Hardewerk, one of the most powerful men of Westphalia.[3] The arrival of

---

[1] See above, p. 16.

[2] Letter of Duodechin, priest of Lahnstein, who was a participant in the crusade. *MGH, Scriptores*, XVII, 28; see below, p. 181, note 1. What he says seems to refer to the German forces and need not necessarily apply to the entire expedition.

[3] "Interea dum haec obsidio [Joppe] ageretur, ducentae naves Christianorum navigio Joppe appulsae sunt, ut adorarent in Iherusalem. Horum Bernardus Witarzh de terra Galatiae, Hardinus de Anglia, Otto de Roges, Hardewerk, unus de praepotentibus Westfalorum, primi et ductores fuisse referuntur." *Liber Christianae expeditionis pro ereptione, emundatione, restitutione sanctae Hierosolymitanae ecclesiae*, in *HC, Historiens occidentaux*, IV, 596. For a discussion of the date see Heinrich Hagenmeyer,

this naval force at Jaffa in 1102 and the part which it played in assisting King Baldwin against his enemies are confirmed by oriental writers,[1] but unfortunately we are entirely without information as to how it had been brought together or what its history had been before its arrival in the eastern Mediterranean.[2]

It is also related by Albert of Aix that in May, 1102, when King Baldwin made his brilliant recovery, after the rout of Ramleh, by escaping through the mountains to Arsuf and then making his way by sea to Jaffa, he took ship with a certain Godric, "a pirate of the kingdom of England."[3] And this Godric has been conjecturally identified with that remarkable figure, St. Godric, the hermit of Finchale,[4] whose so-called hymns have made him a person of note in the history of English versification[5] and whose early life as an active merchant engaged in overseas trade has in recent years been used to illustrate the genesis of mediaeval commerce and of the merchant class.[6] Whether the hermit of Finchale is really to be identified with the English pirate who assisted King Baldwin in 1102 may well be questioned; but in any case his singular

---

"Chronologie du royaume de Jérusalem," in *Revue de l'Orient latin*, XI (1905–8), 457–58. Could *Roges* by any chance be Chocques on the border of Flanders, as the *Zokes* of Albert of Aix has turned out to be? Compare David, *Robert Curthose*, pp. 217–18.

[1] Matthew of Edessa, *Chronique*, in *HC, Documents arméniens*, I, 68; Ibn al-Athir, *Kamel-Altevarykh*, in *HC, Historiens orientaux*, I, 216.

[2] Ekkehard, abbot of Aura, *Hierosolymita*, (ed. Heinrich Hagenmeyer, Tübingen, 1877), p. 275, reports the arrival at Jaffa in September, 1101, of a fleet of thirty ships bearing twelve thousand pilgrims, but he gives no indication whence they came. Hagenmeyer conjectures that they came from Constantinople.

[3] *Liber Christianae expeditionis*, in *HC, Historiens occidentaux*, IV, 595; cf. Fulcher of Chartres, *Historia Hierosolymitana* (ed. Heinrich Hagenmeyer, Heidelberg, 1913), p. 448.

[4] T. A. Archer, in *Dictionary of National Biography* (London, 1885–1900), s.v. *Godric*. He died, evidently at an extreme old age, in 1170.

[5] Julius Zupitza, "Cantus Beati Godrici," in *Englische Studien*, XI (1888), 401–32; J. W. Rankin, "The Hymns of St. Godric," in Modern Language Association, *Publications*, XXXVIII (1923), 699–711.

[6] Henri Pirenne, *Medieval Cities* (Princeton, 1925), pp. 119–24; Walther Vogel, "Ein seefahrender Kaufmann um 1100," in *Hansische Geschichtsblätter*, XVIII (1912), 239–48. The principal source for Godric's life is Reginald of Coldingham or Durham, *Libellus de vita et miraculis sancti Godrici heremitae de Finchale* ([ed. J. Stevenson], London, 1847), being Surtees Society, *Publications*, XX (1845).

career well serves to illustrate the early English maritime
expansion and its crusading contacts with which we are here
concerned. Not to mention his other journeys oversea, he
twice took the cross and went to Jerusalem, and on his way
home from the first of these pilgrimages he visited the shrine
of St. James at Compostela.[1]

Between 1102 and 1112 still other maritime crusading enterprises from both sides of the North Sea can be traced in the
pages of Albert of Aix. He makes a brief mention of three
Flemish ships and their commanders, William, Starcolf, and
Bernard, off the Syrian coast in 1110.[2] And in 1107 he tells of
another body of crusaders who arrived by sea at Jaffa to visit
the Sepulchre. They entered into an arrangement with the
king of Jerusalem to join him in laying siege to Sidon, but
presently the plan was abandoned and they were dismissed.
Of the leaders of this expedition we know nothing, nor are we
able to connect it in any way with the Iberian Peninsula; but
it is said to have been made up of some seven thousand men
from England, besides others from Denmark, Flanders, and
Antwerp.[3] We have a clear impression that the English constituted the preponderant element in it.

The part played by the maritime populations of England
and the Low Countries in the First Crusade can be illustrated
from more abundant sources, but unfortunately they are not
in full accord, and the problem of their correct interpretation
and evaluation is a serious one. According to Ordericus Vitalis,

[1] Reginald of Durham, *op. cit.*, pp. 33–34, 52–58.
[2] *Liber Christianae expeditionis*, in *HC, Historiens occidentaux*, IV, 676: "naves . . .
tres a Flandria et Antwerpia venerant, quibus praeerant Willelmus, Starcolfus, et
Bernardus."
[3] *Ibid.*, p. 631: ". . . plurima multitudo navalis exercitus catholicae gentis Anglorum,
circiter septem milia, navibus quas buzas appellant, cum cetera manu de regno Dano-
rum, Flandriae, et Antwerpiae, longo ambitu maris advecta."
Attention may be drawn in passing to the crusade of that belated viking, Sigurd
of Norway, who set out from his homeland in the autumn of 1107, passed the first
winter in England, the second in Galicia; and then passed on to capture Cintra and
plunder the Moors in Algarve. Later he proceeded to the Balearic Islands, to southern Italy, and finally to the Holy Land, which he reached in 1110. Riant, *Scandinaves en Terre-Sainte*, chap. iv; Dozy, *Recherches sur l'histoire et la littérature de
l'Espagne*, II, 323–26.

a fleet of "almost twenty thousand pilgrims . . . from England and other islands of the Ocean," under the command of Edgar Aetheling,[1] landed at Laodicea in June, 1098, and occupied the city.[2] This looks like a characteristically mediaeval exaggeration of numbers, and there are difficulties in the way of believing that Edgar Aetheling could have reached Syria as early as June, 1098. A somewhat better authority seems to place his arrival in the Holy Land in May, 1102.[3] But the statement of Ordericus Vitalis, in spite of difficulties of detail, may well seem rather more worthy of respect than would be the case were we not familiar with the facts of the Lisbon crusade of 1147 and of the earlier expeditions which have just been passed in review. It can be proved from a strictly contemporary letter that there were English ships and mariners on the coast of Syria, coöperating with the land forces of the First Crusade in 1098.[4] Another letter reveals the presence of English vessels on the coast of Palestine, apparently at Jaffa, in the spring of 1100.[5] And we have an acceptable account by Raymond of Aguilers, himself a participant in the overland expedition, which places the arrival of an important English naval force off the Syrian coast in 1097 in advance of the land forces of the First Crusade. Acting in coöperation with the Greek emperor, these English mariners attacked and captured the port at the mouth of the Orontes River as well as Laodicea, and, together with the Genoese, they rendered vitally important services in the crusade by keeping open communications with the island of Cyprus and by protecting the Greek

[1] Grandson of Edmund Ironside, and claimant to the English throne upon the death of Harold in the Battle of Hastings, 1066.

[2] *Historia ecclesiastica*, IV, 70–71.

[3] William of Malmesbury, *Gesta regum* (ed. William Stubbs, London, 1887–89), II, 310; cf. *ibid.*, p. 449. According to this authority, he was accompanied by another Englishman, a certain Robert, son of Godwin, who played a heroic part in enabling King Baldwin to escape from Ramleh. On this Robert see E. A. Freeman, *The Reign of William Rufus* (Oxford, 1882), II, 118–23, 615–18.

[4] Letter of the clergy and people of Lucca, in *Die Kreuzzugsbriefe aus den Jahren 1088–1100* (ed. Heinrich Hagenmeyer, Innsbruck, 1901), pp. 165–67.

[5] Letter of Dagobert, patriarch of Jerusalem, *ibid.*, p. 176–77; cf. David, *Robert Curthose*, p. 232.

shipping which was engaged in the supply of foodstuffs and equipment. Of the size of this force of maritime crusaders from England, as reported by Raymond, some idea may be formed from his statement that in the winter of 1098–99, when their ships had been reduced by wear and tear from thirty to nine or ten, they abandoned them or burned them and joined the land forces of the crusade in the advance upon Jerusalem.[1]

The problem of naval coöperation in the First Crusade is still further complicated by several passages of Albert of Aix. According to this writer—who is somewhat self-contradictory, it must be acknowledged, and difficult to reconcile with other authorities—when Baldwin, the future king of Jerusalem, arrived in the overland march at Tarsus, near the coast of the Gulf of Alexandretta, in the autumn of 1097, he established contact with a fleet of Christian pirates who had been pursuing their calling for the past eight years; and giving them information concerning the crusade, he secured their coöperation. These pirates hailed from Antwerp, Tiel, Frisia, and Flanders,[2] and they were under the command of a certain Guinemer of Boulogne. It seems impossible to reconcile a number of other statements of Albert of Aix concerning Guinemer and his pirates with other and better authorities for the First Crusade; but it would surely be rash to reject his whole account of these maritime adventurers from the Low Countries and Boulogne in the eastern Mediterranean.[3]

[1] *Historia Francorum qui ceperunt Ierusalem*, in *HC, Historiens occidentaux*, III, 290–91.

[2] In an alternative list Albert reports them as coming from Flanders, Antwerp, Frisia, and other parts of Gaul. See below, note 3. Note that the men of Tiel and Antwerp are mentioned in the London trade regulations of the twelfth century which have been discussed above, p. 14. See *English Historical Review*, XVII (1902), 498, 501.

[3] *Liber christianae expeditionis*, in *HC, Historiens occidentaux*, IV, 348–49, 380, 447. I have discussed at some length the difficult problems of the maritime crusaders from England and the Low Countries in the eastern Mediterranean during the First Crusade in my *Robert Curthose*, Appendix E and *passim*. Much must doubtless remain obscure; but the facts which have been assembled in the present volume incline me to be less drastic in dealing with Ordericus Vitalis and Albert of Aix than I was when my earlier work was written. The latest critic of Albert of Aix gives him a rather better reputation than he has hitherto enjoyed. A. A. Beaumont, "Albert of Aachen and the County of

Many of the foregoing facts, if facts they be, concerning the crusading enterprises of the maritime populations of England and the Low Countries have been gathered from sources of somewhat uncertain value, it may freely be admitted. Nevertheless, their cumulative effect seems impressive. The first half-century of the crusades was a period during which maritime intercourse between the English Channel, the Spanish Peninsula, and the eastern Mediterranean was more active than has commonly been realized. This naval participation in the crusading movement was far from negligible; and had the way not been prepared for the Lisbon enterprise of 1147 by long years of practical experience, it is difficult to believe that it could have achieved so signal a success.

THE MANUSCRIPT OF THE *DE EXPUGNATIONE LYXBONENSI*
AND ITS PROVENANCE

The historical memoir in epistolary form which is commonly known by the title *De expugnatione Lyxbonensi*,[1] and which has long been ascribed without good reason to a certain *Osbernus*,[2] appears to have survived in but a single manuscript, namely, Corpus Christi College, Cambridge, No. 470, folios 125r–146r. The volume forms a part of the famous collection of Archbishop Matthew Parker. Besides the work on the Lisbon crusade, it contains a calendar, some daily offices, the well-known poem of Hildebert of Lavardin on the mass (*De mysterio missae*), the *Hypognosticon* of Lawrence, prior of Durham, and some other unimportant matter. It is written in various hands of the last half of the twelfth and of the thirteenth century; and it is believed by Dr. M. R. James, the latest cataloguer of the Corpus Christi College manuscripts, on the evidence of the calendar which stands at its beginning

---

Edessa," in *The Crusades and Other Essays Presented to D. C. Munro* (New York, 1928), pp. 101–38.

Attention may be drawn in passing to those early English exiles who "fled from the face of William the Bastard" after the Battle of Hastings and entered the service of the Greek emperor. The language of Ordericus Vitalis indicates that they made their way to the East by sea. *Historia ecclesiastica*, II, 172; III, 169, 490.

[1] See below, pp. 52–53, note 1.   [2] See below, pp. 43–45.

and of a pressmark ("N. LXIX") on folio 24r (at the beginning of the poem of Hildebert of Lavardin), to have once been
in the possession of the cathedral priory of Norwich.[1]

But while the arguments of Dr. James seem perfectly valid
as far as they go, they do not warrant the certain conclusion
that that part of the manuscript which contains the account
of the Lisbon crusade necessarily came from Norwich; for the
volume is made up of heterogeneous elements and bears within
itself evidences of having been put together at different times.
Beginning with folio 13r (that is, immediately after the twelve
folios of the calendar) and running through to the end of the
volume, there are quire signatures in the lower right-hand
corners of the recto pages of the first half of each successive
gathering, as follows: *A i, A ii, A iii, B i, B ii, B iii*, etc.
These are written in a hand which, on palaeographical grounds,
may probably be assigned to the fifteenth century[2] and they
seem to offer convincing evidence that the Norwich calendar
was added after the volume had once been complete without
it. Moreover, while the account of the Lisbon crusade evidently formed a part of the volume at the time when the
signatures were inserted, it is practically certain that it had
had a long separate existence before this; for the folios on
which it is written (constituting gatherings *L, M, N,* and *O*)
form a quite distinct section of the volume. The recto of the
first of these folios (125r) is difficult to read and appears worn,
as though it had long been exposed to use without adequate
protection. The vellum also in this section of the manuscript
is of inferior quality and much coarser than that of any other
part of the volume. The leaves must also originally have been
considerably larger than those of the remainder of the volume;
for in being cut down by the binder to match the others, the

[1] M. R. James, *A Descriptive Catalogue of the Manuscripts in the Library of Corpus Christi College, Cambridge* (Cambridge, 1912), No. 470; *idem,* "The Sources of Arch-bishop Parker's Collection of MSS. at Corpus Christi College, Cambridge," Cambridge Antiquarian Society, *Octavo Publications,* XXXII (1899), 5, 12, 74.

[2] According to E. M. Thompson (*Introduction to Greek and Latin Palaeography,* Oxford, 1912, p. 54) signatures of this later mediaeval type did not come into use before the fourteenth century.

margins have been rendered very narrow, indeed in some cases
being almost entirely cut away; and where important marginalia have escaped the binder's knife, they now appear
upon tabs which have been left projecting beyond the edges
of the ordinary leaves. It seems necessary to conclude, therefore, that while the manuscript of the *De expugnatione Lyxbonensi* may once have belonged to the cathedral priory of
Norwich, it is by no means certain that it did so.

Indeed, the early catalogues of the Parker manuscripts may
even raise a passing doubt as to whether the *De expugnatione
Lyxbonensi* was contained in the present volume No. 470 at
the time of the archbishop's bequest. In the inventory, or
register, of the collection which was made at that time and
which exists in three identical copies now in the possession
respectively of Corpus Christi College, Gonville and Caius
College, and Trinity Hall, the present No. 470 appears as the
thirteenth entry under *G* in the following form: *Laurentius
Dunelmensis*, with the *incipit* given as *Omnipotentis sempi-
ternę*.[1] There is, accordingly, no evidence here that the account
of the Lisbon crusade was contained in the volume in 1575.
Moreover, the first printed catalogue of the manuscripts of
Corpus Christi College, which was published by Thomas
James in 1600,[2] contains no indication that the *De expugnatione Lyxbonensi* then formed a part of the volume. Thomas
James mentions the works of Hildebert of Lavardin and
Lawrence of Durham, but at the point where we should expect
to find a mention of the Lisbon crusade we read instead:
Anonymi tractatus theologicus.[3] But any doubts which may be
raised by this silence of the early cataloguers must be set at
rest by the evidence contained within the volume itself. Mention has already been made of the signatures which, if I have
dated them correctly, are alone enough to prove that the
De expugnatione Lyxbonensi was contained in the present

[1] I have examined only the Gonville and Caius copy.

[2] *Ecloga Oxonio-Cantabrigiensis* (London, 1600), p. 74, No. 74.

[3] The account of the Lisbon crusade is mentioned in [William Stanley], *Catalogus
librorum MSS. in bibliotheca collegii Corporis Christi in Cantabrigia . . .* (London,
1722), No. G 13, and in all subsequent catalogues.

volume as early as the fifteenth century. Moreover, on the inside of the flyleaf at the beginning of the volume there is a brief table of contents written in a fine Italic hand, which evidently dates from Archbishop Parker's time and which reads as follows:

> *Kalendarium antiquissimum*
> *Hildebertus de missa in carmine*
> *Ipognosticon ad gervasium in carmine*
> *Historia osberni de expeditione etc.*[1]

And at the end of the volume there are two flyleaves which are described by Dr. M. R. James as follows: "Parts of two leaves of a XIIIth cent. logical (?) MS., with some scribbles: one of these might be in Bucer's hand, another of cent. XIII is: *Robertus surgito cras et ito ad officium.*"[2] Of the merit of Dr. James' suggestion as to Bucer's hand,[3] I am not competent to judge; but the "scribbles" in question are written in a quite recognizable free hand of the sixteenth century[4] and read as follows: "Require hic libellum de missa in carminibus elegiacis. Item expeditionem francorum et variarum nationum ad obsidionem ulyssipponis in portingale contra mauros." In view of these clear, early labels, both at the beginning and the end of the volume, and in view of the still earlier signatures, it may safely be concluded that, whatever the earlier history of the manuscript of the *De expugnatione Lyxbonensi*, it formed a part of the present volume No. 470 when it passed with the Parker bequest to the library of Corpus Christi College, Cambridge.

The folios (125r–146r) which contain the account of the Lisbon crusade are, as already indicated, of rather coarse and

[1] Underneath this is the pressmark of Parker's classification, "G' 13."

[2] *Descriptive Catalogue of the MSS. in the Library of Corpus Christi College, Cambridge*, No. 470 (p. 407).

[3] Martin Bucer arrived in England in April, 1549. He soon became Regius Professor of Divinity at Cambridge, where he died in February, 1551. He lived on terms of intimacy with Parker, who was then vice-chancellor of the university and who preached his funeral sermon.

[4] The hand can be matched with surprising closeness in an entry of 1547 in the Common Paper of the Scriveners' Company of London. See the facsimile in Hilary Jenkinson, *The Later Court Hands in England* (Cambridge, 1927), Plate XIII (i).

uneven vellum. They are sometimes, though not generally, ruled. The pages measure about 15 x 10.7 centimetres, and the space occupied by the writing varies between about 11 x 8.5 and about 12.5 x 9.5 centimetres. The number of lines to the page varies between twenty-five and thirty-four, twenty-seven and twenty-eight being the most usual numbers. The first gathering (125r–130v) contains six folios and is unruled. In the lower right-hand corners of 125r, 126r, and 127r there are signatures as follows: *L i, L ii, L iii*. The second gathering (131r–136v) also contains six folios and (with the exception of the two inner leaves as noted below) is unruled. In the lower right-hand corners of 131r, 132r, and 133r there are signatures as follows: *M i, M ii, M iii*. Folios 133 and 134 (that is, the two inside leaves of this gathering) are made up of two pieces of parchment, which are glued together in such a way that the inner edge of 134 appears between 132v and 133r, adhering to the inner margin of the latter, and the inner edge of 133 adheres to the inner margin of 134r. These two pieces of parchment are not of equal weight and fineness, 134 being much heavier than 133. Both are ruled vertically with a stylus, the lines of writing running directly across the ruling. The third gathering (137r–144v) contains eight folios, of which the following are lightly ruled with a plummet: 139v, 140r, 141v, 142r, 143v, and 144r. In the lower right-hand corners of 137r, 138r, 139r, and 140r there are signatures as follows: *N i, N ii, N iii, N iiii*. The fourth gathering (145r–149v) also once contained eight folios, of which the last three have been cut out. Of those which remain, the following have been lightly ruled with a plummet: 145r, 145v, 146r, 147r, 147v, 148r, 148v, and 149r. In the lower right-hand corners of 145r, 146r, and 147r (but not 148r) there are signatures as follows: *O i, O ii, O iii*. The *De expugnatione Lyxbonensi* ends, as has already been indicated, on folio 146r. Folio 146v is blank; folios 147r to the beginning of 149r are occupied by a sermon. On the rest of 149r there are notes from the *Pastoral Care* of Gregory the Great; 149v is blank.[1]

[1] Compare M. R. James, *Descriptive Catalogue*, II, 407.

Though the manuscript of the *De expugnatione Lyxbonensi* is clear and legible at almost every point and may with some indulgence be classed as calligraphic, it is written with a somewhat disconcerting irregularity. The difference in general appearance between one page and another is in some cases sufficient to raise a doubt whether it may not be the work of more than one hand, but long preoccupation with it has convinced me that this is really not the case.[1] A number of letters, notably *d*, *m*, *n*, *r*, *s*, *i*, and *u*, are freely written in two or more alternative forms, for the most part without any apparent system. Special attention may be directed to *i* and *u* as having some value for dating. Most commonly the ordinary form of *i* is used, and where a confusing series of minims come together, the *i*'s are likely to be distinguished by the addition of oblique hair-lines (í), as modern *i*'s are dotted. But the difficulty is almost as frequently met by the use of *i*-longa (*j*), and this is likely to be the case where two *i*'s come together, *i*-longa being used for the second member of the pair. The ordinary round-bottomed *u* is by far the more common, but a v-shaped form is frequently to be met with, particularly in the latter part of the manuscript. Abbreviations are both abundant and of striking variability. To cite an extreme example, while *autem* is ordinarily written *auť*, three other forms, namely, *á*, *aũ*, and *autẽ*, are to be met with on a single page.[2] A wholly consistent practice is not followed with respect to the abbreviation of such words as *qui*, *quem*, *quod*, and *quia*. The abbreviations of *item* and *iterum* are so variable and irregular as often to cause serious doubt as to which word was intended to be written. In general a distinction is maintained with respect to the value of a horizontal stroke (⁓) and a waved vertical

---

[1] There are two points, viz., fol. 128r, line 13, and 141r, line 24, at which there is the possibility of a change of hand on a single page. The second case is fully accounted for by the fact that the writer was obliged to write more compactly than usual in order to crowd the last five lines on to the page; cf. below, pp. 35–36. The other case is less clear, but I incline to the view that the changed appearance of the hand is due to nothing more than a different pen or some other alteration in the conditions under which the writer was working.

[2] Folio 125v.

stroke (ʼ) as marks of abbreviation, but the practice is far from consistent.

There is much punctuation by means of dots[1] and inverted semicolons (⸴); and the system is used with sufficient regularity to be of great assistance in reading, though not with enough consistency to be an entirely satisfactory guide in the preparation of the modern text. Sentences are often begun with capital letters, but the practice is by no means constant. Where a word is divided at the end of a line, an oblique hairline is usually added with the force of a modern hyphen, but this practice also is not invariable.

On palaeographical grounds the manuscript should, I believe, be assigned to the second half of the twelfth century, and more probably to the fourth quarter than to the third; but this is a point on which there is need to speak with caution, and the possibility that the manuscript is actually contemporary with the events which it records should perhaps be allowed, as should also the possibility that it belongs to the early years of the thirteenth century.[2] The abundance and character of the abbreviations as well as the frequent use of *i*-longa and of the v-shaped *u* would certainly seem to indicate a late rather than an early date. Examples of both *i*-longa and the v-shaped *u* can, of course, be found before the middle of the twelfth century; but I have observed no manuscript in which they occur with such frequency before a considerably later date.

Among the most remarkable features of this manuscript are the erasures, corrections, and marginalia. There are numerous blank spaces, sometimes extending to as much as two and one-half centimetres, where a text has obviously been

---

[1] Apparently no attempt is made to give any particular value to the position of the dot with respect to the line.

[2] According to the editor of the Lisbon Academy edition (*PMH, Scriptores*, I, 391)—doubtless reflecting the opinion of N. E. S. A. Hamilton of the Department of Manuscripts of the British Museum, who made the transcript from which the Lisbon edition was printed—the hand is of the thirteenth century rather than of the twelfth. Professor E. K. Rand of Harvard University, who has had the kindness to make a brief examination of a photostat for me, permits me to say that in his judgment the manuscript cannot be earlier than about 1175.

erased with a scraper. In some cases these erasures certainly seem to have been made as the manuscript was being written, and not afterwards by a corrector. Often the spaces appear to have been left blank for no other reason than that the parchment had been rendered rough and difficult to write upon as a result of the erasure.[1] Elsewhere erasures have been made and altered texts have been written over them, sometimes with the result that these texts have become almost illegible through the spreading of the ink on the injured parchment. In one case the altered text over an erasure extends to nine centimetres, or the equivalent of a full line.[2] Sometimes the corrections are of the simple kind which might well be the work of a corrector in an organized scriptorium,[3] though I incline to the view that they were more probably made by the writer of the manuscript himself; still other corrections seem to be quite obviously his work. For example, on folio 125r, line 8, overlooking the verb, he began to write *exercitus;* but noting his error after he had written *ex*, he made an erasure and then proceeded correctly with *secedit.* The erased letters *ex* are still faintly visible in the manuscript.[4] Still other corrections are incomplete and might well be the work of an author whose task has been left unfinished. Sometimes these involve no more than a change in the tense or mood of a verb;[5] but in other cases a word or more seems wanting to complete the

[1] For example, on fol. 132r, line 22, there is an erasure of 2.5 centimetres over which the attempt was made to write *consuetudinem;* but, the ink spreading badly, the attempt was abandoned after *co* had been written, and the word was begun anew on good parchment beyond the injured place. See below, p. 100, note c.

[2] Folio 134v, lines 8–9.

[3] For example, a syllable such as *pre*, which should normally be abbreviated, was sometimes inadvertently written *in extenso*, then partly erased and a mark of abbreviation substituted for the erased letters. The result is an unsightly gap in the middle of a word.

[4] See frontispiece, line 8. A similar case may be observed on the same page, line 28, where *detenti* was evidently erroneously written before *serenitate*, and then erased. Compare below, p. 54, note a, p. 58, note b.

[5] Examples may be noted on fol. 125r, lines 19 and 20 (see frontispiece). *Retineat* and *confiteantur* seem to have been written first; then the *a*'s were erased with a view to changing from the present to the imperfect subjunctive. In the second case the correction was completed; in the first it was not. Compare below, p. 56, notes c and d.

sense.[1] There are also numerous marginalia. Many of these consist of simple additions of one or more words and may well be due to the omissions of a careless copyist. But others look more like the work of an author. For example, at the beginning of the speech of Hervey de Glanvill there is a mutilated marginal note which seems to say that the text as given is not in Glanvill's exact words but contains the sense of what he said.[2] With this may perhaps be classed another mutilated marginalium which is evidently based on Solinus and which is concerned with the properties of the citron.[3]

William Stubbs was so impressed with the foregoing features of the manuscript that he boldly declared it to be "probably the original copy of the author,"[4] and this view was confirmed without question by Reinhold Pauli after an independent examination of the manuscript.[5] Nevertheless, I venture to believe that this hypothesis is untenable and that an adequate explanation of the characteristics referred to may be found in the supposition that the manuscript is simply the work of a careless or inexpert copyist. None of the erasures or corrections offers any serious obstacle to such a view. Where something is wanting to complete the sense, it may well be that the copyist was unable fully to read the text which he was following. And as for the more extended marginalia which appear as notes to the text rather than as integral parts of it, it seems not unlikely that, originally added as such by the author, they were simply reproduced by the copyist in the form in which he found them.

[1] Attention has been drawn to all such cases in footnotes to the text.

[2] Folio 132v, lines 17–21; cf. below, p. 104, note b.

[3] Folio 131r, lines 12–20; cf. below, p. 92, note e. Another extended marginal note (fol. 129v, lines 10–14; cf. below, p. 84, note c) consists of the beginning of a text of Scripture the end of which had already been written in the manuscript. But here, it must be noted, we have to do with a sermon which, if genuine and not a rhetorical composition of the author, was being copied in any case; and it seems not unlikely that a whole line of the text had inadvertently been omitted and then crowded into the margin with heavy abbreviation.

[4] In the introductory note to his edition of the text, published in 1864. *Itinerarium*, p. cxlii.

[5] *MGH, Scriptores*, XXVII, 6: "autographo cantabrigiensi a. 1880 denuo a me ipso inspecto."

Moreover, quite apart from palaeographical considerations which indicate a date somewhat later than the middle of the twelfth century, the mere external appearance of the manuscript seems irreconcilable with the view that it is the original of a crusading news letter sent home in mid-campaign. On the contrary, it looks like a small volume, a *libellus*, designed to be a permanent record. It is written in a small, compact book hand, and, while it has no great beauty, it is not without adornment. It begins with a large, illuminated red capital *O* (a good one and one-half centimetres in diameter), and four other majuscule letters which stand in the first line, though written in black, are illuminated with patches of red.[1] There is no other use of decorative color in the manuscript; but the separate sections of the text, and particularly the sermons, speeches, and letters, are for the most part introduced with special large capitals (sometimes extending to two lines in height) which were inserted after the ordinary text had been completed. That these special capitals were later additions is proved by the fact that in a number of cases they are wanting, the spaces which were left for them never having been filled.[2]

Moreover, certain features of the manuscript can hardly be explained except upon the theory that it is a copy. Indeed, it looks like a page-for-page copy of an earlier text, for the pages seem not to be allowed to end haphazard at the point which the scribe had reached at the end of his last line. On a number of pages there are additions, varying in length from a part of a word to as much as half a line, suspended by a bracket beneath the latter part of the last line.[3] Evidently the object was to complete the copying of one page of the model before turning to the next page of the copy. A similar purpose

---

[1] Compare frontispiece. The initial *O* is entirely in red. *SB, R*, and *Q* were doubtless originally all colored red within the bows, though the color is no longer visible in the upper halves of *SB*.

[2] Compare below, pp. 70, 90, 96, 114, 120.

[3] Such additions appear on fol. 128r, 131r, 132v, 134v, 135r, 135v, 137r, 138v, 139r, 140r, 142v, 143r. Where the addition consists of a single word, one would at first glance suppose it to be a catchword.

appears sometimes to have been accomplished by mere compression, as may be noted at the bottom of folio 141r. The scribe had evidently been writing with somewhat extravagant disregard for space until he reached the end of the text of a sermon, whereupon he found it necessary so to compress the last five lines of his page as to make them appear almost as if they had been written by another hand.[1] Other indications that the writer was copying are to be seen in some of the erasures and corrections which have already been noted, where it seems evident that his eye had got ahead of his pen and caused him to write words out of their proper order.[2] More striking still is a correction which occurs on folio 145v, lines 24–26. Overlooking the words *donis quosdam reficiens, alios flagellis erudiens*, he wrote the whole of the next sentence. Then, realizing his error, he obviated the difficulty by adding the omitted words at the point which he had then reached and indicating their correct position in the text by inserting a superscribed *.a.* before *donis* and a superscribed *.b.* at the beginning of the previous sentence.[3]

In view of all the foregoing considerations, it seems necessary to conclude that the existing manuscript of the *De expugnatione Lyxbonensi* is almost certainly not the original of a news letter written from Lisbon at the time of the siege, but a copy made at some later date with a view to preserving a permanent record. But if this be the case, where and under what circumstances was the text produced of which it is a copy? And is the text as it exists today substantially in the form in which it was originally written, or has it been subjected to a later revision?[4]

[1] Compare above, p. 31, note 1. There are other places where one, two, or even three lines at the end of a page seem to be somewhat shortened, as if there were space to spare; but these features are far less striking than the cases of addition or compression.

[2] See above, p. 33 and note 4.

[3] Compare below, p. 182, note b.

[4] At one time I so far yielded to the view of Stubbs and Pauli as to think that the existing manuscript might well be the autograph of a revision made by the author himself at some time after his return to England. This view no longer seems to me possible. Compare *Speculum*, VII (1932), 50, note 3. For another possibility see below, p. 40, note 1.

It is not altogether easy to believe that the account of the Lisbon crusade in the form in which it now exists can be that which was actually written from the very scene of action, under the stress and strain of almost daily conflict. No other letter of a crusader which has survived to modern times is to be compared with it for length and elaboration. The epistolary form with which it begins—address, superscription, salutation—is not consistently maintained to the end. After the opening sentences the work has more of the character of an historical memoir than of a letter; and it ends, not with a formal epistolary *Vale*, but with an elaborate hortatory passage strongly resembling the conclusion of a sermon. Moreover, it contains a number of speeches and sermons. Some of these may have been copied from manuscripts supplied the author by those who delivered them. Such may well have been the case with the sermon of Peter, bishop of Oporto, which was preached before the crusaders assembled in his cathedral churchyard and was translated by interpreters into the vernacular languages so that all could understand.[1] It differs markedly in style and literary background from the other sermon which was delivered by a certain priest on the occasion of the dedication of a siege-tower at Lisbon.[2] But other speeches, such as the brief address of King Affonso Henriques to the crusaders upon their arrival at Lisbon, the speeches of the archbishop of Braga and the bishop of Oporto to the Moors, and the reply of the Moorish elder[3] seem much more likely, in their present form, to have been the compositions of the author himself. Indeed, in the case of the impassioned appeal of Hervey de Glanvill,[4] when he was trying to prevent the defection of a part of the Anglo-Norman forces, a mutilated marginal note, which has already been referred to,[5] seems to warn the reader that he has to do, not with a genuine speech, but with the author's invention. Such dis-

---

[1] See below, pp. 70–85.

[2] See below, pp. 146–59. It has been conjectured by Reinhold Pauli that the priest in question was the author of the *De expugnatione Lyxbonensi* himself. Below, p. 146, note 3.

[3] See below, pp. 98–101, 114–25.

[4] See below, pp. 104–11.

[5] See above, p. 34 and note 2.

courses, it may well be argued, would require time and leisure for their composition, such as it would have been difficult to find at Lisbon during the siege, and they seem a little out of place in an ordinary news letter. A similar observation may be made with respect to certain rhetorical passages in the narrative itself, such as the description of the battle of the clouds above the crags of Cintra, which was observed as a good omen as the crusading fleet entered the mouth of the Tagus,[1] or the concluding paragraph of the work, with its numerous quotations from Scripture.[2] Finally, in the geographical passages the author quotes repeatedly from Solinus, and it may well be questioned whether he had a copy of the work of this ancient author in his military baggage.[3]

Such facts as these must surely suggest the possibility of leisurely composition in the first instance or else of a later revision, but on the other hand there are strong indications that the work in its present form must be very nearly contemporary with the events which it records. Not only has the narrative all the vividness and freshness of an account emanating from the very scene of action, but it maintains consistently the point of view of a participant in the crusade addressing himself to a correspondent back at home—a point of view which might easily be lost in the event of a later revision. There are certain expressions which are particularly noteworthy in this connection. In speaking of the fish in the Tagus River, the author says that they retain their richness and natural flavor at all seasons of the year and do not change or deteriorate "as is the case with you" (*ut apud vos est*).[4] And in recording a portent which transpired among the Flemings at Lisbon when, after the completion of the mass, the

---

[1] See below, pp. 88–91.

[2] See below, pp. 182–85.

[3] The passages have all been cited in footnotes to the text.

[4] See below, pp. 90, 91. It should be noted that both Stubbs (*Itinerarium*, p. cliv) and Hamilton (*PMH, Scriptores*, p. 395) read *nos* instead of *vos* in this phrase. It is, of course, often difficult to distinguish between *n* and *u* in mediaeval manuscripts, but that difficulty is not often encountered in the present manuscript, and in this case the reading seems perfectly clear.

blessed bread (*panis benedictus*) was observed to be bloody, he says, "and it has now been seen for many days after the capture of the city" (*et iam post urbis captionem multis diebus visus est*).[1] Finally, perhaps most significant of all is the fact that the latest date mentioned in the narrative is 1 November, 1147,[2] and that it appears to contain no trace of a knowledge of anything which happened after that date. Such consistency seems almost to preclude the possibility of any extensive revision after the author had left Lisbon; but on the other hand, all the characteristics of our narrative seem to find a natural explanation if we suppose that the author spent the winter of 1147–48 in Lisbon and occupied himself with its leisurely composition during that interval, before continuing on his voyage to Jerusalem. And there is good reason for supposing that he did spend the winter in Lisbon. We know that he was there until after All Saints Day;[3] and in the passage above mentioned concerning the portent of the consecrated bread which had a bloody appearance, his words carry the clear implication that he was still in Lisbon many days after the capture of the city which took place on 24 October.[4] Under the conditions of twelfth-century navigation it seems highly unlikely that it would have been practical for him to depart, after so late a date as is here indicated, before the following spring. Moreover, the priest Duodechin of Lahnstein, in speaking of the German contingent, says specifically that they passed the winter at Lisbon until 1 February, and then proceeded on their way to the Sepulchre.[5] It seems not unlikely, therefore, that the *De expugnatione Lyxbonensi* was

---

[1] See below, pp. 134, 135.

[2] The purification of the cathedral and the restoration of the episcopal see of Lisbon on All Saints Day. See below, pp. 180, 181.

[3] Compare note 2 above.

[4] Compare note 1 above.

[5] See below, p. 181, note 1. The author of the *De expugnatione Lyxbonensi* himself says that after the siege had been going on for six weeks (i.e., in about the second week of August), the Anglo-Norman forces drew up their ships on dry land, lowered the masts, and put the cordage under the hatches as a sign that they were spending the winter. This seems to be represented as a *ruse de guerre*; but it may well have been more than that. See below, pp. 136, 137.

composed in Lisbon during the winter of 1147–48 in substantially its present form. The author doubtless had free access to the documents which he quotes, and in some way, we know not how, he had access to the *Collectanea rerum memorabilium* of Solinus. And he had time to perform his task with care and deliberation.[1]

The surviving manuscript is doubtless not free from some copyist's errors; but there seems no good reason to suppose that it does not reproduce with reasonable fidelity the original text of the author.

THE AUTHOR [2]

Concerning the author of the *De expugnatione Lyxbonensi* unfortunately nothing is known beyond what can be inferred from the work itself.* That he was an active participant in the crusade is perfectly apparent. That he was of Norman rather than of English descent has been argued by Ulrich Cosack[3] from the fact that he tends in his narrative to give precedence to the Normans over the English, and by Reinhold Pauli from the fact that he occasionally makes use of a French word, as, for example, *garciones*.[4] A more careful examination of his work seems to justify the conjecture that he was a priest of the virile fighting type that was likely to be attracted by crusading enterprises, that he traveled with the Anglo-Norman contingent from East Anglia, being particularly interested in the deeds of the men of Suffolk, and that he was closely associated with Hervey de Glanvill, principal leader of the Anglo-Norman forces.[5]

---

[1] On such a hypothesis it is conceivable that the existing manuscript is the author's autograph, as Stubbs has said, but for the reasons which have been set forth above this seems to me very unlikely.

[2] Some parts of the following paragraphs have, with the permission of the editors, been reproduced, in greatly revised form, from what I have already written in *Speculum*, VII (1932), 50–57.

[*Since the date of David's Introduction (1936) new views of the author of *De expugnatione Lyxbonensi* have been developed. See pp. 00–00 of the new foreword by Jonathan Phillips.—Ed.]

[3] *Die Eroberung von Lissabon im Jahre 1147* (Halle, 1875: dissertation), p. 7.

[4] *MGH, Scriptores*, XXVII, 5, note 2. But he also uses the Anglo-Saxon *worma*. See below, pp. 66–67, note 2.

[5] Perhaps he served Glanvill as chaplain, though specific evidence on this point is lacking.

The language which he uses throughout his work, and particularly in the passages where he pauses for reflection; his
interest in religious or ecclesiastical events, in churches, relics,
miracles, and sermons; his frequent quotation from the Scrip-
tures all reveal unmistakably the attitude of a priest, though
not of a fanatical or narrow-minded one.[1] The conjecture of
Pauli[2] that he was the "certain priest" who, holding a piece
of the true cross in his hands, preached the sermon on the
occasion of the dedication of an Anglo-Norman siege-tower
at Lisbon appears to be entirely consistent with known facts
and seems to me very probable; though it is difficult to adduce
any positive evidence in its support.[3]

As to his fighting qualities, from the animation of his narrative and the abundance of details which he records, it is difficult to escape the conviction that he took part personally in
the unpremeditated attack of the rank and file of the Anglo-
Normans which resulted in the capture of the western suburb
of Lisbon, and in the heroic struggle by which the Anglo-
Norman siege-tower was successfully defended while it was
being moved up against the wall of the city for the final attack.[4]
His interest in the brave deeds of the men of Suffolk is revealed in his account of the seven youths of Ipswich who defended the siege-tower under the shelter of a "Welsh cat."[5]

---

[1] See below, pp. 60–65, 94–97, 132–35, 146, 147, 166, 167, 174, 175, 182–85.

[2] *MGH, Scriptores,* XXVII, 5, note 3.

[3] Below, p. 146: ". . . sacerdos quidam, sacrosanctam ligni dominici tenens in manibus
particulam, sermonem huiusmodi habuit." I have pointed out in *Speculum,* VII (1932),
52, that the appearance of the sermon in the manuscript (the care with which it is
written, the special capitals with which it is adorned, etc.) may suggest the conscious
pride of the author of an address delivered on an important public occasion, but if, as I
now believe (see above, pp. 34–40), the manuscript is not an autograph, this argument
is without validity—except on the weak assumption that, for an unknown reason, the
copyist was slavishly following the original.

[4] Below, pp. 124–29, 158–65. If it is true, as has been conjectured, that he was the
preacher of the sermon at the dedication of the tower, then the following passage, as
being in his own words, is worthy of especial note: "Ego vero ipse, fratres, in tribulationibus et laboribus vestris particeps premiorumque vestrorum socius sicut vobis
spondeo mihi fieri opto. Deo opitulante in hac machina, huius ligni sacrosancti custos
et comes inseparabilis, vita comite vobiscum manebo." Below, p. 156.

[5] Below, pp. 160, 161.

His interest in Hervey de Glanvill and his close association
with him receive repeated illustration. In the catalogue of the
forces with which he begins his narrative he names him first,
as commander of the ships of Norfolk and Suffolk, among the
four constables (*constabularii*) who were the leaders of the
Anglo-Norman contingents.[1] On a critical day in the negotiations between the crusaders and King Affonso Henriques of
Portugal, when a powerful minority of "about eight ship-
loads of Normans and men from Southampton and Bristol,"
under the leadership of one William Viel, declared their opposition to stopping at Lisbon and their determination to push
onward and practice piracy on "the merchant vessels of Africa
and Spain," their defection was only prevented, according to
the author, by an impassioned appeal from Hervey de Glanvill,
and he reproduces the speech with evident pride and admira-
tion.[2] Again, his language leaves no doubt that after the first
brush with the enemy upon the arrival of the fleet in the Tagus
before Lisbon, he was one of the little band of thirty-nine, who,
with Hervey de Glanvill and Saher of Archelle, lay out on
guard all night in a particularly exposed and dangerous position when there had not yet been time to establish a defensible
camp.[3] And this same close association seems once more to be
revealed in his account of the unpremeditated attack of the
Anglo-Normans upon the western suburb of Lisbon, which
has already been referred to; for in recording the decision of
Saher of Archelle to continue the attack, since a withdrawal
was impractical, he says that he took what men he could get
"from our tent and from his own" (*ex nostro tentorio vel ex suo
proprio*). Hervey de Glanvill happened not to be present on
this occasion, but there can be little doubt that by "our tent"
the author means the Glanvill tent.[4] Perhaps even more in-
structive is the situation revealed when the Moors in Lisbon

---

[1] Below, pp. 54–55.   [2] Below, pp. 104–11.   [3] Below, pp. 96, 97.

[4] Below, pp. 126–27. The full significance of the passage here cited only becomes
clear when it is compared with the passage cited in note 3 above. It is manifest that
the author was a tent companion of Hervey de Glanvill at Lisbon. Pauli, in *MGH,
Scriptores*, XXVII, 5, note 1, was the first to draw attention to these two significant
passages.

had been brought to the point of surrendering the city and a brief truce had been arranged. Five hostages were received from the Moors by Hervey de Glanvill on behalf of the Anglo-Norman forces and by Fernando Captivo on behalf of King Affonso, and by them they were in due course handed over to the king. This action caused grave dissatisfaction to spread among the Anglo-Normans, where the king was distrusted and where it was felt that the hostages ought not to have been delivered into his hands; and at the instigation of a renegade priest of Bristol a mutiny was started among the lower ranks which was directed against Hervey de Glanvill. Our author defends Glanvill with eloquence and animation; and from his language it transpires that he himself was present with Glanvill in the king's camp when emissaries were dispatched to calm the mutineers.[1]

Such, with one exception, are the facts concerning the author which emerge from a careful examination of his work. That exception must now be considered. The opening words of the *De expugnatione Lyxbonensi* as they stand in the manuscript are as follows: *OSB̆. de baldr̄. R̆ sal̄.*[2] It is obvious that we have here the initial formula of a letter which contains the names of the author and his correspondent followed by the word *salutem*. But how shall the abbreviations of the names be extended, and which name is that of the writer and which that of the addressee? Shall *OSB̆.* be extended as *Osbertus* or *Osbernus* to designate the writer, or shall it be extended as *Osberto* or *Osberno* to designate the addressee? And shall *R̆* be extended in the nominative case as *Radulfus*—or some other name beginning with *R*—to designate the author, or shall it be extended in the dative case to designate the addressee? Unfortunately it is impossible to decide.

Since the sixteenth century the author has been known as

[1] Below, pp. 168, 170: "De quibus amplius quadrigentis ex castris proruentes circumquaque armati perscrutantur, licet eum absentem noverint, voce magna clamantes, 'Tollatur impius, puniatur proditor.' Hoc itaque comperto, cum castris interessemus regis, a quibusdam senioribus nostrorum obviam itum est compescendum eorum vehementie initia."

[2] See frontispiece, line 1, and cf. p. 52, below.

Osbern, for, as has already been pointed out, his name so appears in a brief table of contents, evidently dating from Archbishop Parker's time, which is written inside the flyleaf at the beginning of the manuscript volume in which his work is contained;[1] and this name has been repeated in three successive catalogues of the manuscripts of Corpus Christi College, Cambridge,[2] as well as in Cooper's account of the Public Records,[3] and so has become traditional. But since there is nothing to show that the traditional rendering is older than the sixteenth century, it is evident that it is worthy of little respect.

Reasoning from his obvious close connection with Hervey de Glanvill, the present editor once believed that he had found ground for identifying the author with Osbert, clerk of Bawdsey[4] (*Osbertus clericus de Baldreseia*) who, along with three members of the Glanvill family (Osbert, Gerard, and Hervey), attested a charter of Ranulf de Glanvill, the famous chief justiciar of England, in 1171.[5] But critics have shown the weakness of this hypothesis,[6] and it now seems on the whole more likely that, if *OSB. de baldr.* is to be identified with Osbert, clerk of Bawdsey (which is not certain),[7] he was the addressee rather than the writer of the *De expugnatione Lyxbonensi*. It was a rule of mediaeval epistolography that a writer should place his correspondent's name before his own, unless he were addressing a subordinate.[8] In the present case,

---

[1] See above, p. 29.

[2] [Willam Stanley], *Catalogus librorum MSS. in bibliotheca collegii Corporis Christi in Cantabrigia* . . . (London, 1722), No. G 13; James Nasmith, *Catalogus librorum MSS. quos collegio Corporis Christi . . . in Acad. Cantabrig. legavit . . . M. Parker* (Cambridge, 1777), No. 470; M. R. James, *Descriptive Catalogue of the Manuscripts in the Library of Corpus Christi College, Cambridge*, No. 470.

[3] C. P. Cooper, *An Account of the Most Important Public Records of Great Britain* . . . (London, 1832), II, 166.

[4] A village near the southeast coast of Suffolk at the mouth of the River Deben.

[5] *Speculum*, VII (1932), 54–57. The witness list of the Glanvill charter is printed *ibid.*, p. 56, note 2.

[6] C. R. Cheney and J. C. Russell, *ibid.*, pp. 395–97.   [7] *Ibid.*

[8] See, e.g., Alberic of Monte Cassino, in L. Rockinger, *Briefsteller und Formelbücher* (*Quellen und Erörterungen zur bayerischen und deutschen Geschichte*, IX, Munich, 1864), pp. 11, 12.

since the writer was obviously not a person of exalted rank in either church or state, there is no apparent reason for supposing that he was writing to a subordinate. On the contrary, it seems more likely that he would have been addressing some patron who stood above him, or perhaps more likely still (since there is no ground for supposing his correspondent to have been a great person) that he would have been addressing some friend upon terms of equality. Moreover, attention has been drawn to the remarkable contrast between the mere initial $\overset{\text{'}}{R}$, which stands for one name, and the much less drastically abbreviated *OSB. de baldr.*, which stands for the other; and it has been argued that a mediaeval letter-writer would be unlikely to designate his correspondent with a single letter while writing his own name so nearly in full.[1]

It is to be hoped that someone more fortunate than the present editor will light upon some clue or clues which will lead to a solution of these difficult problems. But for the present there appears to be no choice but to leave the author in a kind of perplexing half-world, neither known nor yet wholly anonymous. He is none the less a singularly appealing figure. His Latin style is undoubtedly against him, and his range of reading, so far as can be seen from his work, may hardly have extended beyond the Bible and Solinus; and of the latter he made a not very intelligent use. But his deficiency in book lore finds some compensation in his zest of life and in an interest in experience which extended to details. Surely no more eager or enthusiastic traveler ever journeyed abroad. He was an absorbed observer of the lands which he visited and of the peoples with whom he came in contact, of topography and climate, of soil and its products, of strange habits and customs. His sturdy moral principles and his fair but insular outlook on the continental world were of a quality which may still to this day be properly called English. He was critical of the Germans and Flemings, whose conduct hardly squared with his standards, but he was willing to give them their due; and he did not spare English or Normans when he thought

[1] *Speculum*, VII (1932), 395.

them in the wrong. He was thoroughly loyal to his own cause and his own religion, but he was not fanatical or cruel. He was interested in the religion as well as in the customs of the enemy; and he was moved with sympathy for their sufferings in defeat, though he acknowledged that the ways of God must remain inscrutable. He came far closer than most writers of his epoch to seeing a crusade as it really was.

THE TEXT

In preparing the *De expugnatione Lyxbonensi* for publication the editor has been guided by the belief that mediaeval texts lose much of their value through standardization. But since he hopes that the present text may prove to be of sufficient interest to attract some readers who are not specialists, he has thought it wise to follow a rule of moderation and not place unnecessary difficulties in their way. Specifically this means that the following practices have been adopted:

In the matter of capitalization and punctuation the editor has used discretion, endeavoring to approach an acceptable modern standard without departing any further than seemed necessary from the practice of the manuscript. Since the author's frequent use of fragmentary sentences, divided by full stops, usually causes no serious difficulty, they have generally been allowed to stand unconnected in the printed text. With respect to paragraphing, a few broad divisions are indicated in the manuscript, but they are quite inadequate to the demands of modern taste and convenience. The present division into paragraphs is, therefore, almost entirely the work of the editor. In the spelling of proper names the manuscript has been followed exactly. Apart from proper names the spellings of the manuscript have also been respected, except where the departure from standardized forms seemed so extreme as to give offense or cause difficulties. In such cases the spelling has been regularized in the printed text, and the manuscript reading has been given in a footnote. Thus, for example, *neggligens, supliciter, imfra,* and *columpnia* have been allowed to stand, while *epdomada* (*hebdomada*), *cachymno* (*cachinno*),

reumata (*rheumata*), and *tysis* (*phthisis*) have been standard-ized. Inevitably this has involved the exercise of much dis-cretion; many will doubtless often disagree with the editor's decisions and think them arbitrary (which is acknowledged), but since the true reading of the manuscript will always be at hand, no serious difficulty can arise.[1]

Some peculiar difficulties have arisen in connection with the extension of abbreviations. As a rule there are no diffi-culties, and the editor has taken full responsibility for the extensions; but in a few cases, where there is a reasonable doubt, he has used italics to extend the abbreviations in the form which seemed to him most probably correct. In many cases abbreviations have been extended in spellings which are at variance with classical standards. Here the constant endeavor has been to conform to the spelling of the writer of the manuscript. Thus the preposition *apud*, which is regularly abbreviated by suspension, has invariably been extended as *aput*, since this is proved to be the writer's spelling by a number of examples in which he has written the word in full.

The diphthong *ae* requires special consideration. Apart from three exceptions[2] which may be said to prove the rule, this diphthong is not used in the manuscript. As a rule its place is taken by a simple *e*; but the use of *e*-cedilla (*ę*) is not uncommon. Care has been taken to print *e*-cedilla in the text wherever it occurs in the manuscript; but in the very numerous cases where the manuscript gives only a mark of abbreviation, this has been extended as a simple *e*, in accord with the writer's most usual practice.[3]

[1] Occasional obvious slips of grammar, or in the use of a word, have also been cor-rected and the manuscript reading has been relegated to a footnote, but this practice has been followed sparingly.

[2] *Coniuratae* (fol. 144v, line 22); *lactaentium*, for *lactentium* (fol. 127r, line 12); *uni-vaersitatem*, for *universitatem* (fol. 132v, line 24).

[3] The practice I have adopted in printing *v* to represent consonantal *u* will give offense to some, since it is not in accord with mediaeval usage; but it is a convenience to the modern eye, and it is tolerated by high authority. See H. Maxwell Lyte, "'U' and 'V,' a Note on Palaeography," in Institute of Historical Research, *Bulletin*, Vol. II, No. 6 (1925), pp. 63–65.

The *De expugnatione Lyxbonensi* was first published in 1861 by the Lisbon Academy of Sciences in *PMH, Scriptores*, I, 391–405. This edition was printed from a transcript made by N. E. S. A. Hamilton of the Department of Manuscripts of the British Museum, a number of whose observations on the text were preserved in footnotes marked with the letter *H*. Editorial supervision was undoubtedly by Alexandre Herculano, though his name does not appear in connection with the edition. His comments are often acute and helpful, but no attempt is made to solve most of the editorial problems.

The work was again published in 1864, apparently without knowledge of previous publication, under the editorship of William Stubbs in the introduction (pp. cxlii–clxxxii) to his *Itinerarium peregrinorum et gesta regis Ricardi*, in *Chronicles and Memorials of the Reign of Richard I* (London, 1864–65). The text of Stubbs is usually, though by no means always, preferable to that of Hamilton, but it is still far from satisfactory. The treatment of editorial problems is also less unsatisfactory than in the earlier edition, but is still very inadequate. It seems fair to the memory of Stubbs to say that he evidently regarded the printing of this text as but incidental to more important undertakings, and that he cannot have given it his best attention.

Extracts from the *De expugnatione Lyxbonensi*, edited by Reinhold Pauli, were published in 1885, in *MGH, Scriptores*, XXVII, 5–10. Pauli's text is based on that of Stubbs, but with corrections from the manuscript, of which he had made an independent examination. His editorial comments are slight, but, so far as they go, helpful.

After the *De expugnatione Lyxbonensi*, which stands in a class by itself, the fullest and most satisfactory contemporary

---

[1] For the fullest discussions of the sources for the Lisbon crusade see Alexandre Herculano, *Historia de Portugal* (8th ed., by David Lopes and Pedro de Azevedo, Paris and Lisbon, n.d.), III, 307–10, and Ulrich Cosack, *Die Eroberung von Lissabon im Jahre 1147*

account of the Lisbon crusade of 1147 is contained in three other letters of participants, as follows: (1) *Ein Brief des kölnischen Priesters Winand über den Kreuzzug gegen Lissabon im Jahre 1147*, edited by Ernst Dümmler [Vienna, 1851: privately printed]; (2) a letter of Duodechin, priest of Lahnstein, to Cuno, abbot of Disibodenberg (near Mainz), in *Annales sancti Disibodi*, edited by Georg Waitz (*MGH, Scriptores*, XVII, 27–28); (3) a letter of Arnulf, presumably a Flemish priest, to Milo, bishop of Thérouanne, in *HF*, XIV, 325–27 (also in E. Martène and U. Durand, *Veterum scriptorum . . . amplissima collectio*, Paris, 1724–33, II, 800–802, and in *PMH, Scriptores*, I, 406–407). But apart from their opening formulae, these three letters are so nearly identical that it is evident that in reality they constitute but a single source.[1] For convenience I have referred to it throughout the present work as the "Teutonic Source," meaning thereby to emphasize the fact that it reflects the viewpoint of the German and Flemish elements, as the Anglo-Norman point of view is reflected in the *De expugnatione Lyxbonensi*. Though the two authorities are in remarkably close agreement on most of the points which both treat, I have found no reason to suppose that they are not entirely independent of one another.[2]

There are only two sources of any importance emanating

(Halle, 1875: dissertation), pp. 3–14. Compare Reinhold Röhricht, *Beiträge zur Geschichte der Kreuzzüge* (Berlin, 1874–78), II, 104. The discussion of the sources which was announced by Friedrich Kurth for publication in 1909 in *Neues Archiv der Gesellschaft für ältere deutsche Geschichtskunde* seems never to have appeared. Friedrich Kurth, *Der Anteil niederdeutscher Kreuzfahrer an den Kämpfen der Portugiesen gegen die Mauren*, in Institut für österreichische Geschichtsforschung, *Mitteilungen*, Ergänzungsband VIII (1909), 133, note 4.

[1] The conjecture of Friedrich Wilken (*Die Geschichte der Kreuzzüge*, Leipzig, 1807–32, III, Pt. 1, p. 264, note 1), made more than a century ago, that a single account was composed by one of the crusaders, and then appropriated by several of his fellows who sent it home as their own with but slight alterations and additions, seems plausible. It is approved by Cosack, *Eroberung von Lissabon*, pp. 3–6; cf. W. Wattenbach, *Deutschlands Geschichtsquellen* (6th ed., Berlin, 1893–94), II, 433, note 2.

[2] According to Wattenbach, *loc. cit.*, it has been argued by Widmann ("Dudechin von Lahnstein," in *Rhenus: Zeitschrift für Geschichte der Mittelrheins*, I, 1883, Nos. 9, 10) that the *De expugnatione Lyxbonensi* was a source of Duodechin's work. It has proved impossible to consult a file of *Rhenus* in this country.

from Portugal, viz., the *Indiculum fundationis monasterii beati Vincentii Ulixbone* (*PMH*, *Scriptores*, I, 91–93) and the *Chronica Gothorum* (*ibid.*, 8–17). The former, which is by far the more important, is a foundation history, apparently dating from 1188, of the monastery of St. Vincent de Fora at Lisbon, which was founded by King Affonso Henriques in 1148 to commemorate the great victory over the Moors.

Brief but significant contemporary notices are to be found in the chronicles of Henry of Huntingdon (*Historia Anglorum*, ed. Thomas Arnold, London, 1879, p. 281) and of Helmold (*Cronica Slavorum*, 2d ed., B. Schmeidler, Hanover and Leipzig, 1909: *Scriptores rerum Germanicarum in usum scholarum*, pp. 117–18).

Outside of Portugal the Lisbon crusade has attracted far less attention in modern times than its interest and importance would seem to warrant. I have noted only one English historian of the epoch who has devoted to it as much as two pages.[1] The following works in German[2] are worthy of mention: Ulrich Cosack, *Die Eroberung von Lissabon im Jahre 1147* (Halle, 1875: dissertation); Reinhold Röhricht, *Beiträge zur Geschichte der Kreuzzüge* (Berlin, 1874–78), II, 79–92; Wilhelm Bernhardi, *Konrad III* (Leipzig, 1883), pp. 579–90; Friedrich Kurth, *Der Anteil niederdeutscher Kreuzfahrer an den Kämpfen der Portugiesen gegen die Mauren*, in Institut für österreichische Geschichtsforschung, *Mitteilungen*, Ergänzungsband VIII (1909), 133–59 (also independently as a doctoral dissertation, Innsbruck, 1909). Of the four, that of Kurth is the fullest account of the whole movement; but that of Cosack is the most detailed and critically helpful for the part with which it deals. Unfortunately it is incomplete, stopping short about the middle of July when the siege of Lisbon had barely got under way. The brief sketch of Röhricht is the most readable; and while it is not free from errors, it is for the most part based closely on the sources.

[1] Kate Norgate, *England under the Angevin Kings* (London, 1887), I, 361–63.

[2] Wilken's account (*Geschichte der Kreuzzüge*, III, Pt. 1, pp. 264–69) was written without knowledge of the *De expugnatione Lyxbonensi* and is therefore of but slight value.

The conquest of Lisbon has naturally attracted much attention from Portuguese historians, and to this day perhaps the most satisfactory modern account, though it was written before any of the German works above mentioned, is that by Alexandre Herculano in his *Historia de Portugal* (1846–53, 8th definitive ed. by D. Lopes and P. de Azevedo, Paris and Lisbon, n.d.), III, 7–52. The most extensive work so far devoted to the Lisbon crusade is that of Julio de Castilho, a disciple of Herculano, who has given it a whole volume in his elaborate *Lisboa antiga*, Pt. 2, Vol. II (Coimbra, 1884); but this work is prolix and sadly lacking in the critical rigor and in the insight of the author's master.

Of outstanding importance for the mediaeval topography and fortifications of Lisbon are Augusto Vieira da Silva's *O Castello de S. Jorge: Estudo historico-descriptivo* (Lisbon, 1898) and the same author's *A Cerca moura de Lisboa: Estudo historico-descriptivo* (Lisbon, 1899).[1] These are the work of a military engineer, and are based on archaeological research and accompanied by careful maps and plans. The student of the siege of 1147 will also profit from the use of both the descriptive matter and the maps in the first volume of the elaborate *Guia de Portugal*, which is being published under the auspices of the Biblioteca Nacional of Lisbon (Lisbon, 1924–   ).

[1] Both are off-prints from the *Revista de engenheria militar*.

De expugnatione Lyxbonensi[1]

OSB*ERTO* de Baldr*eseia* R.,[2] salutem.

Qualiter circa nos habeatur magni fore voti aput vos scitu pro certo credimus, idemque de vobis aput nos agi nulla dubitatione teneamini. Itineris ergo nostri vel prospera vel adversa vel que interim facta vel dicta vel visa vel audita, relatu digna fuerint quecumque scripto manifestabimus.

Igitur aput portum de Dertemuðe[3] diversarum nationum et morum et linguarum gentes navibus circiter C. LXIIII.[4] convenere. Horum omnium trifariam partitur exercitus. Sub comite Arnoldo de Aerescot, nepote Godefridi ducis,[5] a Ro-

---

[1] The work is without title in the manuscript. To avoid bibliographical confusion I have retained the title which was ascribed to it in the edition of William Stubbs (see above, p. 48) and which approximates closely to the titles adopted by other editors and cited in the well-known bibliographies of August Potthast and Auguste Molinier.

[2] On the author and his correspondent, see above, pp. 40–46.

[3] Dartmouth, in Devonshire, 27 miles east of Plymouth, long remained a favorite port of departure for crusades and pilgrimages to Spain, Portugal, and the East. It so served for a squadron which came from beyond the North Sea in 1189, *De itinere navali, de eventibus deque rebus a peregrinis Hierosolymam petientibus MCLXXXIX fortiter gestis narratio*, ed. Costanzo Gazzera, in R. Accademia delle scienze di Torino, *Memorie*, 2d ser., II (1840), *Scienze morali, storiche e filologiche*, p. 192; also for the expedition of Counts George of Wied and William of Holland in 1217, *Quinti belli sacri scriptores minores* (ed. Reinhold Röhricht, Geneva, 1879), pp. 29, 59. It was still in use for the maritime pilgrimage to Santiago de Compostela in the middle of the fifteenth century, C. L. Kingsford, *Prejudice and Promise in XVth Century England* (Oxford, 1925), p. 90.

[4] The "Teutonic Source" (see above, pp. 48–49) gives the number of ships at Dartmouth as "almost two hundred," *Ein Brief des kölnischen Priesters Winand über den Kreuzzug gegen Lissabon im Jahre 1147* (ed. Ernst Dümmler [Vienna, 1851]), p. 3; Duodechin, in *MGH, Scriptores*, XVII, 27. According to the Portuguese *Indiculum fundationis monasterii beati Vincentii*, in *PMH, Scriptores*, I, 91, there were one hundred and ninety ships in the besieging fleet at Lisbon. According to the *Sigeberti continuatio Praemonstratensis*, in *MGH, Scriptores*, VI, 453, the total Christian forces at the siege of Lisbon numbered 13,000. Compare Ulrich Cosack, *Die Eroberung von Lissabon im Jahre 1147* (Halle, 1875: dissertation), p. 23, note 1; Friedrich Kurth, *Der Anteil niederdeutscher Kreuzfahrer an den Kämpfen der Portugiesen gegen die Mauren*, in Institut für österreichische Geschichtsforschung, *Mitteilungen*, Ergänzungsband VIII (1909), 135.

The Conquest of Lisbon[1]

TO OSBERT of Bawdsey, R.,[2] greeting.

We confidently believe that you will have a great
longing to know how it goes with us, and you may rest
assured that a like yearning is felt by us concerning you.
Accordingly, we will set forth in writing all the events of our
voyage which have been worth telling, whether fortunate or
adverse, and all that was done or said or seen or heard in its
course.

To begin, then, men of divers nations, customs, and speech
assembled in the port of Dartmouth[3] in about one hundred
and sixty-four[4] vessels. The whole expedition was divided into
three parts. Under Count Arnold of Aerschot, nephew of Duke
Godfrey,[5] were the forces from the territories of the Roman

---

The German squadron set sail from Cologne on 27 April and arrived at Dartmouth
on 19 May. *Brief des Priesters Winand*, p. 3; Duodechin, in *MGH, Scriptores*, XVII, 27.

[5] Arnold III, count of Aerschot (on the River Demer, in the *arrondissement* of
Louvain, province of Brabant, Belgium), nephew of Duke Godfrey I of Lower Lotharingia. Fragmentary information concerning him and his family may be gleaned from
documentary sources. In 1125 he joined with his father, Count Arnold of Aerschot, and
his brother Godfrey in a donation of lands at Buggenhout and elsewhere to the abbey
of Afflighem, when John, another of his brothers, became a monk there: *Cartulaire
de l'abbaye d'Afflighem* (ed. Edg. de Marneffe, Louvain, 1894), pp. 68–69; also in
Albertus Miraeus, *Opera diplomatica* (2d ed. by J. F. Foppens, Louvain, 1723–48), I,
375; II, 817; cf. *Cartulaire d'Afflighem*, p. 109. It was probably in 1146 that he and his
brother Godfrey and a third brother Rainier, who was archdeacon of Liége from 1126
to 1169 (cf. *Analectes pour servir à l'histoire ecclésiastique de la Belgique*, XXXI, 1905,
p. 155; XXXVII, 1911, p. 49), joined in a donation to the abbey of Middelburg:
Bijdragen voor de Geschiedenis van het Bisdom van Haarlem, XXV (1900), 415–16. (On
the date of this charter see *ibid.*, XX, 1895, p. 172, XXV, 1900, pp. 413–15; F.-J.
Raymaekers, "Recherches historiques sur l'ancienne abbaye de Parc," in *Revue
Catholique*, 6th ser., I, 1858, p. 416. For another edition of the charter, by Edg. de
Marneffe, from a late copy, see *Bijdragen tot de Geschiedenis bijzonderlijk van het
aloude Hertogdom Brabant*, ed. P. J. Goetschalckx, Hoogstraten, 2d year, 1903,
p. 427.) Probably at about the same time the three brothers joined in still other benefactions to the abbey of Middelburg: *ibid.*, p. 428; *Bijdragen voor de Geschiedenis . . .
van Haarlem*, XX (1895), 172–73. These and other benefactions of the three brothers
were confirmed by Henry, bishop of Liége, in 1152 and 1157: *ibid.*, XXV (1900),

mani imperii partibus[a] secedit exercitus. Sub Christiano de Gistella[1] Flandrenses et Bononenses. Ceterorum omnium sub constabulariis quatuor. Sub Herveo de Glanvilla[2] Norfolcenses

[a] An erasure of 3 millimetres follows *partibus*. Apparently the first two letters of *exercitus* were written by mistake, and then erased.

416–18; *Bijdragen tot de Geschiedenis . . . van . . . Brabant*, 2d year (1903), 429–30. Sometime between the latter part of 1142 and the early part of 1146 Count Arnold attested the charter of Duke Godfrey III of Lower Lotharingia in which the latter proclaimed that he had received the advocateship of the abbey of Tongerloo from the emperor Conrad III: Miraeus, *op. cit.*, I, 536; cf. Alphonse Wauters, *Table chronologique des chartes et diplômes imprimés concernant l'histoire de la Belgique* (Brussels, 1866–1912), II, 258. That Arnold was the nephew of Duke Godfrey I (d. 1140) of Lower Lotharingia, as the author says, is proved by a charter of 1134 in which the duke recognizes Arnold's brother Rainier as his nephew: *Revue Catholique*, 6th ser., I (1858), 409, note 2. Arnold is said to have had another uncle named Godfrey, his father's brother, who made a career for himself in Hainault: Miraeus, *op. cit.*, II, 814, 820; Alphonse Wauters, in *Biographie nationale de Belgique*, VII, 848; Charles Leyssens, *Geschiedenis van Aerschot* (Aerschot, 1853), p. 13. According to Leyssens, *loc. cit.*, Arnold's grandfather, Arnold, the first count of Aerschot, went on the First Crusade with Godfrey of Bouillon, but I can find no acceptable authority for this. Count Arnold was evidently the most important noble who took part in the Lisbon crusade. The priests Winand and Duodechin, in recording the arrival of the forces from Cologne at Dartmouth, speak almost as if he were the commander of the entire fleet: *Brief des Priesters Winand*, p. 3; *MGH, Scriptores*, XVII, 27.

[1] Christian of Ghistelles (*arrondissement* of Ostend, province of West Flanders) is probably he of the same name who can be traced in chronicles and documents from 1128 to 1168. In the former year he and an unnamed son were fighting on the side of William Clito, son of Robert Curthose, against Thierry of Alsace in the war then being waged over the countship of Flanders: Galbert of Bruges, *Histoire du meurtre de Charles le Bon, comte de Flandre* (ed. Henri Pirenne, Paris, 1891), p. 168, cf. p. 170. His wife, who was a sister of Borsiard (or Burchard), nephew of Bertulf, *prévôt* of Bruges, had the good fortune to escape disinheritance when punishment was visited on those who were implicated in the conspiracy which resulted in the murder of Count Charles the Good in the previous year: *Chronicon Hanoniense quod dicitur Balduini Avennensis*, in *MGH, Scriptores*, XXV, 443. In 1129, 1133, and 1146 he witnessed charters of Thierry of Alsace, count of Flanders: *Chronicon monasterii Aldenburgensis maius* (ed. Ferdinand van de Putte, Ghent, 1843), p. 88; André Duchesne, *Histoire généalogique des maisons de Guines, d'Ardres, de Gand, et de Coucy* (Paris, 1631), Preuves, p. 71; *Chronicon et cartularium abbatiae Sancti Nicolai Furnensis* (ed. Ferdinand van de Putte and Charles Carton, Bruges, 1849), p. 84. In 1151 he witnessed a charter of Walter de Heines, *advocatus* of the church of Saint Pierre of Oudenbourg (*Chron. mon. Aldenburgensis maius*, p. 93) and in 1168 a charter of Philip of Alsace, count of Flanders (*Chartes et documents de l'abbaye de Saint-Pierre au Mont Blandin à Gand*, ed. A. van Lokeren, Ghent, 1868–71, I, 177). Compare [T. Comte de Limburg Stirum], *Le Chambellan de Flandre et les sires de Ghistelles* (Ghent, 1868), pp. 83–84; Henri Pirenne, in *Histoire du meurtre de Charles le Bon*, p. 168, note 3, p. 51, note 3.

Empire; under Christian of Ghistelles,[1] the Flemings and the men of Boulogne. All the others were under four constables: the ships of Norfolk and Suffolk under Hervey de Glanvill,[2]

[2] The family name is probably derived from the Norman village of Glanville, *arrondissement* and canton of Pont-l'Évêque, department of Calvados. It seems impossible to determine the exact relationship of Hervey de Glanvill with Robert de Glanvill who figures prominently as an undertenant in Suffolk at the time of the Domesday Survey. He may have been the father or the grandfather of Ranulf de Glanvill, the famous chief justiciar of England who died at Acre on the Third Crusade. Ranulf's father was without any doubt named Hervey de Glanvill (*The Crawford Collection of Early Charters and Documents*, ed. A. S. Napier and W. H. Stevenson, Oxford, 1895, No. XVI; *Curia Regis Rolls*, London, 1922– , Richard I–2 John, p. 433), and it would seem natural to identify the latter with the Lisbon crusader, were it not for the complicating evidence of a late, and perhaps not wholly reliable, record of a meeting of the county court of Norfolk and Suffolk, held at Norwich between 3 Jan., 1148, and 3 Nov., 1153 (*English Historical Review*, XXXIX, 1924, pp. 569–71; also in *Pinchbeck Register*, ed. Francis Hervey, London, 1925, II, 297–99; cf. *Speculum*, VII, 1932, pp. 54–56). The principal decision of the court is said to have been determined by the testimony of one Hervey de Glanvill, then a man of advanced years, whose memory ran back beyond the reign of King Henry I and who had been attending courts of shire and hundred for fully fifty years; when the decision of the court was agreed upon, it is said to have been made with the assent, among others, of "Hervey son of Hervey and Robert de Glanvill." Though it may not be absolutely necessary to conclude that there were two Herveys de Glanvill, father and son, this is an inference which seems too probable to be ignored. Ranulf de Glanvill may have been the son of either of them, and either may have been the leader of the Lisbon crusade. (A Hervey, son of Hervey, appears, in the accounts for Suffolk, in *The Pipe Roll of 31 Henry I*, ed. Joseph Hunter, reprint, London, 1929, p. 98.) According to W. U. S. Glanville-Richards, *Records of the House of Glanville* (London, 1882), pp. 23–26, *et passim*, the elder Hervey was the crusader, and Ranulf and Hervey, son of Hervey, were two of his nine sons; but little reliance can be placed on this work. There seems to be no possible ground for the suggestion of Jessopp (Thomas of Monmouth, *The Life and Miracles of St. William of Norwich*, ed. A. Jessopp and M. R. James, Cambridge, 1896, p. xxxii, note 3) that the elder Hervey was the grandfather of the Lisbon crusader. A Hervey de Glanvill can be traced in the following documents besides the ones already mentioned: a charter of Stephen, count of Mortain, afterwards king of England (*Calendar of the Charter Rolls Preserved in the Public Record Office*, London, 1903– , I, 46–47), of uncertain date but perhaps between 1113 and 1125 (see William Farrer, *Honors and Knights Fees*, London, etc., 1924–25, III, 438; *idem, Early Yorkshire Charters*, Edinburgh, 1914–16, III, 457; *The Book of Fees, Commonly Called Testa de Nevill*, London, 1920–31, Pt. I, pp. 137–38); the *carta* or return of Nigel, bishop of Ely, to the inquest of knights' fees of 1166, where he appears as the holder of a knight's fee in Suffolk (*Red Book of the Exchequer*, ed. Hubert Hall, London, 1896, Pt. I, p. 365); Ranulf de Glanvill's foundation charter of Butley Priory, 1171 (William Dugdale, *Monasticon Anglicanum*, new ed., London, 1817–30, VI, 380; cf. *Speculum*, VII, 1932, p. 56). There is record evidence of other children of a Hervey de Glanvill, besides Ranulf above mentioned, viz., a son John (*Descriptive Catalogue of Ancient Deeds in*

et Suðfolcenses. Sub Symone Dorobernensi[1] omnes Cantię naves. Sub Andrea[2] Londonienses. Sub Saherio de Arcellis[3] relique omnium naves.

Inter hos tot linguarum populos firmissima concordię atque amicitię pignora;[a] insuper leges severissimas sanxerunt, ut mortuum pro mortuo, dentem pro dente. Pretiosarum vestium omnimodum apparatum interdixerunt. Ne item mulieres[4] in publico prodirent. Pacem servandam omnibus nisi ex indicto iniurias. Ut singulis hebdomadibus[b] capitula serventur, seorsum a laicis, seorsum a clericis, nisi forte magna quedam utrorumque coniunctionem exigerent. Ut singule naves singulos presbyteros haberent, et eadem que in parrochiis observari iubentur. Ut nullus alterius nautam vel servientem in convictu suo retin[er]et.[c] Ut singuli singulis hebdomadibus[b] confiterentur[d] et die dominico communicarent. Et sic per cetera capitula usui nostro necessaria, singulę singulis observationum sanctiones. Constituti sunt preterea de unoquoque milleno duo electi, qui iudices et coniurati dicerentur, per quos ex indicto constabulariorum causarum terminatio peccuniarumque distributio fieret.[5]

---

[a] *pignora* written in margin.
[b] *epdomadibus.*

[c] An uncompleted correction of *retineat.*
[d] A correction of *confiteantur.*

---

the *Public Record Office*, London, 1890–1906, III, 274), and two daughters Alice and Guia (*Curia Regis Rolls*, Richard I–2 John, pp. 155, 433). I know of no evidence that a Hervey de Glanvill held the office of chamberlain under King Stephen, as asserted by Glanville-Richards, *op. cit.*, p. 22.

[1] Probably, though not certainly, of Dover rather than Canterbury. By the twelfth century the word in this ambiguous form seems to have disappeared from documentary and official usage, but the narrative writers still made occasional use of it. Simon of Dover seems to be otherwise unknown.

[2] He may well have been Andrew Buccuinte (*Bucca Uncta*), a very prominent citizen of London during the reigns of Henry I and Stephen. For all that is known about him see J. H. Round, *The Commune of London and Other Studies* (Westminster, 1899), pp. 97–113, and the references there cited. Round has traced him in documents from *ca.* 1125 onward, and has shown that in 1137 he was "justiciar" of London and that in 1139 the king addressed him first as the leading man of London. His identification with the Lisbon crusader of 1147 was first proposed by William Stubbs (*Constitutional History of England*, I, 5th ed., Oxford, 1891, p. 675). Round found it "very tempting"; but he evidently felt constrained to leave the question open, since "*Andreas de Londonia* is found as a witness to a Ramsey charter under Henry I, while Andrew Buccuinte used to attest under his own name."

those of Kent under Simon of Dover,[1] those of London under Andrew,[2] and all the rest under Saher of Archelle.[3]

Among these people of so many different tongues the firmest guarantees of peace and friendship were taken; and, furthermore, they sanctioned very strict laws, as, for example, a life for a life and a tooth for a tooth. They forbade all display of costly garments. Also they ordained that women should not go out in public;[4] that the peace must be kept by all, unless they should suffer injuries recognized by the proclamation; that weekly chapters be held by the laity and the clergy separately, unless perchance some great emergency should require their meeting together; that each ship have its own priest and keep the same observances as are prescribed for parishes; that no one retain the seaman or the servant of another in his employ; that everyone make weekly confession and communicate on Sunday; and so on through the rest of the obligatory articles with separate sanctions for each. Furthermore, they constituted for every thousand of the forces two elected members who were to be called judges or *coniurati*, through whom the cases of the constables were to be settled in accordance with the proclamation and by whom the distribution of moneys was to be carried out.[5]

[3] The family name is presumably derived from the village of Archelle (a short distance inland from Dieppe), commune of Arques, canton of Offranville, department of Seine-Inférieure. Compare Auguste Longnon, *Pouillés de la province de Rouen* (Paris, 1903), pp. 390, 81, 35, 22; *HF*, XXIII, 258. Saher of Archelle appears to have been a feudal lord of somewhat higher rank than Hervey de Glanvill, for the author repeatedly refers to him (below, pp. 126, 127, 128, 129) as *dominus Saherius*, i.e., the lord Saher (one hesitates to say Dom Saher at so early a date; but cf. J. H. Round, *Calendar of Documents Preserved in France*, London, 1899, No. 1212). He witnessed a grant by Gilbert of Ghent to Rufford Abbey [1147–53], *Documents Illustrative of the Social and Economic History of the Danelaw* (ed. F. M. Stenton, London, 1920), No. 348. He was a benefactor of Lincoln Cathedral, where his *obit* (31 May) appears in a list compiled "probably *ca.* 1185": *Statutes of Lincoln Cathedral* (ed. Henry Bradshaw and Chr. Wordsworth, Cambridge, 1892–97), II, p. ccxxxviii. Evidence of two benefactions conferred by him on the Templars, one in Kent and the other at Lusby in Lincolnshire, has been preserved in the Templars' *Inquisitio* or Feodary of 1185: *Records of the Templars in England in the Twelfth Century*, ed. B. A. Lees (London, 1935), pp. 24, 80, 99.

[4] This is the only mention of women in connection with the expedition.

[5] That the responsible members of the expedition were bound together by oath in a formal association is abundantly proved by the tenor of the arguments advanced in

Hiis inibi sic statutis, sexta feria[1] ante ascensionem Domini velificare incepimus.[2] Subsequenti dominica[3] costam Britannie, profunditatis dimensione saltem LXXV. cubitorum et maris nigredine, comperimus.[a] Per biduum vero subsequens aurarum placidissima[b] serenitate detenti, nichil aut parum profecimus. [125v] Quarta feria[4] vento incumbente prospero Balearicam maiorem,[5] scilicet montium Pyreneorum capita, undarum magnitudine et fervore maris, comperimus.[a] Vespere autem te[m]pestate aborta, omnes circumquaque dispersi sumus.[6] Noctis enim[c] supra modum tenebrositas atque insueta maris rheumata[d] nautas etiam audacissimos desperare coge-

---

[a] *er* in this word was first written in full, then erased and a mark of abbreviation substituted—a curious, but not uncommon, practice in this manuscript.

[b] An erasure of one centimetre follows *placidissima*. Apparently *detenti*, which belongs after the next word, had been written by mistake.

[c] *enim* written in margin.   [d] *reumata*.

---

the course of disputes which arose concerning policy at Lisbon. See below, pp. 104, 105, 176, 177. It is highly probable that the author had before him as he wrote the text of the proclamation (*indictum*) which contained the ordinances for the maintenance of order, the distribution of spoils, etc., which were adopted before the fleet sailed from Dartmouth. Some such regulations would seem to have been a necessity for the success of any such enterprise. Those issued by Richard I for the enforcement of discipline in his fleet on its way to the Holy Land in 1190 are, of course, well known. *Gesta regis Henrici Secundi* (ed. William Stubbs, London, 1867), II, 110–11. A brief record also exists of the *leges in exercitu servandae* which were promulgated at Dartmouth and reinforced at Pointe-de-Saint-Mathieu (on the coast of Brittany) for the expedition of Counts George of Wied and William of Holland in 1217. *Quinti belli sacri scriptores minores* (ed. Reinhold Röhricht, Geneva, 1879), pp. 29, 59–60; cf. Gosuinus, "De expugnatione Salaciae carmen," in *Chronica regia Coloniensis* (ed. Georg Waitz, Hanover, 1880), p. 349, lines 29–32. But no other record appears to be extant which is so full or so early as that of the regulations of 1147, and these take on an additional interest from the fact that the Lisbon crusade seems to have been organized upon a more broadly democratic basis than any analogous enterprise of which we possess adequate knowledge. I owe to Professor Henri Pirenne the suggestion (made in private correspondence) that the ordinances of 1147 were in part inspired by laws for the enforcement of peace (*leges pacis*) which are to be met with in certain municipal charters of Flanders and neighboring parts of France and Germany. The charter granted to Saint-Omer in 1127 by William Clito contains the phrase (cap. 20) *oculum pro oculo, dentem pro dente:* A. Giry, *Histoire de la ville de Saint-Omer* (Paris, 1877), pp. 371–75; the charter of Louis VI to Laon in 1128, the phrase (cap. 5) *caput pro capite, membrum pro membro:* L. A. Warnkoenig and L. Stein, *Französische Staats- und Rechtsgeschichte* (Basel, 1846–48), I, Urkundenbuch, pp. 30–34. The *pacis securitas qua Furnenses fruuntur*, which was granted to Poperinghe, and probably also to Arques, in 1147, provided

These ordinances having thus been established, we began to make sail on the Friday[1] before Ascension.[2] On the following Sunday,[3] when in dark water of a depth of at least seventy-five cubits, we sighted the coast of Brittany. But during the two following days we were almost becalmed and made little or no progress. On Wednesday,[4] with the wind blowing favorably, the waves being great and the sea rough, we sighted *Balearica Maior*,[5] that is, the peaks of the Pyrenees Mountains. But as night came on a tempest arose, and we were scattered in every direction.[6] Indeed, the excessive darkness of the night and the unaccustomed tossing of the waves compelled even the

---

(cap. 7) *si quis aliquem occiderit, occidetur:* L. A. Warnkoenig, *Flandrische Staats-und Rechtsgeschichte* (Tübingen, 1835–42), II, Pt. 2, Urkundenbuch, Nos. clxxx, clxxxviii; cf. Henri Pirenne "La Question des jurés dans les villes flamandes," in *Revue belge de philologie et d'histoire,* V (1926), 410–14. Somewhat similar examples of later date have been noted at Arras, Amiens, Péronne, Tournay, and Verneuil in France (cf. Adolphus Ballard, *British Borough Charters,* Cambridge, 1913, pp. cxiii–cxiv, cv–cvii), and at Schwerin in Germany (Wilhelm Jesse, *Geschichte der Stadt Schwerin,* Schwerin, 1913–20, I, 69). Some connection may perhaps also be traced between the *electi qui iudices et coniurati dicerentur* of the Lisbon expedition and the *iurati, iudices electi, coremanni* or *coartores,* that are charged with the administration of the peace in many of the documents above cited. It may also be noted that in the charter granted to Aire in 1188, but containing matter of earlier date, the peace is called an *amicitia. Revue belge de philologie et d'histoire,* V (1926), 414–16. I have found nothing analogous to the continental *leges pacis* in the contemporary municipal history of Great Britain. Compare Ballard, *op. cit.,* pp. cxxxv–cxxxvi, cxiii.

[1] 23 May, 1147.

[2] On the route, cf. the earliest extant mediaeval portolano, preserved in Adam of Bremen, *Gesta Hammaburgensis ecclesiae pontificum* (2d ed., Hanover, 1876), pp. 154–55. See above, pp. 15–16.

[3] 25 May.

[4] 28 May.

[5] I can offer no explanation of the use of the word *Balearica* in this connection. Presumably the reference is to some part of the Picos de Europa. As conspicuous landmarks which, in fine weather, can be seen from more than sixty miles out to sea, they still figure prominently in pilot guides. See U.S. Hydrographic Office, *Bay of Biscay Pilot* (3d ed., Washington, 1926), pp. 434, 472. Los Urrieles, which stand directly south of Llanes and are only a few miles inland and of which Torre de Cerredo (*ca.* 8,786 feet) and Naranjo de Bulnes (*ca.* 8,340 feet) are the most conspicuous peaks, occupy the central, dominant position. See U.S. Hydrographic Office Charts, No. 4379; cf. *Enciclopedia universal ilustrada Europeo-Americana* (Barcelona: J. Espasa, etc. [1912–30]), XXII, 1432–34.

[6] The notorious storms of the Bay of Biscay still claim attention in the pilot guides. *Bay of Biscay Pilot,* pp. 34–35, 371, 414–15.

bat. Audite sunt interim Syrenes, horribilis sonitus, prius cum luctu, postea cum risu et cachinno,[a] quasi insultantium castrorum clamoribus. Per totam igitur dominicę ascensionis noctem[1] laborantibus, consors atque custos divina misericordia affuit, ut castigando castigaret et morti non traderet. Quanti illic penitentes, quanti peccata et neggligentias cum luctu confitentes et gemitu, peregrinationis suę conversionem utcumque inceptam, inundatione lacrimarum diluentes, in ara cordis contriti Deo sacrificabant. Idque adeo actum ut dispensatio divina nullum preteriret, imo etiam cęlestis beneficii singulare privilegium se accepisse unusquisque gratularetur, ut longum sit enumerare per singula quantis visionum imaginibus divina miracula patuerint. Postera igitur die,[2] paululum sedata tempestate, in Hyspania aput portum Sancti Salvatoris, qui dicitur Mala Rupis,[3] feliciter applicuimus. Ibidem enim ecclesia a Mauris ante parum temporis fuerat destructa, monachorum cenobio celeberrima.[4] Distat autem a civitate Oveti

---

[a] *cachymno.*

[1] 29 May. "In vigilia ascensionis et in ipsa die sollemnitatis." *Brief des Priesters Winand*, p. 3; cf. Duodechin, in *MGH, Scriptores*, XVII, 27; Arnulf, in *HF*, XIV, 325.

[2] 30 May.

[3] Presumably the port of Gozón, which is probably to be identified with the modern harbor of Luanco some twelve miles northwest of Gijón and about seven or eight miles from the tip of Cape Peñas, province of Oviedo; although both Cosack (*Die Eroberung von Lissabon*, p. 24) and Kurth (*Niederdeutscher Kreuzfahrer*, in Institut für österreichische Geschichtsforschung, *Mitteilungen*, Ergänzungsband, VII, 1909, p. 138) believed, though with some hesitation, that Gijón was the port designated. The Teutonic Source (*Brief des Priesters Winand*, p. 3; Duodechin, in *MGH, Scriptores*, XVII, 27; Arnulf, in *HF*, XIV, 325) gives *Gozzim* or *Gozzem* (which is certainly to be identified with Gozón) as the landing place, but Kurth (*loc. cit.*) was of the opinion that this designation was not applicable in the case of the ships whose movements are recorded in the *De expugnatione Lyxbonensi*. However, the identification with Gozón is, as will appear below, in some degree supported by the words of the text, *portus Sancti Salvatoris* and *Mala Rupis*. The name Gozón, which now survives only as that of a municipal district (*municipio*) with its capital or administrative centre at Luanco, is derived from the mediaeval castle of Gozón, or Gauzon, which was built in the ninth century by Alfonso III of Asturias as a defense against the Norsemen. The exact location of the castle has apparently not been determined, but there is reason to believe that it stood on Punta del Castillo above Luanco on the north side of Luanco Bay. "Castellum etiam concedimus Gauzonem cum ecclesia S. Salvatoris, quae est intra, cum omni sua mandatione, et cum ecclesiis quae sunt extra illud castellum, videlicet ecclesiam Sanctae Mariae sitam sub ipso castro, monasterium S. Michaelis de Quilonio

bravest of our seamen to despair. At intervals the Sirens were heard, a horrible sound, first of wailing, and then of laughter and jeering, like the clamor of insolent men in a camp. Accordingly, through all the night of Ascension[1] divine mercy was present as companion and protector of our men in travail, to the end that they might be corrected by chastisement but not delivered unto death. How many there were who, becoming penitent and confessing their sins and short-comings with sorrow and groaning and atoning with a flood of tears for the perversion of their pilgrimage, however it had been begun, offered sacrifices to God upon the altar of a contrite heart. Thus it happened that divine grace passed no one by, and, indeed, that everyone congratulated himself upon receiving the singular privilege of a heavenly favor, to such an extent that it would be tedious to relate in detail the divine miracles which were revealed in visions. And so next day,[2] the storm having somewhat abated, we happily made land in Spain at the port of San Salvador, which is called *Mala Rupis*.[3] The church there had recently been destroyed by the Moors—a very famous monastery.[4] It

per suos terminos et locos antiquos . . .," says a charter of donation (dated 875) by the king to the cathedral of Oviedo: Enrique Flórez, *España sagrada* (Madrid, 1747–1879), XXXVII, 330; cf. *ibid.*, p. 215. The church of the Savior within the castle seems to explain the designation *portus Sancti Salvatoris*, and Santa María is still the name of the parish of Luanco, which is quite properly described as *sub ipso castro*. Beside the foregoing mediaeval text should be placed the words of the modern pilot: "Westward of Cabrito point is Luanco Point, rocky, with rocks named Pena Cercada, Lleixe, Pegollo, and Espiga, extending about 600 yards northward of it. The largest of these rocks is Pena Cercada, which is isolated at high water, and on it is a hermitage. Between this point and Punta del Castillo, about ¾ mile to the northward, is Luanco Bay. On Punta del Castillo are the ruins of a castle and off it are some rocks, the outer of which is El Peon, with a reef around it. . . . At the head of the bay is the town and port of Luanco": *Bay of Biscay Pilot*, p. 484; cf. U.S. Hydrographic Office Charts, Nos. 4379, 4380. It seems impossible to identify any of the above named rocks with *Mala Rupis*, but such a name is readily understandable in view of the situation described in the pilot text. Finally, it should be noted that during the fifteenth century the port of Gozón was regularly known to navigators as "Peñas de Gozon," i.e., the Rocks of Gozón. See Konrad Kretschmer, *Die italienischen Portolane des Mittelalters* (Berlin, 1909), p. 574, and the references there cited. See also *Enciclopedia universal*, s.v. Gauzon, Gozón, and Luanco. I have been unable to consult in this country Manuel González Llanos, *Monografía de Gozón*.

[4] This event seems not to be elsewhere reported. Could the monastery referred to be San Miguel de *Quilonio* of the charter quoted above, note 3?

miliaria X.,[1] in qua est ecclesia Salvatoris et totius Hyspanię preciosissimę reliquiarum.[2] Adiacet autem provintia montuosa, ferarum venatibus et frugum generibus multimodis celeberrima, admodum delectabilis nisi propriis inhabitatoribus fedaretur.

Inde navigantes ad ripam Ovies[3] pervenimus, que adiacet Lucanę provintię. Distat autem miliaria XX.[4] a civitate Lucana. Hinc iterum navigantes devenimus Ortigiam.[5] Exin ad turrem Faris,[6] que olim a Iulio Cęsare constructa, admirandi operis, ut ibidem reditus[a] et cause interminabiles totius Britannię et Hybernie et Hyspanie quasi in meditullio commearent. Est enim [126r] adeo sita inter meridionalem et occidentalem plagam ut prima sit littoris appulsio recto tra-

[a] redditus.

[1] Actually more than 25 miles, if the identification of portus Sancti Salvatoris with Luanco is correct. The author's figures of distances are invariably understated, and it would seem that he was using some longer unit than the ordinary mile. The author of the De itinere navali (R. Accademia delle Scienze di Torino, Memorie, 2d ser., II, 1840, p. 193), says more correctly, six leagues.

[2] The fame of these relics, which are listed in detail in the latest guidebook (Marcel Monmarché, Espagne, Paris, 1927, Les Guides bleus, p. 276), still persists, though they must recently have narrowly escaped destruction as a result of political disorders. In October, 1934, the Cámera Santa of the cathedral, in which the reliquary was kept, was besieged by rebels and its incomparable treasures largely reduced to ruins. The Arca Santa, or reliquary, is said to have fallen to pieces, badly crushed and scratched. See London Times, 24 November, 1934, p. 11, col. 1. On the early history of the relics, see Flórez, España sagrada, XXXVII, 279–94.

[3] Rivadeo is situated in the corner of the province of Lugo at the mouth of the River Eo, which in its lower reaches divides the province of Lugo from that of Oviedo and was the boundary of the mediaeval principalities of Asturias and Galicia. The Teutonic Source mentions Vivero, province of Lugo, at the mouth of the River Landrove, as the port of call between Gozón and the mouth of the Tambre: Brief des Priesters Winand, p. 3; Duodechin, in MGH, Scriptores, XVII, 27; Arnulf, in HF, XIV, 325. Evidently all parts of the fleet (perhaps as a result of the storm) did not make the same ports and at the same time.

[4] Actually more than fifty miles.

[5] Either Cape Ortegal, as Stubbs believed (Itinerarium, p. cxlv), or perhaps more probably Ortigueira, both near the northeastern corner of the province of Corunna. Ortigueira is on the Ria de Santa Marta de Ortigueira and affords a harbor which, though now unsatisfactory for any but small boats, would have been adequate in the twelfth century; Cape Ortegal extends into the sea to the west and north of the Ria de Santa Marta, and affords no shelter. The author seems to be giving harbors where shelter could be obtained. See U.S. Hydrographic Office Charts, No. 4391; Enciclopedia universal, XL, 721.

is ten miles[1] distant from the city of Oviedo, in which is located the church of the Savior and the most precious relics of all Spain.[2] Adjacent lies a mountainous province, very celebrated for its hunting and for the varied products of its soil, and altogether delightful, except that it is defiled by its own inhabitants.

Sailing thence we came to Rivadeo,[3] which adjoins the province of Lugo and is twenty miles[4] distant from the city of Lugo. Thence again sailing we came to Ortigueira (?);[5] and thence to the Lighthouse Tower[6] [Corunna], a wonderful work which was formerly built by Julius Caesar in order that it might serve as a centre through which the revenues and the interminable law cases of all Britain and Ireland and Spain might pass to and fro. For it is so situated between the southern

[6] The famous ancient tower, now popularly known as Hercules' Tower, which stands at the extremity of Corunna Peninsula, in the shelter of which the port of Corunna is situated. Compare the charter of Alfonso IX in favor of Santiago, dated 1208: "pro utilitate regni mei novam construo populationem in loco qui dicitur Crunia apud turrim de Faro": Antonio López Ferreiro, *Historia de la santa A. M. Iglesia de Santiago de Compostela* (Santiago, 1898–1909), V, Appendix, No. viii; charter of Ferdinand II, dated 1161, *ibid.*, IV, Appendix, No. xxxi; Flórez, *España sagrada*, XIX, 13–20; Enrique de Vedia y Goosens, *Historia y descripción de la ciudad de la Coruña* (Corunna, 1845), pp. 141–47 and *passim*; Andrés Martínez Salazar, *Antiguallas de Galicia: los nombres de la Coruña* (Corunna, 1899), *passim*; Kurth, *op. cit.*, p. 14. Dio Cassius xxxvii. 53, appears to be the only ancient writer who in any way connects the name of Julius Caesar with the site, and his statement evidently has no bearing on later tradition. The tradition as recorded in the *De expugnatione Lyxbonensi* is substantially repeated in the *De itinere Frisonum* of 1217: "Phare pervenimus, quod est oppidum Galicie dives admodum, portum habens flexuosum, turre sublimi presignata a Iulio Cesare constructa": *Quinti belli sacri scriptores minores*, p. 60 (the editor has mistakenly identified *Phare* with Cabo de Vares). The tower is mentioned as a conspicuous landmark by Paulus Orosius i. 2. 71: "Secundus [Hispaniae] angulus circium intendit; ubi Brigantia Gallaeciae civitas sita altissimam pharum et inter pauca memorandi operis ad speculam Britanniae erigit." It is conspicuously represented and named (*Faro*) on the *mappamundi* in the Beatus manuscript (dated 1086: Timoteo Rojo, "El 'Beato' de la Catedral de Osma," in *Art Studies*, VIII, 1931, Pt. 2, 106, 123) now preserved in the cathedral of Osma: Konrad Miller, *Mappaemundi* (Stuttgart, 1895–98), Heft 1, pp. 34–35, Heft 2, Tafel 3 (where the date is given erroneously as 1203). It is also indicated and named (*al faru*) on the Arabian world map of 1192 ("the Small Idrisi-Map"): Konrad Miller, *Mappae Arabicae* (Stuttgart, 1926–31), I, Heft 3, p. 71, and detached map, II, 104–106. Stubbs has incorrectly identified it with Ferrol, *Itinerarium*, p. cxlv. For a large scale map of the region, see U.S. Hydrographic Office Charts, No. 4391.

mite a Britannia venientium. Ibi vero pons lapideus ex multis arcubus ostenditur, in mari protensus, ex quibus viginti quatuor arcus qui ante biennium non apparuerant iam apparent.[1] Inde relatum est a quodam gentis illius antiquissimo vaticinatum ut dum pontis illius arcus emergerent, destructionem gentium finemque idolatrię[a] in Hyspania imminere. Exhinc ad portum Tambre devenimus vigilia Pentecostes.[2] Distat autem ab ecclesia beati Iacobi miliaria VII.[3] Est autem civitas Hyrię proxima, que nunc Petra Iacobi vocatur, et est sedes episcopalis.[4] Portus autem, multis generibus piscium fecundus, habet in sinu maris insulam.[5] Vidimus inibi, mirabile dictu, piscem tenentis manum stupefacientem; est vero ad modum raię, habens in summitate spinę duas pinnas acutissimas.[6] Provintia adiacens feris abundat, segete sterilis, vite arida, pom[is ab]-und[ans].[b]

Inde pervenimus ad insulam que vulgo Flamba[7] vocatur, in

[a] ydolatrię.

[b] pom . . . und . . . written in margin, the remainder of the words having been clipped away in rebinding. I have adopted the conjectural restoration of Stubbs, *Itinerarium*, p. cxlvi, note 2. Hamilton proposed to read *poma undique*, which seems less satisfactory, *PMH, Scriptores*, I, 393, note 1.

[1] I can offer no explanation of this curious passage.

[2] 7 June.

[3] Actually more than twenty miles, or so it would seem, though *portus Tambre* gives but an indefinite location. From Noya to Santiago de Compostela by road is about twenty-two miles. The Teutonic Source gives the distance as eight miles. It also gives the date of arrival in the Tambre as Friday, 6 June, and records an excursion to the shrine of Santiago, which was reached on the eve of Pentecost: *Brief des Priesters Winand*, p. 3; Duodechin, in *MGH, Scriptores*, XVII, 27; Arnulf, in *HF*, XIV, 325.

[4] The ancient Iria Flavia, modern Padron (province of Corunna), on the right bank of the River Ulla at the point where it is joined by the Sar, about twelve miles from Santiago and somewhat farther from Noya. It was no longer an episcopal see in 1147, having been supplanted by Santiago. The name *Petra Iacobi* by which the author calls it would seem to lend noteworthy support to the view of those who derive the mediaeval and modern name of Padron from the stone to which, according to the legend, the disciples of St. James moored their boat when they landed in Spain with the body of the apostle, and which is supposed still to exist in the inscribed stele which is now preserved beneath the principal altar in the church of Santa María de Iria at Padron. Compare Ambrosio de Morales, *Viaje . . . por orden del rey D. Phelipe II a los reynos de Leon y Galicia y principado de Asturias* (ed. Enrique Flórez, Madrid, 1765), pp. 134–38; Flórez, *España sagrada*, XIX, 1–5; Fidel Fita and Aureliano Fernández-Guerra, *Recuerdos de un viaje á Santiago de Galicia* (Madrid, 1880), pp. 26–31; P. B. Gams, *Die Kirchengeschichte von Spanien* (Regensburg, 1862–79), II, Pt. 2, pp. 374–75.

THE CONQUEST OF LISBON

and the western regions that it offers the first landing place for travelers coming directly over from Britain. A stone bridge of many arches is shown there, extending into the sea, of which twenty-four arches are now visible which were not in sight two years ago.[1] Hence they relate the prophecy of a certain aged man of that people that when the arches of the bridge should emerge, the destruction of the heathen and the end of idolatry in Spain would be at hand. Thence we came to the mouth of the Tambre on the eve of Pentecost.[2] It is seven miles[3] from the church of St. James. And the city of Iria is near at hand, which is now called *Petra Iacobi* [Padron], and is an episcopal see.[4] The harbor, which abounds in many kinds of fish, contains an island.[5] And we saw there, strange to relate, a fish which benumbs the hand of him who holds it; it resembles the ray and has two sharp dorsal fins.[6] The adjacent province abounds in wild animals but is unproductive of corn and sparing of vines, though abounding in fruit trees.

Thence we came to the island which is vulgarly called Tamba (?),[7] in which there are great numbers of rabbits and

[5] Evidently Quiebra Island, located not far below the point where Muros Bay narrows rapidly to the Tambre and Noya channels. "Quiebra Island, a little more than 1 cable S. of Huia point," says the pilot guide, "is high, with rocks extending from its N.W. and S.E. ends, the passage between it and the point being only fit for boats": U.S. Hydrographic Office, *The Northwest and West Coast of Spain and the Coast of Portugal* (Washington, 1874), p. 82. See U.S. Hydrographic Office Charts, No. 4407; British Admiralty Charts, No. 1756. Julio de Castilho, *Lisboa antiga*, Pt. 2, II, 33, mistakenly makes an identification with "a ilhota que demora na bocca da enseada, em cujo fundo jaz Padron, e que se chama hoje Grobo." Apparently he refers to Grobe Peninsula at the mouth of Arosa Bay.

[6] Probably *Torpedo torpedo* (Linn.), also called *T. ocellata*, which is by far the commonest of the electric rays found on the coast of Spain and which differs from the others in having two dorsal fins, pointed rather than rounded. The foregoing information was kindly communicated to me by Mr. J. R. Norman, Assistant Keeper of the Department of Zoölogy of the British Museum.

[7] The manuscript reading seems perfectly clear. Herculano, in *PMH, Scriptores*, I, 393, note 2, cited by Castilho, *Lisboa antiga*, Pt. 2, II, 34, has proposed on the basis of a passage in the *Historia Compostelana*, in Flórez, *España sagrada*, XX, 197, to read *Flamia*, by which name, he says, one of the Bayona Islands (more commonly called Cies Islands) at the entrance to Vigo Bay was known in the twelfth century; but the identification of *Flamia* in the text cited with one of the Bayonas seems very questionable. Perhaps a more likely identification of *Flamba* would be with Tamba (or Tambo)

qua est cuniculorum copia et serpentium;[1] habet etiam folium unde worma[2] tingitur. Insula hec una ex Balearibus est.[3] Provintia a sinistra in continenti vocatur Campis.[4] Habet autem litus maris ab insula usque ad Portugalam fluvium Mineum,[a] super quem civitas Tude. Post hunc fluvius Cad*uv*a,[b] supra quem civitas Braccara.[5] Post hunc fluvius Ava, supra quem ecclesia beati Tyrsi[6] martyris. Post hunc fluvius Leticia.[7] Post hunc fluvius Doyra,[c] supra quem Portugala, ad quam ab insula venimus circiter horam diei nonam.[8] Dicta autem olim a portu Gallorum,[9] habens iam annos reparationis suę circiter LXXX., desolata[10] ab introitu Maurorum et

[a] The manuscript reading is certain, although the word is written over an erasure and the spreading of the ink has rendered it difficult. Hamilton mistakenly read *Onnem* and Stubbs *Ovier*. Herculano, without having seen the manuscript, observed that *Mineum* must be the correct reading. See *PMH, Scriptores*, I, 393, and note 3; *Itinerarium*, p. cxlvi.

[b] Reading doubtful. It seems impossible to decide certainly between *Caduva* and *Cadivia*. Hamilton read the former, Stubbs the latter. See *PMH, Scriptores*, I, 393; *Itinerarium*, p. cxlvi. Clearly the Cávado, the ancient Celadus (?), is meant.

[c] An erasure of 2.5 centimetres follows *Doyra*.

Island, lying far up in Pontevedra Bay, between Marinulos and Pasquera Points, about three miles southwest of Pontevedra. According to the pilot guide, Tamba offers a beach, a spring, and good anchorage: U.S. Hydrographic Office, *The N.W. and W. Coast of Spain and the Coast of Portugal*, p. 102. See U.S. Hydrographic Office Charts, No. 4407; British Admiralty Charts, No. 1758. Compare *Enciclopedia universal*, LIX, 211.

[1] Compare Solinus 23. 10–12, and note 3, below.

[2] The translation of *worma* as "scarlet cloth" is perhaps doubtful; but cf. the following passages: "Ostrum, wurma, read godweb," from a glossary of the eleventh century, in Thos. Wright, *Anglo-Saxon and Old English Vocabularies* (2d ed., London, 1884), I, 460; "Wolcreadum wurman oþþe wealhbasu, bistincto cocco sive vermiculo," from an eleventh-century gloss on St. Aldhelm's "De laude virginitatis," in *Anglia*, XIII (1891), 29; "Vermiculum, rubrum, sive coccineum. Est enim vermiculus ex silvestribus frondibus, in quo lana tingitur, quae vermiculum appellatur," from the eleventh-century grammarian Papias, in Du Cange, *Glossarium mediae et infimae Latinitatis*, s.v. *Vermiculus;* cf. also other passages quoted by Du Cange. Kermes (*coccum*) is mentioned repeatedly by Pliny, twice as a product of Lusitania, once as a means by which the poor of Spain were enabled to discharge half of their tribute. He calls the plant in question *ilex aquifolia parva*, but it must really have been *quercus coccifera*, which resembles *ilex* and abounds in Spain and Portugal. Compare Pliny *HN* ix. 141; xvi. 32; xxii. 3; T. J. Dillon, *Travels through Spain and Portugal* (2d ed., London, 1782), pp. 18–31; Edward Bancroft, *Experimental Researches concerning the Philosophy of Permanent Colours* (Philadelphia, 1814), I, 293–96. It is

snakes.[1] It also has a plant from the leaves of which scarlet cloth[2] is dyed. This island is one of the Balearics.[3] The province to the left on the mainland is called *Campis*.[4] Along the coast from the island as far as Oporto the following rivers empty into the sea: the Minho, on which is the city of Tuy; after this the Cávado, on which is the city of Braga;[5] after this the Ave, on which is the church of the blessed martyr Tyrsus;[6] after this the Leça;[7] and after this the Douro, on which is the city of Oporto, at which we arrived from the island about the ninth hour of the day.[8] Its name was formerly derived from *Port of the Gauls*;[9] and it has now been for some eighty years in process of restoration after its destruction[10]

possible that the author was writing, to some extent, under the influence of Solinus 23. 4.

[3] The erroneous association of Tamba (?) with the Balearic Islands evidently arose from the author's mistaken idea that they were located on the Atlantic side of Spain, an idea which he may have derived from the misleading passage in Solinus 23. 10-12, which in turn is based on an unintelligent reading of Pliny *HN* iv. 119-20; iii. 76-78. Compare below, pp. 86-87, note 6.

[4] I have failed to identify this place name, the application of which to the region in question may have some significance for the much discussed question of the origin of the name Compostela. According to the *Annales Complutenses*, in Flórez, *España sagrada*, XXIII, 312, an attack of the Normans (*Lodormani*) took place in 970 *ad Campos*; cf. R. Dozy, *Recherches sur l'histoire et la littérature de l'Espagne pendant le moyen âge* (3d ed., Paris and Leyden, 1881), II, 295-96. Cosack (*Eroberung von Lissabon*, p. 26, note 3) has drawn attention to the large number of villages in the region which still bear the name Campo; cf. *Enciclopedia universal*, X, 1297 ff.

[5] Actually some three or four miles south of the Cávado on the River Este.

[6] Santo Thyrso (district of Oporto) on the River Ave, some fifteen miles from the sea and about eighteen miles northeast of Oporto.

[7] The Leça is a small river emptying into the sea through the modern harbor of Leixoes, about three miles north of the mouth of the Douro.

[8] According to the Teutonic Source, departure from the Tambre took place on the octave of Pentecost (15 June) and arrival at Oporto on Monday, 16 June: *Brief des Priesters Winand*, p. 3; Duodechin, in *MGH, Scriptores*, XVII, 27; Arnulf, in *HF*, XIV, 325.

[9] The true derivation is believed to be from the port (*portus*) of the ancient Cale, which was located on the left bank of the Douro. See J. Augusto Ferreira, *Memorias archeologico-historicas da citade do Porto* (Braga, 1923-24), I, 9-14; cf. *idem, Porto: Origens historicas e seus principaes monumentos* (Oporto, 1928), pp. 3-6.

[10] The events referred to seem to be otherwise unknown. See Alberto Sampaio, "As Póvoas marítimas do norte de Portugal," in *Portugalia*, II (1905-8), 399-400; Ferreira, *Memorias . . . do Porto*, I, 126; *idem, Porto*, p. 5.

Moabitarum.[1] Habet autem portus a meridie harenas salubres, a prima rupe in introitu usque ad aliam rupem imfra,[2] habentes in latitudine passus XII. ab extremi recessus margine,[3] in quibus involvuntur egroti donec mare superveniens eos abluat ut sic sanentur. Ibidem vero testatus est episcopus predecessorem suum sanatum a livore simili lepre. [126v] De huiusmodi harenis, quod sint in Hyspania, in hystoriis Romanorum invenitur.[4]

Cum autem pervenissemus ad portum, episcopus[5] una cum clericis suis nobis obviam factus est; nam rex longe aberat cum exercitu suo contra Mauros. Ibidem salutatis omnibus ex more gentis suẹ, adventum nostrum se prescisse nobis indicavit; sed et ab heri litteras regias accepisse in hec verba:

"Hyldefonxus Portugalensium rex[6] Petro Portugalensi episcopo, salutem. Si forte Francorum naves ad vos pervenerint, cum omni benignitate et mansuetudine suscipite eos accuratius, et secundum conventionem remanendi mecum quam constitueritis, vos et quos vobiscum voluerint obsides totius conventionis [date];[a] et sic aput Lyxebonam pariter cum eis ad me veniatis. Vale."

Hiis auditis, cum esset iam hora decima, usque in crastinum distulimus respondendum, ut pariter qui in navibus erant omnes mandata regis audirent, et ab episcopo absolutionem peccatorum et benedictionem susciperent. Reliqua diei pars cura rerum familiarium consumpta est.

Summo mane[7] ex omnibus navibus in summitate montis in cimiterio epyscopii[8] coram episcopo omnes convenimus; nam

[a] An erasure of 7 millimetres follows *conventionis*, and something is wanting to complete the sense. I have ventured to supply *date*.

[1] The word, if properly understood, refers to the Almoravides. Dozy, *Recherches sur l'histoire et la littérature de l'Espagne*, II, 375–78, 327.

[2] The sense seems to require *supra*, and I have so translated.

[3] The sandy beach or tide-flat on the left bank of the Douro inside the rock and bar at the mouth of the river has now grown, through accumulating sand, to a width of perhaps an eighth of a mile. See U.S. Hydrographic Office Charts, Nos. 4322, 4407.

[4] I have failed to identify this reference in any ancient author.

[5] Peter Pitões, who can be traced as bishop of Oporto from 1146 to 1152. See Ferreira, *Memorias . . . do Porto*, II, 178–81.

[6] Affonso Henriques (1111–85), or Affonso I, founder of the Portuguese monarchy.

[7] 17 June (?).

at the time of the entry of the Moors and Moabites.[1] The port contains a beach of salubrious sands on the south, extending from the first rock within the entrance to another rock farther up[2] and having an extreme breadth of twelve paces at low tide.[3] The sick are enveloped in these sands until the sea comes in with the rising tide and washes them off, and so they are healed. And the bishop there testified that his predecessor had thus been cured of a black and blue spot resembling leprosy. As for sands of this sort, it is noted in the histories of the Romans[4] that there are such in Spain.

When we had arrived in the port we were met by the bishop[5] and his clergy, for the king was far away with his army on an expedition against the Moors. When everyone had been welcomed in accordance with the custom of his own people, the bishop told us that he had known in advance of our coming and that on the previous day he had received a letter from the king in the following words:

"Affonso, king of the Portuguese,[6] to Peter, bishop of Oporto, greeting. If perchance the ships of the Franks should come to you, take care to receive them with all possible friendliness and courtesy; and, in accordance with the agreement which you may conclude with them to stop with me, [offer] yourself and whoever else they may desire with you as security for its absolute inviolability; and so may you come with them to me at Lisbon. Farewell."

Since, when we had heard these things, it was already the tenth hour of the day, we put off our answer until the morrow, in order that our comrades who were still on shipboard might hear the king's message and at the same time receive absolution and a benediction from the bishop. The rest of the day was taken up with attending to personal affairs.

Early next morning[7] we all gathered from all the ships before the bishop on a hilltop in the cathedral churchyard,[8] for

[8] The cathedral is situated on a prominent hill well over two hundred feet above the river. The exact location of the cemetery has, so far as I know, not been determined. The natural landing place would have been on the low ground slightly down stream but almost directly under the hill, in the neighborhood of the modern Praça da Ribeira, which is to this day the most animated centre of waterside traffic in Oporto.

ecclesia pro quantitate sui omnes non caperet. Indicto ab
omnibus silentio, episcopus sermonem coram omnibus lingua
Latina habuit, ut per interpretes cuiusque lingue sermo eius
omnibus manifestaretur, qui sic incipit:

"'[B]eata* gens cuius est Dominus Deus eius, populus
quem elegit in hereditatem sibi.'¹ Et profecto beata quibus
Deus nescio quo inestimabili privilegio sensum et divitias
contulit: sensum ut vias discipline intelligerent; divitias ut
adimplere possent que pie cuperent. Et certe felix tellus vestra
que tot et tales alumpnos nutrit, que tot et tantos in sinu
matris ecclesie filios unanimes associat societati. Et merito
illius summę benedictionis effectus, qua dicitur, 'Beati qui
me non viderunt et crediderunt,'² in vobis completur.

"Mediator Dei et hominum, Christus, per se in mundum
veniens, paucissimos huius vię viros et pure religionis sectatores
invenit. Unde et a quodam iuvene interrogatus, cum se com-
plesse et observasse legem^b [127r] diceret, quomodo perfectus
esse posset, respondit, 'Vade et vende omnia,' et cetera. Per-
pendite quod^c sequitur, 'Tristatus est, nam erat in possessionibus dives.'³ O quanta est iusticia et misericordia Condi-
toris nostri! O quanta cecitas et duritia mentis humanę! Cum
veritate et de ipsa conferebat iuvenis, vox veritatis in auribus,^d
et quia callose mentis verbo veritatis non emollivit duritia,
iam non est mirum si vacuatam sinceritatis gaudio subintroiit
tristitia. Et quid dicemus ad hec? Quanti hic inter vos hoc
iuvene in possessionibus ditiores, quanti in dignitatum pro-
vectu sublimiores, quanti prole multiplici et fecunda generosi-
tate feliciores, quos constat profecto omnes honorum dignita-
tes, ut eternum a Deo consequerentur premium, felici pere-
grinatione commutasse! Blandos uxorum affectus, inter ubera
lactentium^e pia oscula, adultorum magis dilecta pignora, pa-

---

ᵃ The initial *B* is wanting, space having been left for a capital which was never
inserted.   ᵈ An erasure of 1.4 centimetres follows *auribus*.
  ᵇ *legis*.   ᵉ *lactaentium*. See above, p. 47 and note 2.
  ᶜ *quid*.

¹ Psalms (Vulgate) 32: 12; (English) 33: 12.
² John 20: 29.
³ Compare Matt. 19: 16–22; Mark 10: 17–22; Luke 18: 18–23.

our numbers were so great that the church would not hold us. When silence had been proclaimed of all, the bishop delivered a sermon in Latin, so that it might be made known to everyone in his own language through interpreters. Thus it begins:

"'Blessed is the nation whose God is the Lord, and the people whom he hath chosen for his own inheritance.'[1] And assuredly are they blessed on whom God has by some inestimable privilege conferred both understanding and riches: understanding, in order that they should know the ways of discipline; and riches, in order that they should be able to accomplish that which they piously desire. And truly fortunate is your country which rears such sons, and in such numbers, and unites them in such a unanimous association in the bosom of the mother church. And deservedly is the truth of that highest beatitude accomplished in you, in which it is said, 'Blessed are they that have not seen me and yet have believed.'[2]

"Christ, the mediator between God and men, when he came in person into the world, found very few who were followers of this way and of pure religion; hence, when a certain young man who said that he had fulfilled and kept the law asked him how he could be perfect, he answered, 'Go and sell all,' etc. Weigh carefully what follows: 'He was sad, for he had great possessions.'[3] Oh how great is the righteousness and mercy of our Creator! Oh how great the blindness and the hardness of the human mind! The young man spoke with Truth and about truth, and the voice of Truth was in his ears, and yet, since the hardness of his callous mind was not softened by the word of Truth, it is not to be wondered at if, when his mind had been emptied of the joy of sincerity, sadness entered in. And what shall we say to all this? How many there are among you here who are richer in possessions than this young man! How many who are higher in the rank of honors! How many who are more fortunate in a prolific stock and a numerous off-spring! Yet it is a fact that they have exchanged all their honors and dignities for a blessed pilgrimage in order to obtain from God an eternal reward. The alluring affection of wives, the tender kisses of sucking infants at the breast, the even more

rentum et amicorum affectanda solatia, soli natalis tantum^a
dulci remanente sed torquente memoria, Christum sequuti
reliquere. O admiranda Salvatoris opera! nullo predicante,
nullo admonente, zelum legis Dei in cordibus habentes, impetu
Spiritus ducente, per tot terrarum et marium pericula et longi
itineris dispendia, relictis omnibus,^b nobis primitive ecclesię
filiis huc advecti, hii novissimi crucis mysterium^c represen-
tant. O quanta omnium hilaritas, quibus ad laborem et penam
facies iocundior quam nobis, qui hic heu torpentes segni vaca-
mus otio! Et certe 'a Domino factum est istud, et est mirabile
in oculis nostris.'[1] Ecce, fratres karissimi, crucis improperium
portantes, extra castra exiistis;^d[2] Deum queritis dum inveniri
potest,[3] ut comprehendatis. Non enim videtur mirum homines
ad Deum ire, quia propter homines et inter homines Deus
venit. Iam usque ad vos in terre finibus verbi Dei prolata sunt
semina; nam 'exiit, qui seminat, seminare semen suum.' 'Semen
est verbum Dei';[4] verbum Dei Deus est. Si mentis vestre
sedem conscenderit, bona est igitur mens, nec sine eo. Semina
ista divina corporibus vestris dispersa sunt, que, si boni cul-
tores suscepistis, similes origini fructus prodire necesse est et
pares [127v] hiis ex quibus orti sunt; si mali, non aliter quam
humus sterilis ac palustris necat, ut postea purgamenta pro
frugibus generet. Et Deus bonus 'augeat incermenta frugum
iustitię vestre.'[5]

"Ecce, filii karissimi, novo penitentię renati baptismate,
Christum induistis iterum, vestem innocentię ut immaculatam
custodiatis iterum suscepistis. Videte ne iterum post concu-
piscentias vestras abieritis. 'Auferte malum cogitationum'[6]
de medio vestri. Animum purgate, id est mentem, in sancti-

---

^a An erasure of 7 millimetres follows *tantum*.

^b There is a superscribed *a* at the end of this word and a superscribed *b* over *huc* a
few words farther on. Perhaps the writer meant to indicate that *huc advecti* should be
read before *nobis primitive ecclesie filiis*, and inadvertently inserted the *a* and the *b* in
the opposite order from what he had intended.

^c *misterium.*   ^d *existis.*

[1] Psalms (Vulgate) 117: 23; (English) 118: 23.   [4] Luke 8: 5, 11.

[2] Compare Hebrews 13: 13.   [5] II Corinthians 9: 10.

[3] Compare Isaiah 55: 6.   [6] Isaiah 1: 16.

delightful pledges of grown-up children, the much desired
consolation of relatives and friends—all these they have left
behind to follow Christ, retaining only the sweet but torturing
memory of their native land. Oh, marvelous are the works of
the Savior! Without the urging of any preacher, with the zeal
of the law of God in their hearts, led by the impulse of the
[Holy] Spirit, they have left all and come hither to us, the
sons of the primitive church, through so many perils of lands
and seas and bearing the expenses of a long journey. They
are the most recent proof of the mysterious power of the cross.
Oh, how great is the joy of all those who present a more cheerful
face to hardships and pain than we do, we who, alas, are vege-
tating here in slothful idleness. Verily, 'this is the Lord's
doing, and it is marvelous in our eyes.'[1] Verily, dear brothers,
you have gone forth without the camp bearing the reproach
of the cross;[2] you are seeking God while he may be found,[3] in
order that you may lay hold on him. For it seems not strange
that men should go unto God, since for the sake of man God
also came among men. Even now unto you at the ends of the
earth hath the seed of the word of God been borne, for 'a
sower went out to sow his seed.' 'The seed is the word of God.'[4]
The word of God is God. If it ascend the throne of your mind,
your mind is accordingly good, but not without it. These
divine seeds have been sown in your bodies, and, if you receive
them as good husbandmen, they must needs produce fruit
like unto its source and the counterpart of that from which
it sprang; but, if you prove bad husbandmen, the result can
only be that sterile and swampy ground will destroy the seeds,
and afterwards it will bring forth trash instead of fruit. And
may the good God 'increase the fruits of your righteousness.'[5]

"Verily, dear sons, reborn of a new baptism of repentance,
you have put on Christ once more, you have received again
the garment of innocence to keep it stainless. Take care lest
you wander away again after your own lusts. 'Put away the
evil of your doings'[6] from your midst. Purge your souls, that
is, your minds, to be a temple sanctified unto God. Now the

ficatum Deo templum. Mentis vero habitus sub quolibet pon-
dere nequit deprimi,[a] si eam innocentię puritas comitetur. Et
ut pura sit innocentia mentis, penitus exstirpetur[b] invidia.
Cavendum est igitur maxime per mundi precipitia iter agen-
tibus ab huius [ge]neris [v]itio[c] quo aliena perduntur et sua
consumuntur[d] bona. Verum enim dum conspecta felicitas tor-
quet invidos et afficit pena contortionis[e] nequiores reddit;
aliorum bona que habere non possunt si diligerent, utique
fecissent sua. Vestra utique sunt bona sociorum que etsi imi-
tari non valetis, diligite in alios, et vestra fient que amantur
in socios. Excludite ergo invidiam que caritatem eicit et dis-
cordiam nutrit, que[f] corpus corrodit et macerat, nec ipsum
in sua valetudine[g] atque vigore stare permittit, quia dum
pestis invidię mentem lacerat corpus consumit, et quicquid in
se habere videtur boni interimit. Unde scriptum est, 'Vita
carnium sanitas cordis, putredo ossium invidia.'[1] Per livoris
vitium ante Dei oculos pereunt, etiam que humanis oculis
fortia videntur. Ossa quippe per invidiam putrescere est,
quedam etiam robusta deperire. Est autem invidia quasi odium
occultum, inde dicitur invidia, id est invisibile odium. Hoc est
tolerare et odisse, quod non est virtus mansuetudinis sed ve-
lamentum furoris. Sollerti igitur custodia muniendus est mentis
aditus, et eo observandum callidius quanto in ipso tempta-
tionis articulo fallacius[h] surrepit.[i] Necessaria est igitur ad
hec dilectionis[j] operatio, que inter malos non dilectio[k] sed
simultas proprie dicitur. Non est ergo dilectio[k] nisi inter bonos,
quia non est dilectio[k] valida [128r] nisi ex utraque parte affectus pendeat. Dilectionis[j] huius vel caritatis custos est innocentia, que tante virtutis et gratie creditur, ut Deo et homini-

---

[a] *deprimi* written in margin.   [b] *extyrpetur.*

[c] *generis vitio* written in margin and partly clipped away in rebinding.

[d] *consummuntur.*

[e] *contortionis* written over an erasure and rendered almost illegible by the spreading
of the ink. Stubbs, *Itinerarium*, p. cxlviii, read *extortionis.*

[f] An erasure of 6 millimetres follows *que.*   [g] *valitudine.*   [h] *fallatius.*

[i] *subripit.* Both here and on p. 76, line 13, below the writer uses *surripio* when the
sense seems to require *surrepo.* I have ventured to emend with *surrepo* in both instances,
as Stubbs (*Itinerarium*, p. cxlix) has done in the latter.   [j] *dileccionis.*   [k] *dileccio.*

[1] Proverbs 14: 30.

disposition of the mind cannot be depressed under any weight
whatsoever, if the purity of innocence attend it; and in order
that the innocence of your minds be perfect, envy must be
entirely cast out. Therefore, it is very necessary for those who
are traveling through the dangerous places of the earth to be
on their guard against this vice, whereby other people's welfare is lost and their own is destroyed. For, verily, while observed felicity [in others] wracks and torments the envious,
it renders them more base; [but] if they were to love the welfare
of others which they cannot have, they would inevitably make
it their own. The welfare of associates is yours in any case:
love it in others, even though you cannot imitate it, and it
will become your own, even as when loved in colleagues.
Therefore, put away envy which casts out love and nourishes
discord, which corrupts and wastes the body and prevents
it from enjoying its proper health and vigor. For while the
plague of envy tortures the mind, it consumes the body and
destroys whatever good appears to be in it. Hence it is written,
'A sound heart is the life of the flesh, but envy the rottenness
of the bones.'[1] Even those things which appear mighty to
the eyes of men, through the vice of envy come to nothing in
the eyes of God. Indeed, for the bones to rot through envy
means that certain things, strong though they be, do yet waste
away. Envy is, so to say, a hidden rancor, for which reason
it is called *invidia*, that is, invisible hate. To be envious is
to hate and to endure, which has not the virtue of mildness
but is a cover of fury. The entrance to the mind must therefore be guarded with sagacious care and so much the more
artfully watched as [envy] the more stealthily creeps in at the
very moment of temptation. Now for these things the working
of love is essential, which between evil men is properly called
not love but faction. Accordingly, there is no love except between the good, for love is without strength unless there be
affection on each side. The guardian of this love or affection
is innocence, which is believed to be endowed with such virtue
and grace in order to be pleasing both to God and men. That
is true innocence which harms neither itself nor another, and

bus placeat. Vera est hec que nec sibi nec alteri nocet, et cum valet, prodesse satagit. Innocentia vero ferrum retundit, acies hebetat, hostes comprimit, malorum precogitata refellit; nam miro modo divine animadversionis iudicio, quos prave mentis inquinat conscientia, hos proculdubio adversus innocentiam sequitur actionis difficultas.

"Sit vobis inter cetera temperatio gule, et ut breviter dicam, satietur caro ut in bono opere famulari nobis sufficiat. Sit itaque vobis ars quedam satiari, ne unusquisque per satietatem carnis ad iniquitatem prorumpat turpitudinis. De similitudine et collateralitate[a] et de hiis que in ea breviter annotavi,[1] eadem in[b] rectitudinis cautela teneatur; nam sepe pro virtutibus vitia surrepunt.[c]

"Auditum satis partibus vestris credimus, quod divina ultio superincumbentibus Mauris et Moabitis totam Hyspaniam in ore gladii percusserit;[2] paucis in ea Christianis admodum et in paucis urbibus sub gravissimo servitutis iugo relictis. Sed et ea que ad vos sola fame notitia[d] pertulit, ea proculdubio iam luce clariora certius subiecta visibus patent. Proh dolor! ut vix in tota Galletia et Aroganum regno et Numantia,[3] ex innumeris urbibus, castris et vicis et sanctorum sedibus, nisi sola ruinarum signa et iam facte desolationis indicia iam pareant. Ista etiam nostra quam cernitis, olim inter celebres, nunc ad instar parvuli redacta viculi,[4] iam nostra memoria multotiens a Mauris spoliata est. Verum enim ante hoc septennium ab eis adeo afflicta est, ut ab ecclesia beate Marie virginis, cui Dei gratia qualiscumque deservio, signa, vestes, vasa, et omnia ecclesie ornamenta, captis clericis aut occisis, asportarent. Sed et ex civibus captivos et ex circumquaque

[a] An erasure of 2.5 centimetres follows *collateralitate*.

[b] An erasure of 8 millimetres follows *in;* perhaps *hac* should be supplied.

[c] *surripiunt;* cf. p. 74, note i, above.   [d] *noticia*.

[1] I am unable to explain the meaning of this passage.

[2] Compare IV Kings (Vulgate) 10: 25; II Kings (English) 10: 25.

[3] The use of this word appears to be wholly rhetorical. "El nombre de Numancia quedaba en Edad Media sólo como recuerdo del heroismo celtibérico; pero se desconcía su emplazamiento que muchos colocaban en Zamora," *Enciclopedia universal*, XXXIX, 3; cf. Flórez, *España sagrada*, VII, 282–85.

when it is strong it is content to be useful. Indeed, innocence blunts iron, dulls blades, holds back enemies and confounds the well-laid plans of evil men; for in a marvelous way by the judgment of divine animadversion, a difficulty of action against innocence assuredly pursues those whom the consciousness of a base mind defiles.

"For the rest, be temperate in your eating, and, to speak briefly, let the flesh be satisfied, in order that it may suffice to serve us in a worthy enterprise. And so may you have a certain art of being satisfied, lest any of you through satiety rush headlong into some shameful iniquity. With respect to similitude and collaterality and the points which I have briefly noted under them,[1] let the same care for rectitude be exercised; for vices often steal in under the guise of virtues.

"We believe it has already become well enough known in the countries from which you come that through the presence of the Moors and Moabites divine vengeance has smitten all Spain with the edge of the sword,[2] and that but few Christians, resident in but a few cities, have been left in it, [and these] under the yoke of a grievous servitude. But these matters, of which a knowledge was brought to you by fame only, now most certainly lie open to your view more clear than day. Alas, that in all Galicia and the kingdom of Aragon and in Numantia,[3] of the numberless cities, castles, villages, and shrines of the saints there should now remain hardly anything to be seen but the signs of ruin and marks of the destruction which has been wrought! Even this city of ours which you see, once among the populous, now reduced to the semblance of an insignificant village,[4] has within our memory repeatedly been despoiled by the Moors. Indeed, but seven years ago it was so oppressed by them that from the church of the blessed Virgin Mary, which according to my poor talents by God's grace I serve, they carried away the insignia, the vestments, the vessels, and all the ecclesiastical ornaments, after they

[4] The phrase is evidently rhetorical, but there is little reason to suppose that Oporto in 1147 was any considerable centre of population. See Alberto Sampaio, "As Póvoas marítimas do norte de Portugal," in *Portugalia*, II (1905–8), 216–32, 393–401.

iacentibus territoriis usque ad ecclesiam beati Iacobi apostoli innumeros fere in patriam suam secum transtulere, non sine nobilium nostrorum sanguine, igne et gladio cetera consumentes^a omnia.[1] Quid enim litus Hyspanię vestris aliud obtutibus nisi sue desolationis memoriam quandam^b et ruinę ostendit indicia? Quot in eo urbium [128v] et ecclesiarum desolationes visu et indigenarum indiciis didicistis? Ad vos autem mater [e]cclesia^c iam quasi truncis brachiis et deformi facie clamat, sanguinem filiorum et vindictam per manus vestras requirit. Clamat, certe clamat! 'Vindictam facite in nationibus, increpationes in populis.'[2] Nulla ergo itineris incepti vos festinationis seducat occasio, quia non Iherosolimis fuisse sed bene interim invixisse laudabile est;[3] non enim ad eam nisi per opera eius pervenire potestis. Ex bono opere vero ut ad finem gloriosum quis perveniat meretur. Iacentem igitur et depressam Hyspanorum ecclesiam ut boni emulatores erigite; fedam et deformem vestibus iocunditatis et leticie reinduite. Ut boni filii, nolite spectare turpitudinem patris, et matri nolite dicere, 'Munus quodcumque est ex me tibi proderit.'[4] Federa societatis humane nolite parvipendere, quia, ut ait beatus Ambrosius, 'Qui a sociis et fratribus si potest non repellit iniuriam, tam est in vitio quam ille qui facit.'[5]

"Et vos boni filii matris ecclesię vim atque iniuriam propulsate; nam iure hoc evenit ut quis que ob tutelam sui corporis fecerit iure fecisse arbitretur. Vos fratres, arma deposuistis, arma scilicet quibus rapiuntur aliena. (De quibus dicitur, qui

---

^a *consummentes.*

^b *desolationis* and *quandam* written in margin at bottom of the page.

^c *ecclesia* written in margin and partly clipped away in rebinding.

---

[1] This raid of 1140 would seem to have followed upon the capture of Leiria by the Moors in that year, though Portuguese historians seem to have ignored this evidence that it was carried so far northward. Compare A. Herculano, *Historia de Portugal* (8th definitive ed. by D. Lopes and P. de Azevedo, Paris and Lisbon, n.d.), II, 180–81. Sampaio (*op. cit.*, p. 400) interprets it, perhaps correctly, as a maritime raid by Saracen pirates.

[2] Psalms 149: 7.

[3] Reinhold Röhricht, *Beiträge zur Geschichte der Kreuzzüge* (Berlin, 1874–78), II, 104, note 99, has pointed out that this is a play on the words of St. Jerome *Epistolae* 58.

had slain the clergy or made them captive. And from among the citizens and from the surrounding territory as far as the church of St. James the Apostle, they bore away with them into their own country almost innumerable captives, though not without bloodshed on the part of our nobles; and everything that remained they destroyed with fire and sword.[1] Indeed, what does the coast of Spain offer to your view but a kind of memorial of its desolation and the marks of its ruin? How many cities and churches have you discovered to be in ruins upon it, either through your own observation or through information given you by the inhabitants? To you the mother church, as it were with her arms cut off and her face disfigured, appeals for help; she seeks vengeance at your hands for the blood of her sons. She calls to you, verily, she cries aloud. 'Execute vengeance upon the heathen and punishments upon the people.'[2] Therefore, be not seduced by the desire to press on with the journey which you have begun; for the praiseworthy thing is not to have been to Jerusalem, but to have lived a good life while on the way;[3] for you cannot arrive there except through the performance of His works. Verily, it is through good work that anyone deserves to come to a glorious end. Therefore, as worthy rivals [strive together] to raise up the fallen and prostrate church of Spain; reclothe her soiled and disfigured form with the garments of joy and gladness. As worthy sons, look not on the shame of a father nor say to a mother, 'It is a gift by whatsoever thou mightest be profited by me.'[4] Weigh not lightly your duty to your fellow men; for, as St. Ambrose says, 'He who does not ward off an injury from his comrades and brothers, if he can, is as much at fault as he who does the injury.'[5]

"Now, as worthy sons of the mother church, repel force and injury; for in law it happens that whatever anyone does in self-defense he is held to have done lawfully. Brothers, you have laid aside the arms [of violence] by which the property of others is laid waste—concerning which it is said, 'He that

---

2 (ad Paulinum): "non Hierosolymis fuisse, sed Hierosolymis bene vixisse laudandum est."   4 Matt. 15: 5.   5 Ambrose De officiis i. 36.

gladio percutit gladio peribit,[1] scilicet qui, nulla superiore ac
legitima potestate vel iubente vel concedente, in sanguinem
fratris armatur.) Sed nunc Deo inspirante arma fertis, quibus homicidę et raptores dampnentur, furta cohibeantur,
adulteria puniantur, impii de terra perdantur, parricide vivere
non sinantur, nec filii impie agere. Vos igitur fratres, cum hiis
fortitudinem armis suscipite, eam scilicet que vel bello tuetur
a barbaris patriam vel domi defendit inimicos vel a latronibus
socios; nam plena est iusticię. Huiusmodi vero opera vindicte
officia sunt que boni bono animo implent. [129r] Nolite, fratres,
nolite timere. Non enim in huiusmodi actionibus homicidio
vel taxatione alicuius criminis notabimini; imo rei propositi
vestri deserti iudicabimini. 'Non est vero crudelitas pro Deo
pietas.'[2] Zelo iusticię, non felle ire, iustum bellum committite.
'Iustum vero bellum,' dicit Ysidorus noster, 'quod ex indicto
geritur de rebus repetendis aut hostium pulsandorum causa';[3]
et quia iusta est causa homicidas et sacrilegos et venenarios
punire, non est effusio sanguinis homicidii. Et item non est
crudelis qui crudeles perimit. Vel qui malos perimit, in eo
quod mali sunt et habet causam interfectionis, minister est
Domini. Profecto filii Israel contra Amorreos iustum bellum
commisere, quibus transitus negabatur innoxius. Et vos ergo
populus Israel et filii Christi et servi crucis, numquid hec
libertas permittenda adversariis crucis ut impune vobis insul-
tent? Absit. Audite quid super hiis Augustinus dixerit ad
Donatum presbyterum: 'Non est permittenda mala voluntas
sue libertati, sicut nec Paulo permissum uti pessima voluntate,
qui persecutus est ecclesiam Dei.'[4] Item Crisostomus, *super*
Matheum, homilia[a] xvii: 'Occidit Finees hominem, "et repu-
tatum est ei ad iusticiam";[5] Abraham non solum homicida,
sed quod gravius parricida effectus, magis magisque Deo

---

[a] *omelia.*

[1] Compare Matt. 26: 52.
[2] Jerome *Epistolae* 109. 3 (ad Riparium).
[3] Isidore of Seville *Etymologiae* xviii. 1, 2.
[4] Compare Augustine *Epistolae* 173. 3 (ad Donatum).
[5] Psalms (Vulgate) 105: 31; (English) 106: 31.

strikes with the sword shall perish with the sword,'[1] that is, he who, without the command or consent of any higher or legitimate power, takes up arms against the life of his brothers —but now by God's inspiration you are bearing the arms [of righteousness] by means of which murderers and robbers are condemned, thefts are prevented, acts of adultery are punished, the impious perish from the earth, and parricides are not permitted to live nor sons to act unfilially. Therefore, brothers, take courage with these arms, courage, that is to say, either to defend the fatherland in war against barbarians or to ward off enemies at home, or to defend comrades from robbers; for such courage is full of righteousness. Indeed, such works of vengeance are duties which righteous men perform with a good conscience. Brothers, be not afraid. For in acts of this sort you will not be censured for murder or taxed with any crime; on the contrary you will be adjudged answerable if you should abandon your enterprise. 'Indeed, there is no cruelty where piety towards God is concerned.'[2] Engage in a just war with the zeal of righteousness, not with the bile of wrath. 'For a war is just,' says our Isidore, ' which is waged after a declaration, to recover property or to repulse enemies';[3] and, since it is just to punish murderers and sacrilegious men and poisoners, the shedding of their blood is not murder. Likewise he is not cruel who slays the cruel. And he who puts wicked men to death is a servant of the Lord, for the reason that they are wicked and there is ground for killing them. Certainly the children of Israel waged a just war against the Amorites when they were refused a peaceful passage [through their borders]. And you, therefore, being people of Israel, sons of Christ, and servants of the cross, shall it be permitted to the adversaries of the cross to insult you with impunity? God forbid! Hear what Augustine has said on this subject to Donatus the priest: 'An evil will must not be allowed its liberty, even as Paul, who persecuted the church of God, was not permitted to carry out his worst intentions.'[4] Again, Chrysostom, *On Matthew*, Homily XVII: 'Phinehas killed a man, "and it was counted unto him for righteousness."'[5] Abra-

placuit.'[1] Item Ieronymus ad Ripoarium: 'Legi siromasten[a] Finees, austeritatem[b] Heliȩ, zelum Symonis Cananei, Petri severitatem Annaniam et Saphiram trucidantem, Pauli constantiam qui Elimam magum viis Domini resistentem eterna cecitate[c] dampnavit.'[2] Unde in lege dicitur, 'Si frater tuus et amicus et uxor que est in sinu tuo te depravare voluerit a veritate, sit manus tua super eos et effunde sanguinem ipsorum.'[3] Tale quid in vobis spiritualiter completum est. Percussit in vobis Dominus Saulum et erexit Paulum. Eandem Sauli et Pauli carnem, non eundem mentis affectum sed immutatum. Ecce quam pius, quam iustus, quam misericors Deus! Nichil vobis detraxit Deus. Eadem patriȩ vestre opera, sed affectu solum mutato vobis concessit. Armis et gladio [129v] utebamini; predas agebatis et cetera militantium facinora de quibus non est modo dicendum per singula.[4] Vos, ut videtur, arma portatis et rei militaris insignia, sed diverso affectu, ut superius dictum, non mutantes actum sed voluntatem, attendentes illud apostoli consilium, 'Sicut exhibuistis membra vestra servire immunditiȩ ad iniquitatem, ita exhibete membra vestra,'[5] et cetera. Sed quoniam armati venistis, eia! ut boni milites agite, quia non est peccatum militare, sed propter predam peccatum est militare. Suscipite ergo vobis et vestris beati Augustini[d] salubre consilium ad Bonefacium comitem.[6] Arripite manibus arma, oratio aures pulset Auctoris; quia quando pugnatur Deus apertis oculis spectat, et partem quam inspicit iustam ibi dat palmam. Et vere adimplebitur in vobis prophetia qua ad laudem et honorem[e] virtutis et gloriȩ filiorum Dei dictum est, 'Quomodo perse-

---

[a] *chyromachen.*

[b] *auctoritatem.* I have emended to read in accordance with Jerome.

[c] *severitate.* I have emended to read in accordance with Jerome.

[d] *Augustinus.*

[e] *ad laudem et honorem* written over an erasure, in different ink.

[1] Chrysostom *In Matthaeum*, Homil. xvii. 5.

[2] Jerome *Epistolae* 109. 3.

[3] Compare Deut. 13: 6.

[4] The thinness of the line dividing a crusade from piracy is fully recognized by the bishop.

[5] Romans 6: 19.

ham becoming not only a murderer, but, what is graver still, the slayer of his child, was more and more pleasing to God.'[1] Again, Jerome to Riparius: 'I have read of the javelin of Phinehas, the austerity of Elijah, the zeal of Simon the Canaanite, the severity of Peter in slaying Ananias and Sapphira, the constancy of Paul who damned with perpetual blindness Elymas, the sorcerer, when he resisted the ways of the Lord.'[2] Whence it is said in the Law, 'If thy brother and thy friend and the wife of thy bosom wish to pervert thee from the truth, let thy hand be upon them and shed their blood.'[3] It is something like that which is being spiritually fulfilled in you. In you the Lord hath smitten Saul and raised up Paul. The flesh of Saul and Paul was the same, but not the disposition of the mind, for it was completely transformed. Behold how pious, how just, how merciful is God! God has taken nothing from you: he has permitted the same enterprises on behalf of your country, only your purpose has been changed. You were employed with arms and the sword; you were committing acts of pillage and other misdeeds of soldiers, concerning which there is no need now to speak in detail.[4] You are [still], as is apparent, bearing arms and the insignia of war, but with a different object, as above said; having changed your purpose without changing your acts, you are heeding that counsel of the apostle [which says], 'As ye have yielded your members servants to uncleanness unto iniquity, even so now yield your members,'[5] etc. But since you have come with arms upon you, up then, quit you like good soldiers; for the sin is not in waging war, but in waging war for the sake of plunder. Therefore, take unto yourselves the salutary counsel of St. Augustine to Count Boniface:[6] take arms in your hands and let your prayer smite the ears of the Creator; for, when a battle is fought, God looketh on with open eyes, and to the side which he seeth to be righteous he giveth the palm. And truly will that prophecy be fulfilled in you in which to the praise and honor of the valor and glory of the sons of God it is said, 'How one should chase a thousand and two put ten thousand to

---

[6] Augustine *Epistolae* 189. 4–6 (ad Bonifatium comitem).

quebatur[a] unus mille, et duo fugarent X. M.'[1]; et iterum,[b] 'Persequentur V. de vobis C. alienos et C. ex vobis X. milia;[c] cadent inimici vestri coram vobis gladio.'[2] Nam bellum quod Deo auctore gerendum suscipitur, recte suscipi dubitare fas non est.

"De cetero, filius noster dilectus et frater vester et in tribulationibus particeps, Hyldefonxus rex noster, contra Olixebonam diebus iam decem retroactis cum omni expeditione sua exiit. Vestrum adventum prenoscens, nos hic vos expectatum stare iussit, ut vos vice eius alloqueremur. Si forte Deus cordibus vestris immiserit, vos ut cum omni navigio vestro eum adeatis, et cum illo donec Deo auctore et vobis cooperantibus civitas Lyxbonensis caperetur maneatis; peccunie vero sponsionem, si vobis placet, proinde facturi vestris, prout fisci regie potestatis facultas sequetur. Nos vero inde et quos volueritis vobiscum obsides habeatis sponsionis persolvende. Quid vero placuerit sanctitati societatis vestre responsionem expectabimus.

"Sit iam in manibus vestris consilium pium, modestum, iustum, honestum, ad laudem et honorem nominis eius et sanctissime sue genitricis, qui cum Deo Patre et Spiritu Sancto vivit et regnat per omnia secula seculorum. Amen."

Completo sermone, post expletionem misse deliberatum est ab omnibus ut Christianus dux Flandrensium et comes de Aerescot et naves plurime que nondum ex dispersione con-[130r]venerant expectarentur, et advocaretur Iohannes archiepiscopus Braccarensis.[d3]

Congregatis igitur ex dispersione navibus, deliberatum est ut episcopi una nobiscum in navibus aput civitatem venirent Lixbonensem, ut illinc a rege illorum audiremus presentes, que absentibus mandabantur.

[a] *persequebatur* written over an erasure, in different ink.

[b] *et iterum* inserted at the end of the line, in different ink, apparently at the time the marginalium was added. See note c, below.

[c] *Persequentur . . . X. milia* written in margin, in different ink.

[d] A letter is erased between *r* and *e*, as if *Braccariensis* had first been written.

[1] Deut. 32: 30. [2] Leviticus 26: 8.

flight';[1] and again, 'Five of you shall chase an hundred, and an hundred of you shall put ten thousand to flight; and your enemies shall fall before you by the sword.'[2] For when a war has been entered upon by God's will, it is not permitted to doubt that it has been rightly undertaken.

"For the rest, our dear son and your brother and fellow in tribulation, our king, Affonso, has already departed ten days ago with all his forces on an expedition against Lisbon. Knowing in advance of your coming, he commanded us to remain here to await you, in order that we might speak with you in his place. If perchance God should put it into your hearts that you with all your fleet should go to him and remain with him until by God's will and your coöperation the city of Lisbon be taken, we will promise money to your forces so far as the resources of the royal treasury will permit. And as hostages for the fulfillment of the promise you may keep us with you, and any one else whom you may desire. We will await the reply which it shall please the honor of your association to make.

"And now, may there be among you pious, humble, upright, and honest counsel, to the praise and honor of His name and of His most holy Mother—the name of Him who with God the Father and the Holy Spirit liveth and reigneth for ever and ever. Amen."

When the sermon was over and the mass completed, it was decided by all to await Christian, leader of the Flemings, and the count of Aerschot and a number of ships which had been scattered by the storm and had not yet arrived, and to send for John, archbishop of Braga.[3]

Accordingly, when the fleet had been reassembled after the dispersion, it was decided that the bishops should come with us on the ships to Lisbon, and that we should there hear from the king in person the proposals which had been made to us by commission in his absence.

[3] John Peculiar (*Peculiaris*) was archbishop of Braga 1138–75; he had previously been bishop of Oporto. See Fortunato de Almeida, *Historia da igreja em Portugal* (Coimbra, 1910–), I, 607, 631.

Die vero quasi decima sequen[ti],[a1] impositis sarcinis nostris, una cum episcopis velificare incepimus, iter prosperum agentes. Die vero postera ad insulam Phenicis distantem a continenti quasi octingentis passibus[2] feliciter applicuimus. Insula[b] abundat cervis et maxime cuniculis[3]; liquiricium habet. Tyrii dicunt eam Erictream, Peni Gaddir, id est sepem,[4] ultra quam non est terra; ideo extremus noti orbis terminus dicitur. Iuxta hanc sunt II. insule, que vulgo dicuntur Berlinges,[5] id est Baleares lingua corrupta[6]; in una quarum est palatium admirabilis architecture et multa officinarum diversoria, regi cuidam, ut aiunt, quondam gratissimum secretale hospicium.[7] Habentur autem in continenti a Portugala usque ad insulam flumina et castra. Est castrum quod dicitur Sancte Marie[8]

---

[a] *sequenti* written in margin and partly clipped away in rebinding.

[b] An erasure of 8 millimetres before, and of 1.8 centimetres after, *insula*.

[1] About 26 June. The Teutonic Source seems to date the departure from Oporto 27 June. It also records the "fair market of wine and all other delights" with which they were provided through the king's good will during their sojourn at Oporto: *Brief des Priesters Winand*, p. 4; Duodechin, in *MGH, Scriptores*, XVII, 27; Arnulf, in *HF*, XIV, 326.

[2] The channel has long since sanded up, so that the former island has become Peniche Peninsula, "a rocky headland 110 feet in height, 1.5 miles in length east and west, and a little more than a mile in width, . . . connected with the mainland by a sandy isthmus a mile in length, rather more than 1,000 yards in width, and so low that it is completely overflowed by high tides with strong northerly or southerly winds:" U.S. Hydrographic Office, *East Atlantic Pilot* (4th ed., Washington, 1929), p. 141; cf. Biblioteca Nacional de Lisboa, *Guia de Portugal* (Lisbon, [1924–]), II, 574–82; U.S. Hydrographic Office Charts, No. 4322.

[3] Compare Solinus (whom the author used) 23. 12, who in turn misinterprets Pliny *HN* iii. 78.

[4] The passage is based on Solinus 23. 12: "insula . . . quam Tyrii a Rubro profecti mari Erythream, Poeni lingua sua Gadir id est saepem nominaverunt" (which in turn is derived from Pliny *HN* iv. 120), the author erroneously identifying Peniche with Gades (modern Léon), the island on which Cadiz is located.

[5] Burling Islands, about six miles northwest of the extremity of Peniche Peninsula. See *East Atlantic Pilot*, pp. 143–44; *Guia de Portugal*, II, 582–87; J. Daveau, "Excursion aux Iles Berlengas et Farilhões," Sociedade de geographia de Lisboa, *Boletim*, 4th ser., I (1883), 409–12.

[6] The confusion of the Burlings with the Balearic Islands is not surprising in view of the author's idea that the latter were located on this side of Spain—an idea which, as above noted, p. 67, note 3, he may have derived from a misleading statement of Solinus, which in turn was based on an unintelligent reading of Pliny. That the author is not alone in his confusion is demonstrated by the fact that on the *mappamundi* of

About the tenth day afterwards,[1] our baggage having been replaced on board, we set sail with the bishops and had a prosperous voyage. And next day we landed safely on the island of Peniche, which lies about eight hundred paces off the mainland.[2] The island abounds in deer and especially in rabbits;[3] it also produces liquorice. The Tyrians call it *Erythraea;* the Carthaginians *Gadir,* that is, a barrier,[4] beyond which there is no land. For this reason it is called the farthest limit of the known world. Near it lie two [other] islands, which are vulgarly called the Burlings,[5] that is, the Balearics in corrupt speech;[6] on one of which there is a palace of wonderful construction, with many stalls for workshops, formerly, they say, the most grateful private retreat of a certain king.[7] On the mainland from Oporto as far as the island [of Peniche] there are both rivers and castles. There is the castle which is called St. Mary's [Feira],[8] between the River Douro and the forest

---

the Beatus manuscript of Osma (1086) the Balearics are located very nearly in the position of the Burlings. Compare Miller, *Mappaemundi,* Heft 1, p. 35, Heft 2, Tafel 3 (here not legible, but see *Art Studies,* VIII, 1931, Pt. 2, 154: "Baleares hii sunt").

[7] Nothing appears to be known of ancient ruins on the Burling Islands. Can it be that the author's imagination was at work on the words of Solinus 23. 12, apropos of the island of Gades: "in hac Geryonem aevum agitavisse plurimis monumentis probatur"? Compare Pliny *HN* iv. 120.

[8] Feira, district of Aveiro, some twenty miles south of Oporto. This identification was given as probable (*vermutlich*) by Cosack (*Eroberung von Lissabon,* p. 30, note), citing Brandão (in Bernard de Brito, *Monarchia Lusytana,* [Alcobaça] and Lisbon, [1597]–1727, III, 12, 116). Flórez (*España sagrada,* XXI, 43) has cited Rodrigo da Cunha (*Catalogo dos bispos do Porto,* Oporto, 1623, Pt. 1, pp. 13, 16, 185) as authority for the tradition that the eleventh-century warrior bishop of Oporto, Sisnandus I, dedicated his conquests, of which Feira was one, to the Virgin, calling them *terrae de Santa Maria.* The arms of Feira represent the Virgin with the infant Jesus in her arms, upon a cloud over a castle ("a imagem da Virgem com o menino Jesus nos braços, sobre uma nuvem pousada em um castello"): Manoel Pinheiro Chagas, *Diccionario popular, historico, geographico, mythologico, biographico, artistico, bibliographico, e litterario* (Lisbon, 1876–90), Supplement, I, s.v. *Feira.* According to the modern guidebook (F. Muirhead, *Southern Spain,* London and Paris, 1929, p. 245) the territory between Feira and Oporto is to this day known as *Terras de Santa Maria.* The castle of Feira, said to have been taken from the Moors by Affonso Henriques, is described as "an archaeological marvel," *Enciclopedia universal,* XXIII, 566. According to the pilot guide (*East Atlantic Pilot,* p. 133), "The town and castle of Feira, on rising ground, 6 miles inland, . . . may be distinguished from sea in clear weather."

inter fluvium Doira et silvam que dicitur Medica[a] in frigore,[1] in cuius territorio requiescit beatus Donatus[2] apostoli Iacobi discipulus. Et post silvam fluvius Vaga. Et post, civitas Colymbria super fluvium Mundego. Ultra quam est castrum Soyra.[3] Et post, castrum quod dicitur Mons Maior.[4] Et post, castrum Lora, super fluvium qui dividit episcopatum Lyxbonensem a Colymbriensi.[5] Et post, silva que vocatur Alchubez[6] lingua eorum, circa quam eremi[b] vastitas[7] usque ad castrum Suh*r*ium, quod distat a Lyxebona miliaria VIII.[8]

In insula vero predicta cum pernoctassemus, summo mane velificare incepimus, iter prosperum agentes donec fere ad ostia[c] Tagi fluminis ventus procumbens a montibus Such*r*iis naves tam admirabili tempestate concuteret ut pars batellorum cum hominibus absorberetur. Perseveravit autem tempestas usque ad introitum portus fluminis Tagi. Nobis vero portum intrantibus signum admirabile in aere visum est. Nam ecce a Galliarum partibus nubes candide magne nobiscum venientes, nubibus quibusdam magnis nigredine conspersis a continenti venientibus concurrere vise sunt; atque in modum acierum ordinatarum sinistris cornibus inter se iunctis admirabili impetu confligere, [130v] quedam in modum velitum, dextra levaque impressione facta, in aciem resilire, quedam ut aditum invenirent ceteras girare, quedam ceteras penetrare easdemque penetratas ad modum vaporis inanire, quedam sursum quedam deorsum levari, nunc pene aquis contigue

[a] Just before *Medica* there is a reference to the margin, where one reads *id est mei* (the last two letters doubtful), the remainder of the marginalium being clipped away in rebinding.　　　　[b] *heremi.*　　　　[c] *hostia.*

[1] I have failed to identify this place. Stubbs, *Itinerarium*, p. cliii, note 1, has proposed *Mezanfrio*, by which he presumably meant Mesao-Frio; but this lies to the north of the Douro and some thirty-five miles almost directly east of Oporto. There seems to be no justification, beyond mere geographical position, for Cosack's identification (*loc. cit.*) with the modern Serra Gralheira.

[2] He is mentioned again below, pp. 116–17, as one of the *sequaces* of St. James, but is apparently otherwise unknown to tradition. The only other Donatus whom I have found in any way associated with Portugal is the martyr of Concordia in Italy (17 February) whose martyrdom is assigned to Thomar (district of Santarém) in the year 145 by the false Dexter (early seventeenth century). Migne, XXXI, 333–34.

[3] Evidently Soure, some fifteen miles southwest of Coimbra. Compare *Enciclopedia universal*, LVII, 691.

called *Medica in frigore*,[1] in the land of which lies the blessed Donatus,[2] a disciple of St. James the Apostle; and after the forest, the River Vouga; and after this, the city of Coimbra on the River Mondego, beyond which is the castle of Soure;[3] and after this, the castle called Montemor;[4] and after this, the castle of Leiria, on the river which divides the diocese of Lisbon from that of Coimbra;[5] and after this, the forest called Alcobaça[6] in their tongue, around which a wilderness[7] extends as far as the castle of Cintra, which is eight miles from Lisbon.[8]

When we had passed the night on the aforesaid island, we set sail at dawn and had a prosperous voyage until, when we were almost at the mouth of the Tagus River, a squall came down from the hills of Cintra and struck the ships with such amazing violence that several of the smaller boats were sunk with the men on board. And the squall continued until we entered the shelter of the Tagus River. As we were entering the port a wonderful portent appeared to us in the air. For behold, great white clouds coming along with us from the direction of the Gauls were seen to encounter other great clouds bespattered with blackness coming from the mainland. Like ordered lines of battle with left wings locked together they collided with a marvelous impact, some in the manner of skirmishers attacking on right and left and then springing back into line, some encircling others in order to find a way through, some going right through the others and reducing them to a void like vapor, some being pressed downwards and now almost touching the water, others being lifted

[4] Montemor-o-Velho, on the right bank of the Mondego, some sixteen miles below Coimbra and ten miles from the sea. It is plainly indicated on the world map of Idrisi (1154), Miller, *Mappae Arabicae*, II, 104, 106-7. The author is much confused as to the relative positions of Montemor and Soure. The former is almost ten miles north and slightly west of the latter. Compare *Enciclopedia universal*, XXXVI, 560.

[5] Leiria is in fact on the River Lis, which, in its lower reaches, formed the dividing line between the dioceses of Lisbon and Coimbra. Compare *Enciclopedia universal*, XXIX, 1526; *Guia de Portugal*, II, 655-57.

[6] Alcobaça, about twenty-nine miles southwest of Leiria and some five or six miles from the sea. Compare *Enciclopedia universal*, IV, 279-80; *Guia de Portugal*, II, 611-12.

[7] On the character of this region see Herculano, *Historia de Portugal*, II, 152.

[8] Cintra is actually about seventeen miles from Lisbon.

nunc ab oculis in sublime ferri. Cum tandem nubes magna a nostris partibus veniens omnem aeris impuritatem secum trahens, ut ad modum azoli purissimi citra hanc videretur, ceteras omnes a continenti venientes impetu suo reprimens, quasi victrix coram se predas agens, aeris sola principatum tenuit, ceteris omnibus vel inanitis vel si qua paucula remanserit aput urbem visa est confugere, nobis acclamantibus: "Ecce nubes nostra devicit! Ecce nobiscum Deus! Dispersa est hostium potentia! Confusi sunt, quoniam Dominus dissipavit[a] eos!" Et sic demum tempestatis cessavit omnis quassatio. Igitur post parum temporis, circiter horam diei X., pervenimus ad civitatem que non multum distat ab ostio fluminis Tagi.[1]

[E]st[b] autem Tagus fluvius subterlabens, a Toletanis partibus fluens, in cuius ripis sub primo vere, dum in alveo se recolligit, aurum invenitur;[2] cuius etiam tanta piscium copia ut due partes aque tertia piscium ab incolis credatur. Conchiliis abundat ut harena. Hoc autem precipue, quod huius aque pisces omni tempore pinguedinem suam et saporem innatum retinent, non alternantes vel degenerantes, ut aput vos est, ulla rerum vicissitudine.[3] A meridie huius est Elmada[4] provintia, que abundat vineis et ficis et pomis granatis. Segete adeo fertilis ut bis ex uno semine fructificet; celebris venatibus, melle abundans. Similiter in ea parte castrum Palmella.[5] A septentrione fluminis est civitas Lyxibona in cacumine montis rotundi; cuius muri gradatim descendentes[c] ad ripam fluminis Tagi solum muro interclusi pertingunt. Sub nostro adventu opulentissima totius Affrice et magne partis Europe commeatibus. Est autem sita super montem Artabrum,[6] per-

[a] *dissipabit.*
[b] The initial *E* is wanting, space being left for a capital which was never inserted.
[c] *descentes.*

[1] Lisbon is actually some eight or nine miles from the sea.
[2] The passage is evidently inspired by Solinus 23. 6, which in turn is based on Pliny *HN* iv. 115.
[3] The modern traveler still shares the author's enthusiasm for the fish and shellfish, not only of the Tagus, but of all the coast of Portugal.
[4] Almada is located on the opposite bank of the Tagus directly south of Lisbon.
[5] Palmela is situated southeast of Lisbon at a distance of some seventeen or eighteen

upwards and now borne from view in the firmament. When at last the great cloud coming from our direction and carrying with it all the impurity of the air, so that all on this side appeared as purest azure, pressed back all the others which were coming from the direction of the mainland, and, as a victress driving the booty before her, held all alone the mastery of the air, and all the others had either been reduced to nothing, or, if some fragments remained, they appeared to be in flight towards the city, we all shouted, "Behold, our cloud has conquered! Behold, God is with us! The power of our enemies is destroyed! They are confounded, for the Lord has put them to flight!" And so at last the squall ceased. And a short time afterwards, about the tenth hour of the day, we arrived at the city which is not far from the mouth of the Tagus.[1]

The Tagus, gliding by, is a river which flows down from the region of Toledo. Gold is found on its banks in the early spring after it has returned to its channel.[2] It contains fish in such quantities that it is believed by the natives to be two parts water and one part fish; and it abounds in shellfish like the sands [without number]. This also is especially to be noted, that the fish in this river retain at all seasons their richness and natural flavor, neither altering nor deteriorating, as happens with you, under any circumstances.[3] To the south of it lies the province of Almada,[4] which abounds in vines and figs and pomegranates. So fertile is the soil that two crops are produced from a single seeding. It is celebrated for its hunting and abounds in honey. Also on this side is the castle of Palmela.[5] On the north of the Tagus is the city of Lisbon, situated on the top of a round hill; and its walls, descending by degrees, extend right down to the bank of the river, which is only shut out by the wall. At the time of our arrival [it was] the richest in trade of all Africa and a good part of Europe. It is situated on *Mons Artabrum*,[6] a promontory which extends to

---

miles, on one of the northernmost spurs of the Serra da Arrabida; it is in full view from Lisbon in fine weather. Compare *Enciclopedia universal*, XLI, 409; *Guia de Portugal*, I, 645–48.

[6] In attaching the name *Artabrum* to this promontory, the author follows Solinus

tingentem mare Occeanum Gaditanum; celum, terras, maria distinguit a terris, eo quod ibi litus Hyspanie finiat, et quod a circuitu eius incipit [131r] Gallicus Occeanus et fons septentrionalis, Occeano Atlantico et occasu terminatis ibidem.[1] Quo ab Ulyxe oppidum[a] Ulyxibona conditum creditur.[2] Territoria eius circumquaque adiacentia optimis comparanda nulli postponenda, frugique soli copia, sive arborarios sive vinearum proventus respicere velis. Omni materia affluit, aut quę pretio ambitiosa aut usu necessaria. Aurum et argentum habet; ferrariis numquam deficit. Vincit olea; nichil in ea otiosum[b] vel sterile, nec quod omnimodam messem neget. Non coquunt sales sed effodiunt. Ficis abundat, adeo ut vix a nobis portio consumi[c] quiverit. Vigent pabulis etiam arida.[3] Venatibus multimodis celebris. Non habet lepores. Aves habet multigenas. Aere salubris. Habet autem civitas hec balnea calida.[4] Iuxta quam est castrum Suchtrium, distans quasi miliaria VIII.,[5] in quo fons est purissimus, usus cuius tussim phthisimque[d] sedare dicitur; unde si incole tussientes audierint, non esse indigenas deprehendant. Habet etiam poma citrea.[e] In cuius pascuis eque lasciviunt mira fecunditate. Nam aspirate favoniis vento concipiunt, et postmodum sitientes cum maribus coeunt; sic aurarum spiritu maritantur.[6]

---

[a] *opidum.*   [b] *ociosum.*   [c] *consummi.*   [d] *tysimque.*

[e] *cetria.* The reading of the first two letters is somewhat doubtful. Apparently *cedria* was first written; then the first three letters were partly erased; then *t* was written over the partly erased *d*. A marginal note is added, now only partly legible, which appears to be as follows: *quodammodo . . . odorem . . . rentia . . . catur arb[or] medica cong* (?) *. . . ven[enum] dicitur.* Stubbs (*Itinerarium*, p. clv, note 1) read *quodammodo odorem . . . rentia . . . catur de v . . . medici eorum . . . ver . . . dicitur.* This is certainly based on Solinus 46. 4–6, and appears to be concerned with the odor of the citron and with its supposed virtue as an antidote for poison.

---

23. 5, who follows Pliny *HN* iv. 113, who seems to be in error. See D. Detlefsen, *Die Anordnung der geographischen Bücher des Plinius und ihre Quellen* (Berlin, 1909), p. 72.

   [1] The extreme confusion of this passage arises from the fact that the author was using Solinus, evidently in a very corrupt text, which rendered the clear statement of Pliny unintelligible. The pertinent texts of Pliny and Solinus seem to require quotation. Pliny *HN* iv. 113–14: ". . . promunturium . . . Artabrum . . . terras, maria, caelum disterminans. Illo finitur Hispaniae latus et a circuitu eius incipit frons. Septentrio hinc oceanusque Gallicus, occasus illinc et oceanus Atlanticus." Solinus

the Ocean of Cadiz [and forms a landmark], dividing the land, the sea, and the heavens; for the side of Spain ends there, and with the rounding of the promontory its northern front and the Gallic Ocean begin, the Atlantic and the West having there been terminated.[1] It is the site where the town of Lisbon is believed to have been founded by Ulysses.[2] The surrounding country is second to none and comparable with the best, rich in products of the soil, whether you are looking for the fruit of trees or of vines. It abounds in everything, both costly articles of luxury and necessary articles of consumption. It also contains gold and silver and is never wanting in iron mines. The olive flourishes. There is nothing unproductive or sterile or which refuses to return a harvest. They do not boil their salt but dig it. Figs are so abundant that we could hardly eat a fraction of them. Even the dry places are productive of forage.[3] The region is celebrated for many kinds of hunting. There are no hares, but many kinds of birds. The air is healthful, and the city has hot baths.[4] About eight miles away is the castle of Cintra,[5] in which there is a spring of purest water, the use of which is said to stop coughs and allay consumption. Hence, if the inhabitants should hear anyone coughing, they might discern that he was not a native. The region also produces citrons. In its pastures the mares breed with a wonderful fecundity; for, being blown upon by the west winds, they conceive from the wind, and afterwards, being in heat, they are joined with their mates, and so they are impregnated by the breath of the breezes.[6]

---

23. 5: "Artabrum . . . Hoc caelum terras maria distinguit: terris Hispaniae latus finit: caelum et maria hoc modo dividit, quod a circuitu eius incipiunt Oceanus Gallicus et frons septentrionalis, Oceano Atlantico et occasu terminatis." In translating I have substituted *latus* for *litus* and *frons* for *fons*.

[2] Derived from Solinus 23. 6.

[3] The entire passage *Territoria eius . . . etiam arida*, with the exception of the sentence *Ficis abundat . . . consumi quiverit*, is based very closely on Solinus 23. 1–4, where it is applied to Spain generally.

[4] Hot sulphur springs near the Praça de S. Paulo in Lisbon are exploited commercially at the present day.

[5] See above, p. 89, note 8.

[6] The author's evident difficulty doubtless arose from a conflict between legend and

Constitit vero sub nostro adventu civitas LX. M. familiarum aurum reddentium, summatis circumquaque suburbiis, exceptis liberis nullius gravedini subiacentibus. Cingitur autem muro rotundo cacumen montis, dextra levaque descendentibus muris urbis per declivum usque ad Tagi ripam.[1] Dependentibus sub muro suburbiis vicorum vice in rupibus excisis, ut unusquisque vicus pro castro haberetur munitissimo, tot enim[a] difficultatibus cingitur.[2] Populosa supra quod existimari nequit. Nam sicut postmodum urbe capta ab eorum alcaie, id est principe, didicimus, habuit hec civitas centum quinquaginta quatuor milia hominum, exceptis parvulis et mulieribus: annumeratis castri Scalaphii[3] civibus, qui in hoc anno a castro suo expulsi, novi hospitesque morabantur, de Suchtria et Elmada et Palmella optimatibus cunctis; ex omnibus Hyspanie partibus et Affrice mercatoribus[b] multis. Sed cum tanti essent, solum armaturam XV. milium habebant in lanceis et scutis, et cum hiis egrediebantur adinvicem, sicut ex indicto principis constitutum fuerat. Edificia vero eius artissime conglobata, ut vix nisi in vicis mercatoriis vicus inveniri quiverit amplioris quam VIII. pedum latitudinis. Causa tante multitudinis erat quod nullus ritus religionis inter eos erat; nam quisque sibi lex erat, utpote qui ex omnibus mundi partibus [131v] flagitiosissimi quique quasi in sentinam confluxerant, totius libidinis atque immunditie seminaria. Sub temporibus regum Christianorum priusquam Mauri eam obtinuissent,[c] trium martyrum memoria iuxta urbem in loco qui dicitur Compolet[4] celebrabatur, scilicet Verissime et Maximi et Iulię virginis,[5] quorum ecclesia a

---

[a] *enim* written in margin.　　[b] *mercatoribus* written in margin.　　[c] *optinuissent.*

the facts of observation. The passage is an elaboration of Solinus 23. 7, which in turn is elaborated from Pliny *HN* iv. 116; viii. 166. Compare Virgil *Georg.* iii. 273–75:

> Ore omnes versae in Zephyrum stant rupibus altis
> Exceptantque levis auras et saepe sine ullis
> Coniugiis vento gravidae . . .

[1] See plan facing p. 130.

[2] A literal translation of this sentence seems impossible. *Vicus* as used in the second instance may be approximately equivalent to the Portuguese *calçada* as it is applied to steep and narrow streets in modern Lisbon.

At the time of our arrival the city consisted of sixty thousand families paying taxes, if you include the adjacent suburbs, with the exception of the free ones which are subject to the exactions of no one. The hilltop is girdled by a circular wall, and the walls of the city extend downward on the right and left to the bank of the Tagus.[1] And the suburbs which slope down beneath the wall have been so cut out of the rocks that each of the steep defiles which they have in place of ordinary streets may be considered a very well fortified stronghold, with such obstacles is it girt about.[2] The city was populous beyond what can readily be believed; for, as after its capture we learned from their alcayde, that is, their governor, it contained one hundred and fifty-four thousand men, without counting women and children, but including the citizens of Santarém,[3] who had this year been expelled from their castle and were sojourning in the city as newcomers, and all the aristocracy of Cintra and Almada and Palmela, and many merchants from all parts of Spain and Africa. But although they were so numerous, they had equipment in lances and shields for but fifteen thousand; and with these they went out by turns as the proclamation of the governor had determined. The buildings of the city were so closely packed together that, except in the merchants' quarter, hardly a street could be found which was more than eight feet wide. The cause of so great a population was that there was no prescribed form of religion among them, for everyone was a law unto himself; for the most depraved elements from all parts of the world had flowed together as it were into a cesspool and had formed a breeding ground of every lust and abomination. In the time of the Christian kings, before the Moors took it, the memory of three martyrs was celebrated beside the city in a place called Campolide,[4] namely, the martyrs Verissimus and Maxima and Julia the Virgin,[5] whose

---

[3] Santarém, the ancient Scalabis, is situated on the Tagus about forty-six miles northeast of Lisbon. It was taken from the Moors by Affonso Henriques on 15 March, 1147 by a surprise assault in the night. See Herculano, *Historia de Portugal*, II, 216–22; *Enciclopedia universal*, LIV, 222–25; *Guia de Portugal*, II, 344–45.

[4] The name still survives as that of one of the quarters in the northwest of Lisbon.

[5] The three martyrs of Lisbon whose feast is celebrated on 1 October; supposed to

Mauris solotenus destructa tres tantum adhuc lapides in signum ruine sue ostendit, qui numquam abinde potuere sustolli. De quibus alii dicunt eos fore altaria, alii bustalia. Hec de civitate ad presens sufficiant.

[V]igilia[a] igitur beati Petri apostoli[1] post prandium, cum ibi hora quasi prandii venissemus,[2] quidam ex nostris in littore iuxta civitatem ex navibus progrediuntur. Contra quos Mauri,[b] sed nostrorum impetum non valentes ferre, non sine ipsorum detrimento, usque ad portam que suburbium respicit fugati sunt. Sed Saherius de Arcellis nostros ab impetu, dolum succensens hostium, revocat, gratias agens Deo quod dissimiles prioribus qui ante huc advenerant[3] casus iam in operis[c] principio experti sumus. Advocatis qui aderant tentoria in supercilio montis supereminentis urbem quantum est fere baculi iactus figi jubet, inhonestum ratus iam primo congressu, ne cedere hostibus videremur, terram relinquere. Cuncti qui aderant favent. Adveniente itaque prima noctis vigilia, nisi duo tantum tentoria, Hervei de Glanvilla et Saherii de Arcellis usquam apparuere, ceteris omnibus ad naves regressis. Nos vero cum paucis admodum XXXIX. tota nocte non sine metu excubavimus, ut Sancti Petri vigilias solempnes loricis induti celebraremus.[4] Mane autem facto, ut citius quis potuit tentorium terra defigit, ac si nostri casus nichil prescissent.

Episcopi vero qui nobiscum advenerant regem suum adeunt,

[a] The initial *V* is wanting, space having been left for a capital which was never inserted.

[b] A small erasure at the beginning of *Mauri.*　　　[c] *operis* written in margin.

have been a brother and two sisters, and to have suffered martyrdom in the famous persecution of 304 under the emperor Diocletian, when Dacian was governor (*praeses*). Compare Flórez, *España sagrada*, XIV, 190–93, 384–86. They are mentioned again on pp. 118–19, below. The author is inconsistent in spelling the names of the first two of the trio, as are also the early Mozarabic calendars which have been edited in parallel columns by Dom Marius Férotin, *Le Liber ordinum en usage dans l'église wisigothique et mozarabe d'Espagne du cinquième au onzième siècle* (Paris, 1904), pp. 480–81. I have translated in accordance with what is now the accepted tradition. Dom Férotin, *loc. cit.*, note 1, cites an inscription of the sixth century indicating that at that time the relics of the martyrs were in the altar of the church of St. Stephen near Zafra in Andalusia.

[1] 28 June. Compare *Brief des Priesters Winand*, p. 4; Duodechin, in *MGH, Scriptores*, XVII, 27; Arnulf, in *HF*, XIV, 326.

church, though razed to the ground by the Moors, still reveals, in sign of its ruin, just three stones which it has never been possible to carry away; concerning which, some say they may have been altars, but others gravestones. Let this suffice for the present concerning the city.

On the vigil of St. Peter the Apostle,[1] after lunch, since we had arrived at about the lunch hour,[2] some of our men disembarked upon the shore beside the city. Against whom the Moors [advanced]; but, not being able to withstand our attack, and not without losses, they were put to flight back to the gate which opens on the suburb. But Saher of Archelle, incensed at the craftiness of the enemy, recalled our men from the attack, though he thanked God that at the very beginning of our enterprise we had had a different experience from that of our predecessors who had come here previously.[3] Calling together those who were present, he commanded that tents be pitched on the brow of a hill which overlooked the city at a distance of about a stick's throw; for he thought it disgraceful to give up ground after the first encounter, lest we appear to be yielding to the enemy. All who were present approved; and yet as the first watch of the night came on only two tents were anywhere to be seen, namely, those of Hervey de Glanvill and Saher of Archelle, for the rest of the men had returned to the ships. But we, with a small force of thirty-nine men, and not without fear, lay out on guard all that night, so that we celebrated the solemn vigils of St. Peter with our corslets on.[4] But in the morning everyone pitched his tent as quickly as he could—as if he had had no previous knowledge of our dangerous situation.

The bishops who had come along with us went to the king

[2] Somewhat later than midafternoon; cf. above, pp. 90, 91, where it is said that they arrived about the tenth hour of the day.

[3] The reference is evidently to the northern crusaders who had failed in an attack upon Lisbon five years before. See below, pp. 102, 103. This was perhaps the attack which is described in the *Chronica Gothorum* under the date 1140: *PMH, Scriptores*, I, 13–14; cf. Herculano, *Historia de Portugal*, II, 186; III, 18.

[4] The author was evidently of this party; cf. above, p. 42, and below, pp. 126–27, note 2.

ut, sicut nobiscum constituerant, eum nobis obviam facerent.
Qui brevi cum eo redeunt, nam per dies plus octo in provintia commoratus nostrum adventum existimans expectaverat.
Audierat enim per nostros de nostro adventu, qui, in navibus
V. a nostra societate segregati, V. dierum navigatione a portu
de Dertemuðe advenerant ante dies VIII. Adveniente itaque
rege, omnes fere pariter, ut in tali tumultu fieri solet, divites
et pauperes, obviam facti sumus. Cum percunctasset vero
rex[a] qui essent ex nobis primates aut quorum consilia in
nobis precellerent aut si cuiquam totius exercitus responsum
commisissemus,[b] breviter responsum est nos primates habere
hos et hos, et quorum precipue actus et consilia preminerent,
sed nondum deliberatum cui responsionis officia committerent.
Si ab ipso primitus audissent, inter tot summe prudentie
viros brevi reperturos, qui pro omnibus communi omnium
consilio responderet. [132r] Ad hec rex pro tempore pauca
respondit:
"Scimus satis et compertum habemus vos fortes et strenuos
magneque industrię viros fore, et verum aput nos non vos
vestri presentia quam fama minores fecit. Non enim quod inter
tot tanteque divitię viros nostra sponsio suffecerit, ut nostris
scilicet ditati muneribus ad urbis huius obsidionem nobiscum
maneatis, vos convenimus. A Mauris enim semper inquietatis,
numquam peccunias adunare quibus quandoque secure non
contigit vivere. Sed quoniam facultatem nostram et bone mentis erga vos affectum vos ignorare nolumus, sponsioni nostre
non imferendam iniuriam, imo quicquid terra nostra possidet
vobis mancipatum censemus. Certi vero super hiis, quod vos
magis pietas vestra ad laborem studiumque tanti operis in-
vitabit, quam nostre sponsio peccunię ad premium provocabit.
Sed ne populorum conclamationibus vestrorum nostra tur-
betur oratio, ex vobis eligite quos volueritis ut ab invicem sece-

---

[a] *rex* written over an erasure.   [b] *commississemus.*

in order to have him come to meet us in accordance with their agreement with us. They soon came back with him, for he had remained in the neighborhood for more than a week in anticipation of our arrival. For he had learned in advance of our coming from some of our people who had been detached from our association in five ships, and who had made the voyage from Dartmouth harbor in five days, and had arrived a week before us. As the king approached we almost all went out to meet him, rich and poor mixed up together as usually happens in such a crowd. And when the king inquired who our chiefs were or whose counsels were preëminent among us or if we had commissioned anyone to answer for our whole army, he was briefly informed that such and such were our chief men and that their acts and counsels carried especial weight, but that we had not yet decided on anyone on whom authority should be conferred to make answer for all. If first we should hear from him, among so many men of great prudence someone would quickly be found who with the common assent of all would make answer for all. To this the king for the moment made a brief reply:

"We have fully understood that you would be brave and strenuous men of great industry; and truly your presence here has not proved you to be less so than your reputation had led us to expect. We have not come to you in the belief that our promise to enrich you with gifts would suffice to induce men as wealthy as you are, and as numerous as you are, to remain with us at the siege of this city. For having been constantly harassed by the Moors, so that sometimes not even our life has been safe, it has surely not been our fortune to accumulate [great] wealth. But since we do not want you to be ignorant of our resources and of the affection of a good mind towards you, our promise shall be fully kept: indeed, whatsoever our land possesses, we account it as delivered to you. But beyond this, we feel certain that your piety will invite you to the labor and exertion of so great an enterprise more than the promise of our money will incite you to the recompense of booty. But, lest our discourse be disturbed by the shouting of your people,

dentes benigne placideque sponsionis nostre causam utrimque super hiis que proposuimus diffiniamus. Sicque inter nos diffinita, in commune coram omnibus explicetur, ut omnibus deinde utrimque assensum prebentibus, certo federe certisque pignoribus ad Dei questum rata fiat."

Ad hec omnes responsuri una in concilium veniunt. Quid vero in hoc quisque prout animi lingueque facilitas abundabat dixerit, nichilque aliud nisi aerem verberare conferret,[a] cum parum auctoritatis constet in fabula, non inconvenienter pretereundum puto. Sed cum multi multa supervacua proferrent, usque post prandium differtur consultum quid potius eligendum esset. Sed interim, quo pacto nescio quibusve internuntiis, Flandrenses regis sponsionibus acquiescunt; nam, ut estimo, quos[b] rei familiaris inopia urgebat, hos proculdubio peccuniarum spes capescendarum facilius ad[c] consuetudinem suam reducit. Dum iterum in concilio ventum est, quos paulo ante existimabamus coniurationis socios, nunc regis advocatos in concilio reperimus, hoc solum semper coram nobis excipientes quod a rege pactionem ullam non solum non susciperent, immo nec audirent, sed moris semper ubique terrarum fuisse in hanc[d] partem favere potius qua impetus animi magis duceret. Seque cum rege manere velle si omnibus complaceret sociis neque restare aliquid quin hoc potius fieret aiebant.

Interea quisque prout arbitrabatur prudentior sententiam rogatus, diversi diversa protulere. Inter quos Willelmus Vitulus,[1]

[a] *confferret.*

[b] *quibus* was written first; then partly erased and changed to *quos.*

[c] An erasure of 2.5 centimetres follows *ad.* Over this the attempt was made to write *consuetudinem;* but it was abandoned after the first two letters because of the spreading of the ink, and *consuetudinem* was begun afresh beyond the erasure.

[d] An erasure of 5 millimetres follows *hanc.*

[1] The name *Vitulus* should possibly be Englished as "Calf." The position and influence of this nautical family, which was on the side of the Empress Matilda and Earl Robert of Gloucester against King Stephen in the civil strife in England, is indicated by William of Malmesbury (*Gesta regum*, II, 594) in a curious passage apropos of the earl's return from Normandy and his contemplated attack on Southampton in December, 1142: "Cogitaverat primo ad Hamtunam appellere, ut dispendio burgensium simul et domini eorum iniurias suas ulcisceretur; sed flexerunt eius impetum precibus multis Vituli, qui arctissimarum necessitudinum parentes, quos apud Hamtunam habebant, aerumpnis ceterorum involvi timerent. Genus hominum nauticorum est

choose from among you those whom you wish, in order that we may withdraw together and, quietly and in good temper, mutually define the conditions of our promise with respect to the proposals which we have made. And when they have been so defined, let them be explained in the presence of all, in order that, with the mutual assent of all, they may finally be ratified by an unequivocal treaty and sure pledges, for the profit of God."

To frame a reply to this we all assembled in council. But what on this occasion everyone said in proportion as he abounded in cocksureness and glibness of tongue, and in so saying profited nothing except to beat the air, I think may not inconveniently be passed over, for there is no authority in talk. But when a large number had put forward many superfluities, the decision as to what course it were preferable to take was put off until after lunch. But in the meantime, by what agreement and through what intermediaries I know not, the Flemings acquiesced in the king's proposal—because, as I suppose, those who were feeling the pinch of want the hope of money-snatching reduced the more easily to its sway. When we again assembled in council, those whom a little while before we had esteemed loyal members of our sworn association we now discovered to be advocates of the king, who persistently maintained this one position before us, that they had not only not entered into any agreement with the king, nay, that they had not even heard of such a thing, but that it had ever been a universal custom to favor the party towards which the impulse of the reason the more strongly inclined. And they said that they wished to remain with the king, if that should be agreeable to all their associates, and that no circumstances stood in the way of this as the preferable course.

Meanwhile, as each one who was thought to be a man of unusual prudence was asked for his opinion, some proposed one thing and some another. Among whom William Viel,[1]

---

quos Vitulos vocant; qui quia fidi clientes comitis sunt, preces eorum non negligendas arbitratus, coepto destitit." A charter of Henry II in favor of the abbey of Saint-

adhuc spirans minarum cedisque piraticę,[a1] [132v] et Radulfus frater eius et omnes fere Hamtunenses et Hastingenses,
cum hiis qui ante hoc quinquennium urbem Ulyxibonam obsi-
dendam convenerant,[2] omnes uno ore regis [s]ponsionem[b] accipere nichil aliud quam proditionem aiebant; plurima etiam
super hiis retractantes, que vel ficta, vel si qua[c] vera fuerint,
eorum magis deputanda insipientię quam alterius pravitati,[d]
aut ea que magis patebant, longi dispendia laboris in obsidione nolle pati. Insuper maximo questui fore si costam
Hyspanie sub festinatione transcurrerent, ac perinde multas
peccunias ab Affrice navibus et Hyspanie mercatoriis leviter ex-
torquerent; ventumque insuper plurimum eo tempore in Iherusalem navigantibus aptum commemorant; nec se quosquam
expectaturos si solum VIII. vel X. naves socias habuerint;
et multa hiis similia que potius fortune casibus subiacent
quam virtuti. Sed nostrorum maior pars, omni occasione re-

[a] *pyraticę.*

[b] *sponsionem* written in margin and partly clipped away in rebinding.

[c] An erasure of 6 millimetres follows *qua;* apparently *ficta* was repeated by mistake
and then erased.

[d] *pravitati* was first written without abbreviation; then the second and third letters
were erased and replaced by a mark of abbreviation.

Étienne of Caen [1156–61] reveals that a Ralph *Vitulus* had houses in Caen which
owed custom to the abbey, except in the case of one which enjoyed an exemption under
a charter which had been granted by King William (evidently William the Conqueror
or William Rufus)—an exemption which may indicate that the *Vituli* had been in the
service of the Anglo-Norman ruling family since the eleventh century. Léopold Delisle
and Élie Berger, *Recueil des actes de Henri II, roi d'Angleterre et duc de Normandie,
concernant les provinces françaises et les affaires de France* (Paris, 1909–27), I, 266.
Another charter of Henry II [before 1172–73] grants to Ralph, *serviens suus,* and to his
heirs, freedom from customs throughout all the king's dominions: "quietanciam omnium consuetudinum per omnes terras meas, tam in terra quam in mari et in portu
maris, et nominatim de tallagio et de omnibus consuetudinibus et auxiliis et rebus ad
me pertinentibus. . . . Quare volo et precipio firmiter quod ipse et heredes sui et
omnia catella sua propria quieta sint per omnes terras meas ab omni consuetudine.
Et prohibeo super forisfactum meum ne quis eum vel res suas propter aliquam consuetudinem disturbet." *Ibid.,* p. 474. The frequent employment of the *Vituli* in the
transport service of Henry II is evidenced by the following summary of payments to
them out of the royal revenues, as recorded in the Pipe Rolls: 1157–58, to Ralph
Vitulus, de itinere de Walia, £19 17*s.* 6*d.* (*The Pipe Rolls of 2–3–4 Henry II,* London,
1930, being a facsimile reproduction of the edition by Joseph Hunter of 1844, p. 175);
1164–65, to Walter *Vitulus* and Ralph, Jr., for the cost and equipment (*in custamento*

yet breathing out threatenings and piratical slaughter,[1] and his brother Ralph and almost all the men of Southampton and Hastings, together with those who had come to besiege Lisbon five years before this,[2] all with one voice declared that they took the king's promise to be nothing but treachery; and, bringing up many points against it which were either false or, if in any respect true, to be imputed to their own foolishness rather than to the king's baseness, or things which were even more obvious, [they said] that they were unwilling to bear the expense of a long labor in the siege. Moreover, it would be more profitable if they should sail quickly past the coast of Spain and then extort much easy money from the merchant vessels of Africa and Spain. And, besides, they recalled that the wind at that season was very favorable for voyagers to Jerusalem. And they said that they would not wait for anyone, if only they should have eight or ten ships associated with them, and many other similar things which depend upon the turn of fate rather than upon virtue. But the

---

et apparatu) of two ships, £35 6s. 8d. (Pipe Roll Society, *Great Roll of the Pipe*, 11 Henry II, p. 102); 1167–68, to Walter *Vitulus*, for an *esnecca*, or yacht, £10 (*ibid.*, 14 Henry II, p. 92); 1172–73, to Walter *Vitulus*, for an *esnecca* for the last fifteen days during which he was in the king's service when the Young King, eldest son of Henry II, last crossed over to Normandy, £7 10s. (*ibid.*, 19 Henry II, p. 51); 1173–74, to Ralph *Vitulus*, for his ship which bore the archbishop to England, 2 marks, also for the hire of his ship for the transport of the royal treasure over sea, 50s., also for his ship which joined in the transport of the earl of Leicester and other prisoners to Normandy, 50s. (*ibid.*, 20 Henry II, pp. 132, 134, 135); 1174–75, to Ralph *Vitulus*, ground of payment not indicated, 10 marks (*ibid.*, 21 Henry II, p. 187); 1175–76, for four ships, of which that of Ralph *Vitulus* was one, which accompanied the *esnecca* "when the Young King crossed over," £7 15s. (*ibid.*, 22 Henry II, p. 199); 1176–77, to Ralph *Vitulus*, Jr., for his ship in the service of Walter, archdeacon of Oxford, 50s., to William *Vitulus*, for his ship in the service of Thomas Bardul, 50s., and to Ralph *Vitulus*, Sr., for his ship in the service of Richard Giffard and Robert Pikenot, 40s. (*ibid.*, 23 Henry II, p. 177); 1177–78, to Ralph *Vitulus*, for the transport of treasure in his ship, "because of the absence of the *esnecca*," 50s. (*ibid.*, 24 Henry II, p. 112); 1178–79, to Ralph *Vitulus*, for his ship to carry the harness (*hernasium*) of Stephen de Toron, seneschal of Anjou, when he came to England, 50s. (*ibid.*, 25 Henry II, p. 108); 1179–80, to Ralph *Vitulus*, Jr., for his ship which carried the king's harness to Normandy, 50s. (*ibid.*, 26 Henry II, p. 148); 1187–88, for the repair of the ship of John La Werre which the king gave to Ralph *Vitulus*, £11 3s. 9d. (*ibid.*, 34 Henry II, pp. 14–15).

[1] Compare Acts 9: 1.   [2] See above, p. 97, note 3.

mota, assensum remanendi prebet, Colonensibus, Flandrensibus, Bolonensibus, Britonibus, Scottis in hoc idem libentissime assentientibus; ceteris cum Willelmo Vitulo, quasi navibus octo Normannorum, Hamtonensium et Bristowensium adhuc in hac pertinacia^a immobiliter durantibus. Interim Flandrenses et Colonenses et Bolonenses ad orientalem civitatis partem cum classe sua secedunt. Iterum post parum perversos exhortatum in concilio venimus, ut exhortationibus blandisque promissis eos nobiscum retineremus, vel quasi fidei iuramentique transgressores coniurateque societatis ab omni nostrorum et a sancte matris ecclesie communione segregaremus.¹ Hinc illinc acclamantibus cunctis, Herveus de Glanvilla, vix nactus silentium, orationem huiusmodi habuit^b:

"Pie recordationis memoria qua tot nationum populos pieque eruditionis viros cruce dominica insignitos pridie aput Portugalam me vidisse recolo animum licet mestissimum maxime relevaret, si hanc universitatem^c gentium sub unitatis sincere vinculo scirem posse restringi. Ad hoc enim quemque nostrum summa ope deceret eniti, ut cum iam tanta gentium diversitas sub coniuratę unitatis lege nobiscum astringitur, nichilque in ea quod merito accusari vel derogari queat in contingenti perpendamus, ne in nos eiusdem sanguinis generisque socios vitabunda infamie in posterum macula cohereat. Imo ut antiquorum virtutum memores nostrorum, laudem et gloriam generis nostri accumulare potius quam imfamatam malitie pannusculis obvelare. Insignia enim veterum a posteris in memoriam reducta, et amoris et honoris indicia^d sunt. [133r] Si boni emulatores veterum fueritis,

---

^a *pertinatia.*

^b A mutilated note in margin which, so far as legible, appears to be as follows: [*no*]*n hiis verbis sed hoc* . . . *o*(?) . . . *per sua* . . . *sibus in modo* (?). Hamilton (*PMH, Scriptores*, I, 397, note 1) read, *in hiis verbis sed hoc* . . . *per sua* . . . *tibus modo;* Stubbs (*Itinerarium*, p. clviii, note 1), *non his verbis sed hoc* . . . *d persua* . . . *ribus in modo;* Pauli (*MGH, Scriptores*, XXVII, 7, note a), the same as Stubbs. Apparently the author means to explain that the speech, as he gives it, is not in Glanvill's exact words.   ^c *univaersitatem.* See above, p. 47.   ^d *inditia.*

¹ Stubbs, *Itinerarium*, pp. clviii–clxiv, has dated this council and subsequent events until the attack of the Anglo-Normans on the suburb as having occurred on 29 June;

greater part of our force, setting aside every objection, agreed
to remain, and the men of Cologne, Flanders, and Boulogne,
the Bretons, and the Scots very willingly gave their consent;
but the rest of the Normans and the men of Southampton
and Bristol, together with William Viel—about eight ships
in all—held out immovably in their stubborn opposition.
Meanwhile, the Flemings and the men of Cologne and Boulogne
withdrew with their ships to the eastern side of the city. Again
a little while afterwards we assembled in council to labor with
the objectors, in order that through exhortation and fair
promises we might retain them with us or else cut them off
from all communion with ourselves and with the holy mother
church as violators of sworn faith and of our oath-bound association.[1] With everybody all around shouting, Hervey de Glanvill obtained silence with difficulty, and then spoke somewhat
as follows:

"The grateful memory with which I recall that but recently
I saw so many peoples of divers nations and so many men of
devout learning signed with the sign of the divine cross at
Oporto would greatly relieve the sadness of my mind, if I
but knew that this association of peoples could be constrained
under the yoke of a genuine unity. For now that so great a
diversity of peoples is bound with us under the law of a sworn
association, and considering that we find nothing in its dealings which can justly be made a subject of accusation or dis-
paragement, each of us ought to do his utmost in order that
in the future no stain of disgrace shall adhere to us who are
members of the same stock and blood. Nay more, recalling
the virtues of our ancestors, we ought to strive to increase
the honor and glory of our race rather than cover tarnished
glory with the rags of malice. For the glorious deeds of the
ancients kept in memory by posterity are the marks of both
affection and honor. If you show yourselves worthy emulators

---

but it seems more likely that they should be assigned to the 30th. The extra time seems
a logical necessity, and the Teutonic Source dates the capture of the suburb July 1st:
Brief des Priesters Winand, p. 4; Duodechin, in *MGH, Scriptores*, XVII, 27; Arnulf, in
HF, XIV, 326.

honor et gloria vos insequitur[a]; si mali, dedecus improperii.
Normannorum genus quis nesciat usu continuate virtutis
laborem recusare nullum?—quorum scilicet in summa asperi-
tate semper durata militia, nec in adversitate cito subvertitur,
nec in prosperitate, tot difficultatibus exercitata, segni valet
otio subici, nam semper otii vitia discutere negotiis didicit.
Sed quonam perversitatis modo nescio, quasi glorie honorisque
cupidine, in nos pedissequa subreppit invidia, et dum generis
alieni viros nobiscum nequit inficere, in nosmetipsos maximam
veneni sui partem transfundit. Attendite, fratres, et recolite
corrigendo mores vestros. Exemplum e vicino in confusionem
vestram sumite.[b] Colonenses Colonensibus non dissident;
Flandrigene Flandrensibus non invident. Quis enim Scottos
barbaros esse neget? Numquam tamen inter nos legem debite
excesserunt amicitię. Et quid aliud nisi prodigiosum quiddam
in vobis conspicitur, cum nos omnes unius matris filii simus,
ut si lingua palato, os ventri, pes pari, manus manui, mutue
servitutis neget officium? Et vos hinc abire vultis, et ut bene
fiat optamus. Nos vero, ut iam ab omnibus in commune
decretum est, vobis solum paucis exceptis, quod non sine
dolore cogor dicere, hic remanemus. Deo non vos inde iniuriam
facitis, sed vobis. Si enim vos hic remanseritis, non augetur ex
vobis Dei potestas. Si abieritis, non imminuitur. Si civitas
hec a nobis capiatur, quid dicetis ad hec? Et ut de piaculo
violate societatis taceam, vos ubique terrarum infames et
ignominiosi venietis. Gloriose mortis metu vires vestras a sociis
subduxistis vestris. Prede solam nondum adepte cupidinem

[a] *innsequitur.*   [b] *summite.*

of the ancients, honor and glory will be yours, but if unworthy, then disgraceful reproaches. Who does not know that the race of the Normans declines no labor in the practice of continuous valor?—the Normans, that is to say, whose military spirit, ever tempered by experience of the greatest hardships, is not quickly subverted in adversity, and in prosperity, which is beset by so many difficulties, cannot be overcome by slothful idleness; for it has learned how with activity always to frustrate the vice of idleness. But because, by I know not what manner of perverseness—as it were through lust of honor and glory—envy has crept in among us as a handmaid, while she cannot infect the men of alien race who are here with us, she pours out the largest part of her poison among our very selves. Brothers, take heed, and attend to the reform of your morals. Take an example from your neighbors for your own confusion. The men of Cologne are not at cross purposes with their fellows of Cologne, the Flemings do not look askance at Flemings. Who, indeed, would deny that the Scots are barbarians? Yet among us in this enterprise they have never overstepped the bounds of due friendship. And what else can be said except that something abnormal appears in you, since we are all sons of one mother—as if the tongue should deny to the palate, or the mouth to the stomach, or one foot to the other, or one hand to its mate, the office of mutual service? You wish to depart hence, and well may it be with you. But we are certainly remaining here, as has already been decided by common consent, with the exception only of your small number, a thing which I am compelled to say not without sorrow. You do no injury to God by this conduct, but only to yourselves. For, if you should remain here, God's power is not augmented by your presence; if you should depart, it is not diminished. If this city should be taken by us, what will you say to that? Even though I remain silent concerning the sin of a violated association, you will become the objects of universal infamy and shame. Through fear of a glorious death you have withdrawn your support from your associates. The mere desire for booty yet to be acquired, you have bought at the cost of

eterno comparastis obprobrio. Genus vestrum innoxium hoc vestro crimine obnoxium tenebitur. Et certe pudet quod generis nostri mater Normannia et immerito a tot nationum que hic adsunt gentibus perpetuum vestri facinoris sustinebit obprobrium.

"Nunc de cetero. Quamobrem vos et vestra perditum itis? Certe peregrinatio vestra non videtur karitate fundata, quia non est in vobis dilectio. Si enim in vobis vere dilectionis esset affectus, profecto maiori fiducia[a] ea erga nos uteremini. Non litteras didici, nec populo sermonem facere novi. Didici tamen et scio quod qui vult peccatis dimitti oportet peccata ceteris dimittere. Hic enim officium diligentis implet, qui hiis a quibus est appetitus ignovit. Hec enim ideo de peccatis dimittendis et malis tolerandis intersero, [133v] quia superius in excusatione huius operis quedam de rege improbanda proposuistis. Iterum de questu navigantibus proventuro, quis novit si in concupiscendo aliena perdamus nostra? De itinere festinando, quis novit si illa spe questus festinatio fiat tardatio? Malo vero hic aliquid bene operando mea consumere,[b] quam vagabundus et anceps certa pro incertis mutare, et me et mea casibus fortuitis et in malos usus committere. De rege etsi aput vos culpabilis foret, ut superius proposuistis, pro Deo tolerandus esset, ut aliquid lucri maioris a vobis fieret. Ipse tamen, ut nobis refert, totius pravę actionis erga vos immunem se asserit, purgandum iudicio vestrorum. Miseremini ergo sociorum[c] vestrorum. Parcite generis infamie vestri. Assentite consiliis honoris vestri. Ego vero in primis si placet cum omnibus meis, genibus

---

[a] *fidutia.*　　　　　[b] *consummere.*　　　　　[c] *sotiorum.*

eternal dishonor. The race of your innocent colleagues will
be held responsible for this your crime; and it is certainly a
shame that Normandy, the mother of our race, must bear,
and that undeservedly, in the eyes of so many peoples who
are here represented the everlasting opprobrium of your out-
rageous action.

"Now for another aspect of the matter. Wherefore are you
going forth to waste yourselves and your substance? Your
pilgrimage certainly appears not to be founded on charity,
for love is not in you. For if the affection of true love were in
you, you would surely manifest it in a greater confidence
towards us. I am not educated nor do I know how to make
public addresses. Yet I have learned and I know that he who
wishes to have his trespasses forgiven ought to forgive the
trespasses of others. And he performs the part of the charitable
who pardons those by whom he has been assailed. Now it is
for this reason that I am adding these matters concerning the
forgiveness of sins and the toleration of faults, namely, because
you in justification of your conduct have maintained that
certain actions of the king were reprehensible. Again, as to
the profits in store for those who sail on, who knows whether
in coveting the goods of others we may not lose our own? As
to hastening the journey, who knows whether by that hope
of gain haste may not be turned to delay? Truly, I prefer to
consume my substance here in doing something worth while,
rather than as a vagabond with a divided mind to exchange
certainties for uncertainties and commit myself and my goods
to fortuitous chances and in evil uses. As for the king, even
if he may have been to blame in his conduct towards you, as
you have previously asserted, for God's sake let him be borne
with in order that you may accomplish something of greater
profit. Nevertheless, as he reports to me, he declares himself
to be guiltless of any base action towards you and offers to
clear himself by the judgment of your men. Therefore, have
mercy on your comrades. Spare shame to your race. Yield to
the counsels of honor. Indeed, if you wish, I myself who am
among the first, together with all my men, on bended knees,

flexis, vinctis manibus, omnia mea in manibus vestris tradens, dominium vestri libentissime solum maneatis nobiscum suscipiam. Et si non vultis socios,[a] exhibete vos saltem nobis dominos."

Et cum hec ad ultimum pre lacrimis vix dixisset, pedibus Willelmi Vituli humiliari voluit, optimatibus astantium militum et ceterorum idem facientibus. Sed non sunt permissi ab eo et a cause sue sociis[b] circumstantibus. Acquievit[c] tandem Willelmus et socii[d] eius nobiscum manere quantum sibi victualia suppeterent, nec amplius die uno, nisi regis vel nostrorum stipendiis teneretur. Et lacrimati sunt omnes pre gaudio dicentes, "Deus, adiuva nos."[1]

Electi sunt ex optimatibus nostris una cum Colonensibus et Flandrensibus, per quos inter nos et regem sponsionum et conventionum fieret diffinitionis terminatio. Qui, una cum rege et archiepiscopo et coepiscopis et clericis et laicis, testamentum confirmationis pactionum postea coram omnibus prolatum in hec verba fecerunt:

"Notum sit omnibus ecclesię filiis, tam futuris quam presentibus, conventionis pactum inter me et Francos. Quod scilicet ego Hydefonxus, rex Portugalensium, omnium meorum assensu, ut perpetuo sit aput posteros in memoria, testamento confirmationis assigno: Quod Franci qui ad urbis Lyxbonensis obsidionem una mecum mansuri sunt, hostium possessiones in omnibus in suam ditionem et potestatem transferant et habeant, omnibus meis et me omnimodo expertibus. Hostes captos si qui ut vivant redimi voluerint, redemptionis peccunias libere habeant, mihi insuper captivos reddant. Urbem, si forte ceperint, habeant et teneant donec facto scrutinio spolietur, tam in omnium redemptionibus quam in ceteris.

---

[a] *sotios.*   [b] *sotiis.*   [c] *aqquievit.*   [d] *sotii.*

[1] The motto or battle cry of crusaders which had come into use, beside the original *Deus vult*, during the First Crusade. See Fulcher of Chartres, *Historia Hierosolymitana* (ed. Heinrich Hagenmeyer, Heidelberg, 1913), p. 299 and note 33. Its popularity among pilgrims to Santiago is indicated by its appearance in the refrain of the marching song which is doubtfully ascribed to Aymery Picaud and which Professor King has conveniently called "The Little Hymn of St. James." G. G. King, *The Way of St. James* (New York and London, 1920), III, 533–35.

with hands bound and surrendering all my goods into your possession, will gladly accept your lordship, if only you will remain here with us. And, if you do not want us as associates, at least exhibit yourselves to us as lords."

And when he had spoken these words at the end with difficulty on account of tears, he wished to humble himself at the feet of William Viel; and the leaders of the knights and of the others who were standing by did likewise. But William and his supporters who were standing near did not permit it. Finally, William and his associates consented to remain with us so long as sufficient provisions were in store for them, but not a day longer, unless they should be retained as stipendiaries of the king or of ourselves. And everyone wept for joy and said, "God help us!"[1]

Representatives were chosen from among our leaders and from the leaders of the men of Cologne and the Flemings, through whom the terms of the engagements and agreements between ourselves and the king should be defined. And afterwards they, in association with the king, the archbishop, his fellow bishops, and the clergy and laity, caused the charter of confirmation of the agreements to be made known before all in the following words:

"Let the covenant of agreement between me and the Franks be known to all the sons of the church, both present and to come. To wit, that I Affonso, king of the Portuguese, with the assent of all my men, in order that it may be forever held in memory by future generations, grant by this charter of confirmation that the Franks who are about to remain with me at the siege of the city of Lisbon may take into their own power and possession, and may keep, all the possessions of the enemy, myself and all my men having absolutely no share in them. If any shall wish to have enemy captives redeemed alive, they shall freely have the ransom money, and they shall turn the said captives over to me. If perchance they should take the city, they shall have it and hold it until it has been searched and despoiled, both through putting everyone to ransom and otherwise. And so, at last, after it has

Sicque demum ad eorum voluntatem perscrutatam mihi tradant. Postea vero civitas et terrę subactę, [134r] me presidente, partiantur secundum conditiones suas sicut quosque melius noveri[m],[a] tenende secundum consuetudines et libertates Francorum honestissimas, mihi solum in eis remanente advocationis dominio.[1] Naves insuper et res eorum vel heredum eorum qui ad urbis Lyxbonensis obsidionem una mecum fuere ab omni consuetudine mercatoria que vulgo pedatica dicitur, a modo et in perpetuum per totam terram meam firmiter et bona fide concedo. Hiis testibus: Iohanne archiepiscopo Bracarensi, episcopo Petro Portugalensi, episcopo Lameccensi,[2] episcopo Viseos,[3] Frinando Menendiz socero regis,[4] Frinando Captivo,[5] Gunzalvo Roderici,[6] Gocel*ino*[b] de Seusa,[7] Menendo Hyldefonxi dapifero,[8] Mutio de Lamega,[9] Petro Pelagio,[10] Iohanne Rainno,[c][11] Gocelvo Sotheri,[d][12] et multis quorum non novimus nomina."

Huius conventionis dati sunt ex parte regis obsides certi XX. per fidem et iuramentum, tam episcopi quam laici. Super hiis iuravit rex conventionem et testamentum prescriptum ser-

---

[a] The end of *noverim* clipped away in rebinding.

[b] Perhaps *Gocelmo*.   [c] An erasure of 4 millimetres follows *Rainno*.

[d] A small erasure between the last two letters of *Sotheri*. Apparently the author first wrote *Sothere*, and then erased the last letter and replaced it with *i*.

[1] Compare Helmold, *Cronica Slavorum*, ed. F. B. Schmeidler (Hanover and Leipzig, 1909), p. 118: "Rex Galaciae rogavit peregrinos ut darent sibi civitatem vacuam, divisa prius inter eos socialiter preda."

"Advocate" is used in the sense of the French *avoué* or the German *Vogt*, a sense which was current in English in the eighteenth century.

[2] Menendus, bishop of Lamego, *ca.* 1144–*ca.* 1176. Compare F. de Almeida, *Historia da igreja em Portugal*, I, 625, 182, 187–88.

[3] Odorius, bishop of Viseu 1144–66(?). Compare Almeida, *op. cit.*, I, 636, 182, 187.

[4] Fernando Menendes was in fact the king's brother-in-law, having married his sister Sancia. The king's father-in-law was Amadeus III, count of Maurienne and Savoy. See *Cartulaire général de l'ordre du Temple, 1119(?)–1150* (ed. Marquis d'Albon, Paris, 1913), No. 359; PMH, *Leges et consuetudines*, I, 368–70; Castilho, *Lisboa antiga*, Pt. 2, II, 118–19; Herculano, *Historia de Portugal*, II, 213.

[5] One of the king's principal ministers. He appears repeatedly in contemporary documents, sometimes as *alferes* or *dapifer*. See Herculano, *op. cit.*, III, 40; Castilho, *op. cit.*, Pt. 2, II, 117; *Cartulaire général de l'ordre du Temple*, Nos. 356, 359; PMH, *Leges et consuetudines*, I, 372, 373, 380, 383, 385.

been ransacked to their full satisfaction, they shall hand it over to me. And afterwards the city and subjugated lands shall, with me presiding, be divided among them in accordance with their respective ranks, as each may be best known to me, to be held according to the most honorable customs and liberties of the Franks, I myself retaining in them only the overlordship of an "advocate."[1] Moreover, I release, absolutely and in good faith, the ships and the goods of those who were with me at the siege of Lisbon, and of their heirs, from all the merchant toll which is commonly called *pedatica*, from now henceforth in perpetuity throughout all my lands. These being witnesses: John, archbishop of Braga; Peter, bishop of Oporto; the bishop of Lamego;[2] the bishop of Viseu;[3] Fernando Menendes, the king's father-in-law;[4] Fernando Captivo;[5] Gonsalvo Rodrigues;[6] Gocelino de Seusa;[7] Menendo Alfonsi, the steward;[8] Mutio of Lamego;[9] Peter Pelagius;[10] John Rainno;[11] Gocelvo Sotheri;[12] and many others with whose names we are unacquainted."

For the keeping of this convention twenty sure hostages were given on the king's part, under pledge and oath, some of them being bishops and some laymen. Besides these, the king took oath to observe the convention and charter as

---

[6] He can be traced in contemporary documents. See *Cartulaire général de l'ordre du Temple*, Nos. 359 (1145), 403 (1146).

[7] I have been unable to identify him in contemporary documents. Cosack (*Eroberung von Lissabon*, p. 40, note) has proposed to identify him with Gonçalo de Sousa (Gonsalvus de Sausa), who is represented as *maior domus* of Affonso Henriques and a witness of an early charter by that king in favor of the monastery of St. Vincent de Fora at Lisbon: *Indiculum fundationis*, in *PMH, Scriptores*, I, 93. Gonçalo de Sousa also attests the donation by Affonso Henriques of the castle of Soure to the Templars on 14 March, 1129. *Cartulaire général de l'ordre du Temple*, No. 24.

[8] He appears in contemporary documents, but, so far as I have noted, without the title of *dapifer*. See *Cartulaire général de l'ordre du Temple*, Nos. 356 (June, 1145), 439 (April, 1147); cf. Castilho, *op. cit.*, Pt. 2, II, 118.

[9] I have been unable to trace him in contemporary documents.

[10] He is represented as the king's *alferes* (steward) and a witness of the charter in favor of St. Vincent de Fora which is cited above, note 7.

[11] A Iohannes Raina or Rania appears in documents of *ca.* 1128–30, *Cartulaire général de l'ordre du Temple*, Nos. 19, 24.

[12] I have been unable to trace this witness in any contemporary document.

vare. Insuper autem a nobis non discessurum nisi imfirmitate ultima cogente, aut si hostibus terra eius occuparetur,[a] nec inde fallendi occasionem querere erga nos ullo modo.[1] Nos vero similiter pactionis tenende iuramentum fecimus, datis inde obsidibus similiter viginti.

Hiis ita omnibus confirmatis, communi omnium consilio decretum est ut legatarii ad urbem hostes conventum mitterentur, ne eos nisi inviti videremur impugnare. Archiepiscopus igitur Braccarensis et episcopus Portugalensis cum paucis ex nostris ad urbem mittuntur. Dato utrimque signo, ipso civitatis alcaie super murum cum episcopo[2] et primiceriis civitatis stantibus pax induciarum,[b] ut quid velint dicant, utrimque sancitur;[c] cum sic archiepiscopus exorsus orationem habuit:

"[D]eus[d] pacis et dilectionis velamen erroris a cordibus vestris auferat, et ad se vos convertat. Et nos igitur de pace loquuturi ad vos pervenimus. Concordia enim res parve crescunt, discordia maxime dilabuntur. Sed ut hec inter nos non regnet perpetuo, huc ad vos conciliatum venimus. Sic enim nos ex uno eodemque principio natura progenuit, ut federe societatis humane et vinculo matris omnium concordie aliis alios non ingratos fieri deceret. Nos vero ad hanc quam possidetis urbem non vos expugnatum hinc neque exspoliatum, si vultis, venimus. Habet enim hoc semper Christianorum innata benignitas, ut, licet sua repetat, aliena non rapiat.

"Urbis huius sedem nostri iuris fore vendicamus; et certe si in vobis iusticia naturalis profecerit, inexorati cum omnibus

---

[a] occupparetur.   [b] indutiarum.   [c] sanccitur.

[d] The initial *D* is wanting, space having been left for a capital which was never inserted. Stubbs, *Itinerarium*, p. clxi, read *Spiritus*, but I find no justification for this in the manuscript. Hamilton (*PMH, Scriptores*, I, 398) read *Deus*, but with a query.

[1] Herculano, *Historia de Portugal*, III, 20, saw in this provision a virtual acknowledgment on the king's part that he had deserted the northern crusaders during the earlier attack upon Lisbon. Compare pp. 96, 97, 102, 103, above.

[2] A Mozarabic bishop of Lisbon, according to Herculano, *op. cit.*, III, 20, 48. He is mentioned again on pp. 176, 177, below, but he seems to be otherwise unknown. Herculano's view has been challenged, though unsuccessfully as it seems to me, by Castilho, *Lisboa antiga*, Pt. 2, II, 105–106, 204–205. F. de Almeida, *Historia da igreja em Portugal*, I,

written. And, furthermore, he swore that he would not withdraw from us unless compelled by a mortal sickness or unless
his territory should be occupied by enemies, and that he would
on no account seek an opportunity in these provisions of prac-
ticing deception upon us.[1] And in like manner we also took
an oath to observe the compact, and likewise gave twenty
hostages.

giving hostages.

When these matters had been thus confirmed, it was decided by the common counsel of all that commissioners should
be sent to parley with the enemy, so that we might not appear
to be attacking them except unwillingly. Accordingly, the
archbishop of Braga and the bishop of Oporto and a few of
our men were sent to the city. After signals had been exchanged,
as the alcayde stood in person on the wall with the bishop[2]
and chief men of the city, a truce was mutually ratified in
order that on each side they might say what they wished.
Then the archbishop made the following speech:

"May the God of peace and love remove the veil of error
from your hearts and convert you to himself. And therefore
have we come to you to speak of peace. For in concord small
things grow great, in discord the greatest go to ruin. But, in
order that discord may not forever reign between us, we have
come hither to you with a message of conciliation. For Nature
so begat us from one and the same principle that, by reason of
the common bond of humanity and the chain of harmony derived from the mother of all, one ought not to be unacceptable
to another. And, if you will, we have come hither to this city
which you possess not to subdue you and drive you out and
despoil you. For the inborn kindliness of Christians ever holds
to this principle, that, while it seeks its own, it seizes not the
property of others.

"We demand that the see of this city shall be under our
law; and surely, if a natural sense of justice had made any
progress among you, you would go back unbidden to the land

162, accepts the view of Herculano without question. There evidently were Mozarabs
resident in Lisbon (as Herculano, *op. cit.*, III, 48–51, has contended), who suffered the
same fate as the Moors after the taking of the city. See below, pp. 180–81 and note 3.

sarcinis vestris, peccuniis, et pecculiis, cum mulieribus et imfantibus, patriam Maurorum repeteretis unde venistis, linquentes nobis nostra. Sed compertum habemus iam satis quod inviti vel coacti talia faceretis. [134v] Sed date operam ut libenter faciatis. Nam si que petimus libenter suscipitis, acerbissimam peticionis partem iam effugistis. Quęnam aliter inter nos concordia fieri posset nescio, cum sors ab initio unicuique data proprio possessore careat. Vos ex[a] Mauris et Moabitis Lusitanię regnum regi vestro et nostro fraudulenter subripuistis. Urbium et vicorum et ecclesiarum desolationes innumere ab illo tempore usque in presens et facte sunt et per dies fiunt. In uno fides vestra, in altero societas humanitatis,[b] lesa est.

"Civitates nostras et terrarum possessiones iniuste retinetis, iam annis CCC. et eo amplius LVIII.,[1] ante vos a Christianis habitas, quos non ad fidem gladius exactoris addixit, sed quos verbum predicacionis in filios Dei adoptavit,[c] sub apostolo nostro Iacobo et eius sequacibus, Donato, Torquato, Secundo, Endaletio, Eufrasio, Tesiphonte, Victorio, Pelagio,[2] et pluribus apostolicorum signorum viris. Testis est in urbe ista sanguis martyrum pro Christi nomine sub Ageiano[3]

[a] In the margin beside *ex Mauris* something was written, of which the last letter appears to have been *o*. The rest has been clipped away in rebinding.

[b] *hummanitatis.*

[c] *quos non ad fidem . . . in filios Dei adoptavit* written in different ink over an erasure of 9.5 centimetres.

[1] The date 789 does in fact indicate a time when the Muslim domination had been consolidated and greatly strengthened as a result of the efforts of Abd-ar-Rahman I (756–88).

[2] The word *sequax* is unfortunately ambiguous. That the author intended it to mean "disciple" in the case of Donatus seems proved by the phrase *Donatus apostoli Iacobi discipulus* on p. 88, above. On Donatus see *ibid.*, note 2. Torquatus, Secundus, Indalecius, Euphrasius, and Ctesephon are five of the "Seven Apostolic Men" who, according to tradition, were ordained bishops in Rome by Peter and Paul and sent to preach the gospel in Spain, and who, in the account of the translation of the body of St. James from Jerusalem to Galicia, in the Codex Calixtinus or Book of St. James (which is very nearly contemporary with the Lisbon crusade: see J. Bédier, *Les Légendes épiques*, 3d ed., Paris, 1926–29, III, 42–114), are neatly included among the disciples (*discipuli*) of St. James. See López Ferreiro, *Historia de la santa A. M. iglesia de Santiago de Compostela*, I, 51–53, 187; cf. *ibid.*, pp. 47, 166, 167, 193, 200, 206; L. Duchesne, "Saint Jacques en Galice," in *Annales du Midi*, XII (1900), 164–66; Flórez, *España sagrada*,

of the Moors from whence you came, with your baggage, money, and goods, and your women and children, leaving to us our own. However, we already know full well that you would only do such a thing unwillingly and as a result of force. But consider a voluntary departure; for, if you yield willingly to our demands, you have already escaped the bitterest part of them. For how otherwise there could be peace between us I know not, since the lot assigned to each from the beginning lacks its rightful possessor. You Moors and Moabites fraudulently seized the realm of Lusitania from your king and ours. From then until now there has been desolation of cities, villages, and churches without number, and it still goes on. On the one side in this struggle your fealty, on the other human society itself, has been violated.

"You are holding our cities and landed possessions unjustly—and for three hundred and fifty-eight years[1] you have so held them—which before that were held by Christians; Christians whom not the sword of the oppressor compelled to their religion, but whom the preaching of the word caused to be adopted among the sons of God, under our apostle James and his disciples and successors, Donatus, Torquatus, Secundus, Indalecius, Euphrasius, Ctesiphon, Victorius, Pelagius,[2] and many men of apostolic distinction. A testimonial thereof in this very city is the blood of the martyrs shed for the name of Christ under Dacian,[3] the Roman prince, that is to say,

---

III, 380–84; *Le Liber ordinum*, ed. M. Férotin, pp. 462–63. Victor and Pelagius appear to be otherwise unknown to any tradition connecting them with St. James. The former may perhaps be identified with St. Victor of Braga (12 April); but it is difficult to see why this youthful catechumen, though he is said to have suffered martyrdom in one of the early persecutions, should be included in such a list as the foregoing. See Flórez, *op. cit.*, XV, 268–73; Férotin, *op. cit.*, pp. 460–61 and note 12. Even greater difficulties attend the identification of Pelagius with San Pelayo, who is said to have been a native of the diocese of Tuy and to have suffered martyrdom at the age of thirteen in Cordova in the year 925 at the hands of the Moors: Flórez, *op. cit.*, XXIII, 106–32, 231–36; Férotin, *op. cit.*, pp. 468–69 and note 26.

[3] Either the emperor Diocletian or the *praeses* Dacian (*Dacianus*) who figures in hagiographic literature as the instrument of the emperor's cruel persecution in Spain. Compare *Vita Sanctae Leocadiae*, in Flórez, *España sagrada*, VI, 320–23; Gams, *Kirchengeschichte von Spanien*, I, 298–300, 346–50, and *passim*. It may well be

Romano principe effusus, Maxime scilicet et Verissimi et Iulię virginis.[1] Requirite concilium Toletanum sub glorioso nostro et vestro rege Sisebuto. Testis est inde Ysidorus Hyspalensis archiepiscopus, et ecclesie Lyxbonensis eiusdem temporis episcopus Viericus cum CC. et eo amplius totius Hyspanię coepiscopis.[2] Testantur adhuc in urbibus ecclesiarum ruine indicia[a] manifesta. Sed quia iam usu longo et generis propagatione urbem occupatam tenuistis, utimur ad vos solito bonitatis affectu: solum vestri munimentum castri in manus nostras tradite; libertates huc usque habitas habeat vestrum unusquisque; nolumus enim vos tam antiquis exturbare sedibus. Secundum mores suos unusquisque vivat, nisi gratuito ex vobis augeatur ecclesia Dei.

"Predives est, ut videmus, et satis felix urbs vestra, sed multorum aviditati exposita. Quot enim castra, quot naves, que hominum in vos coniurata multitudo! Parcite desolationi agrorum et fructuum. Parcite peccuniis vestris. Parcite saltem sanguini vestro. Pacem dum felix est[b] suscipite; nam dubium non est quin sit felicior pax numquam lacessita quam que multo reparatur sanguine. Etenim felicior sanitas inconcussa quam ex gravibus morbis et extrema minantibus vi quadam et exactione in tutum reducta. Gravis est morbus et preceps qui vos infestat, alterum faciet: nisi salubre sumatis[c] consilium, aut extinguetur aut extinguemini. Cavete, nam terminum festinat velocitas. Studete incolumitati vestre dum tempus habetis. Vetus est enim proverbium, gladiatorem in area capere consilium.[3] Vos deinceps respondeatis si placet." [135r]

[a] *inditia.*

[b] *dum felix est* written over an erasure of 1.8 centimetres. Spreading of the ink has rendered the words barely legible. [c] *summatis.*

doubted whether the author had any very clear idea as to whom he was referring.

[1] See above, p. 95, note 5.

[2] The author is confused as to the true facts. No council is known to have been held at Toledo during the reign of Sisebut (612–21). An important council, over which Isidore, bishop of Seville (600?–636) presided, was held in Seville in 619; but there is no evidence that Viaricus, bishop of Lisbon (633, or earlier, to 638) had anything to do with it. See *Sacrorum conciliorum nova et amplissima collectio* (ed. J. D. Mansi, Florence and Venice, 1759–98), X, 555–70; C. J. von Hefele, *Histoire des conciles d'après les documents originaux* (Paris, 1907–), III, 256–58. Probably the reference is to the

of the martyrs Maxima, Verissimus, and Julia the Virgin.[1] Inquire of the Council of Toledo under the glorious Sisebut, our king and yours. A witness of these things is Isidore, archbishop of Seville, and Viaricus, at the same time bishop of the church of Lisbon, together with more than two hundred of their fellow bishops from all Spain.[2] They are further attested at this day in the cities by the visible signs of the ruin of churches. But since by the spread of your race and uninterrupted occupation you have now held the city for a long time, we are displaying towards you our usual benevolence: only surrender into our hands the stronghold of your castle, and each of you may preserve the liberties which he has hitherto enjoyed; for we do not wish to drive you out from such ancient seats. Let each one live according to his own customs, unless some of you should voluntarily be added to the church of God.

"We observe that your city is very rich and prosperous, but it stands exposed to the greed of many men. For how numerous are the camps and the ships, and what a multitude of men has gathered against you in an oath-bound association. Preserve your fields and crops from devastation. Spare your money. At the least, spare your blood. Accept peace while it is propitious, for there is no doubt that a peace which has never been broken is more propitious than one which has been reestablished after much bloodshed. For truly health which has never been broken is better than health which has been restored by any force or regimen after grave and threatening diseases. Grave and dangerous is the malady which threatens you, and it will have one of two results: unless you take counsel of safety, either you or it will be destroyed. Take care, for the end rushes on apace. Consider your safety while there is time; for it is an old adage that the gladiator decides in the arena.[3] Now give us your answer, please."

Fourth Council of Toledo, held in December, 633, during the reign of Sisenand (631–36). This was presided over by Isidore of Seville, and Viaricus of Lisbon was present. Sixty-two bishops attended, not, as the author says, more than two hundred. See Mansi, *Concilia*, X, 611–43; Hefele, *Histoire des conciles*, III, 266–77.

[3] The sentence is quoted almost verbatim from Seneca (*Epistulae*. xxii. 1), except that the latter uses *harena* in place of *area*.

Ad hec quidam ex senioribus circumstantibus responsum huiusmodi dedit:

"[V]ideo[a] verba vos satis in potestate habere; non oratio vestra vos effert, nec longius quam destinavistis protraxit. Ad unum finem, scilicet capescende nostre civitatis, vestra respexit oratio. Sed de vobis satis admirari nequeo, cum una silva vel provintia multis elephantibus vel leonibus sufficiat, vobis autem nec mare nec terra sufficit. Non enim vos rerum inopia, sed mentis cogit ambitio.

"Quod enim superius de sorte unicuique data proposuistis, vos sortem nostram inquietatis; ambitionem vestram rectitudinis zelum dicentes, pro virtutibus vitia mentimini. Iam enim adeo in immensum vestra cupiditas exiit, ut non solum vobis turpia delectent sed etiam placeant; et iam fere locus remedio fieri desiit, quia vestre cupiditatis consummata infelicitas iam pene modum naturalem transiit. Inopes et exules nos fieri iudicatis, ut gloriosi efficiamini. Huiusmodi gloriatio, iners diffinitur ambitio. Cupiditas vero vestra dum modum excessit in se ipsam strangulata semper emarcuit. Quotiens iam nostra memoria cum peregrinis et barbaris nos hinc expugnatum advenistis?[1] Numquid vero vobis vestra placent aut ullam domi contrahitis[b] culpam totiens migrantes? Et certe frequens migratio vestra ex innata animi instabilitate fore convincitur, quia nec animum continere qui nec corporis fugam sistere valet.

"Urbem nostram vel vobis quietam tradi vel in ea manentes vobis subici, nondum nostri consilii fuit. Nondum adeo magnanimitas nostra processit ut certa pro incertis relinquamus. De magnis enim rebus magno animo iudicandum est. Urbs

---

[a] The initial *V* is wanting, space having been left for a capital which was never inserted.   [b] *contraitis.*

To this one of their elders who were standing by replied in this wise:

"I perceive that you have your words very well under control. You are not transported by your speech, nor has it carried you further than you meant to go. It has been directed to a single end, namely, to the taking of our city. But I cannot wonder enough concerning you, for, while a single forest or a district suffices for many elephants and lions, neither the land nor the sea is enough for you. Verily, it is not the want of possessions but ambition of the mind which drives you on.

"As to what you have advanced above concerning the lot assigned to each, truly, you interfere with our destiny. Labeling your ambition zeal for righteousness, you misrepresent vices as virtues. For your greed has already grown to such proportions that base deeds not only please you but even delight you; and now the opportunity of effecting a cure has almost passed, for the consummate infelicity of your cupidity has almost exceeded the bounds of natural measure. You adjudge us to exile and destitution in order that you may become famous. This kind of vainglorious boasting is defined as crass ambition. But your greed, when it has grown beyond measure, has always been smothered in itself and dwindled away. How many times now within our memory have you come [hither] with pilgrims and barbarians to subdue us and drive us hence?[1] But do your possessions give you no pleasure at all, or have you incurred some blame at home, that you are so often on the move? Surely your frequent going and coming is proof of an innate mental instability, for he who is unable to arrest the flight of the body cannot control the mind.

"Not yet have we decided to hand over our city unconditionally to you or to remain in it and become your subjects. Not yet has our magnanimity advanced to the point where we would give up certainties for uncertainties. For in large affairs decisions must be made with largeness of view. This

[1] Evidently there had been other attacks upon Lisbon in which northern crusaders had engaged besides the one referred to above, pp. 96, 97, 102, 103. Compare below, p. 124, lines 5–6.

vero hec, ut estimo, vestris olim fuit; nunc autem nostra, in futuro forsitan vestra. Sed et hoc divini muneris erit. Cum voluit Deus, habuimus; cum noluerit, non habebimus. Nullus enim contra voluntatis eius arbitrium inexpugnabilis est murus. Placeat ergo nobis quicquid Deo placuerit, qui totiens sanguinem nostrum de manibus vestris eripuit; ipsumque ideo et merito suaque mirari non desistimus in hoc quod vinci non potest, et quod mala omnia sub se teneat, et quod, ratione qua nichil prestantius, casus et dolores et iniurias nobis subigit.

"Sed vos hinc abite, non enim aditus vobis patet ur[bis][a] n*isi* ferro experiendus. Non enim minę vestre et barbarorum tumultus multi vel magni aput nos constant,[b] [qu]orum virtutem satius quam linguam novimus. Quod vero perniciosa et mala irrefragabilia promittitis, ex futuro si quandoque futura sunt pendent; et certe dementia est nimis angi futuris, nec aliud quam sibi sponte miserias accersere. Admovendum est igitur optimum consolationis officium, [135v] et differendum que, licet nequeant discuti, animi autem nostri timiditas omnia experiri suadebit. Nam timor assiduus et acer et extrema queque minitans, ad audaciam[c] torpentes excitat; et eo acrior virtus efficitur, quanto inevitabili necessitate extunditur.

"Sed quid vos longius protraham?[d] Facite quod valetis. Nos quod divini muneris erit."

Ad hec episcopus Portugalensis:

"Si fieri potest ut propitiis[e] auribus vestris loquar, dicam, si minus, iratis.

"Vos, ut moris est vestri, in hoc solum obstinationis vestre causam et finem figentes rerum et malorum eventus nostrorum expectatis. Sed fragilis spes et imbecillis que non ex proprie

---

[a] The end of *urbis* clipped away in rebinding.

[b] An erasure of 1.3 centimetres follows *constant*, and the sentence continues with . . . *orum*. Evidently a correction was begun and not completed. I follow Stubbs, *Itinerarium*, p. clxiii, in supplying *qu* to make *quorum*.

[c] *audatiam*.   [d] *protraam*.   [e] *propiciis*.

city did indeed, as I believe, once belong to your people; but now it is ours. In the future it will perhaps be yours. But this shall be in accordance with divine favor. While God willed we have held it; when he shall have willed otherwise, we shall no longer hold it. For there is no wall which is impregnable against the arbitrament of his will. Therefore, let us be content with whatsoever shall please God, who has so often saved our blood from your hands. And for this reason, and rightly, we cease not to marvel at him and his powers, namely, because he cannot be conquered, and because he may hold all evil under his feet, and because—than which reason nothing can be more extraordinary—he overcomes misfortunes, sorrows, and injuries for us.

"But get you hence, for entry into the city lies not open to you except through trial of the sword. For your threats and the tumults of barbarians, whose strength we know better than their language, are not highly valued among us. And as for the calamities and the unconquerable ills which you promise, they depend upon the future, if and when they ever come to pass; and it is surely senseless to be too anxious about the future and voluntarily to invite nothing but miseries upon oneself. Therefore the highest office of consolation must be advanced, and all those expedients must be put off which, although they cannot be entirely removed, the timidity of our minds will persuade us to make trial of. For fear which is persistent and poignant and threatens all extremities stirs the sluggish to audacity; and courage is the keener in proportion as it is aroused by inevitable necessity.

"But why should I delay you longer? Do what you can. We will do what the divine will determines."

To this the bishop of Oporto replied:

"If I can speak to your friendly ears, I will do so, but, if not, then I will speak to your angry ones.

"In accordance with your custom, and in this alone you fix the cause and end of your obstinacy, you are awaiting the outcome of events and of our calamities. But frail and foolish is the hope which depends not upon trust in one's own valor but

virtutis fiducia[a] sed ex aliena pendet miseria. Iam enim causa vestra, quasi timida aut infirmata, testimonium condempnationi dare videtur. De incerto et futuro loquuti; sic aput nos fore decretum experiemini, ut rei cuius totiens eventus incertus fuerit, ut aliquando procedat, sepius temptandum. Sed cum totiens, ut dicitis, erga vos nostra cassata sint initia,[b] experiendum adhuc aliquid adicimus. Sed quis vos inde finis maneat, experti cognoscetis.

"Ut estimo, in discessu nostro ab urbe ista nec salutabo vos, nec salutabor a vobis."

Igitur legati nostri omni spe civitatis potiunde ab hostibus frustrati ad nos revertuntur.

Rex cum omnibus suis ad urbis septentrionem in summitate montis distantis a nobis quasi passibus quingentis secedit.[1]

Mane iterum facto,[2] iterum constabularii nostri et optimates nostre partis curiam regis adeunt circiter horam diei nonam, ut supradicte conventionis obsides traderent et plura obsidioni necessaria providerent; cum interim garciones nostri fundiferi hostes irritando ad campum progredi faciunt, ut sic eminus iactu lapidum irritatis, maioris accessionis provocatio fieret. Nostris subinde paulatim arma capientibus imfra suburbium[3] se hostes[c] concludunt, prohibentes nostros ab introitu iactu lapidum a tectis domorum que ad instar muri circumquaque septa erant. Nostri vero undique patulos si qui[d] forent querentes aditus, usque ad medium suburbii, quo in devexo montis muro cingebatur, eos proturbant. Ibi vero nobis fortiter restitum[e] est. Nostris paulatim subcrescentibus, fit acrior impetus. Multi interim sagittarum et balistarum[4] ictibus cadere, nam

[a] *fidutia.*

[b] An erasure of 3 millimetres in this word between the initial *i* and *it*. Apparently *inimicitia* was first written and then changed to *initia.*

[c] The words *se hostes* are inadvertently repeated.　　[d] *qua.*　　[e] *restitutum.*

[1] Castilho, *Lisboa antiga*, Pt. 2, II, 111, has conjectured that the royal camp was established on the Monte da Graça (also called the Monte de S. Gens). See plan facing p. 130.

[2] 1 July. Compare *Brief des Priesters Winand*, p. 4; Duodechin, in *MGH, Scriptores*, XVII, 27; Arnulf, in *HF*, XIV, 326.

[3] Evidently the suburb beneath the western wall of the Monte do Castello in the quarter called the *Mouraria* (neighborhood of the churches of S. Cristóvão and S. Lourenço). Compare Castilho, *Lisboa antiga*, Pt. 2, II, 122–23.

upon another's misfortune. For already your case, as it were through timidity and weakness, seems to give testimony for its own defeat. You have spoken of the uncertainties of the future; you will find out that we have decided that an undertaking of which the outcome has so often proved uncertain requires repeated endeavors in order that it may sometime succeed. But since, as you say, our enterprises against you have so often been brought to naught, we add that another attempt must yet be made. And what end awaits you from it, by experience you will learn.

"I suppose that as we depart from this city I will not salute you nor will you salute me."

And so our commissioners returned to us, having been frustrated by the enemy in every hope of obtaining the city.

The king withdrew his forces to a position on a hilltop to the north of the city at a distance of about five hundred paces from us.[1]

On the morrow[2] about the ninth hour of the day our constables and the chief men on our side went again to the king's court to deliver the hostages which were required by the aforesaid convention and to make a number of arrangements which were necessary for the prosecution of the siege. In the meanwhile our slingers by harassing the enemy made them advance into the open, in order that, being thus aroused at a distance by the pelting of stones, they might be provoked to a greater encounter. Then, as more and more of our forces took up arms, the enemy shut themselves within the suburb[3] and hindered our entrance by hurling stones from the roofs of the houses, which were enclosed all around with parapets. But our men, seeking everywhere for open approaches, if any should exist, pushed them back as far as the middle of the suburb where it was enclosed on the hillside by a wall. But there we met with strong resistance. As our forces were gradually reinforced from below, the attack became more fierce. Meanwhile, many fell wounded by arrows and shots from ballistae,[4] for the bom-

---

[4] *Balista*, as used in the Middle Ages, was a word of variable and uncertain meaning. Here it evidently refers to the missiles, rather than to the instruments from which they

propius accedendi licentiam lapidum prohibebat emissio. Sicque diei pars magna consumpta est. Tandem vero sub solis occasu per quosdam vix etiam inermibus anfractus[a] pervios quandam collis partem maximo belli discrimine nostri preoccupavere. Quo comperto hostes in fugam versi sunt. Nam longe a munimento superioris urbis aberant.

Interim hiis auditis, dominus Saherius de Arcellis a rege et a constabulariis nostris nos retroagendum missus est. Deliberatum enim aput eos fore aiebant, ut in crastino a rege et ab omnibus undique civitas invaderetur, ne inter paucos dampni maioris occasio fieret. [136r] Sed cum usque ad nos pervenisset, iam fere omnes nostri ex navibus confluxerant et iam ade[o][b] in urbe[1] cum hostibus, ut vix[c] nisi armorum varietate dinosci possent. Iam fer[e][d] nox aderat. Comperto vero quod retroagi nisi nostrorum detrimento maxime nequiremus, iub[entur][e] omnes a domino Saherio ex castris proruere, episcopo Portugalensi omnes benedicente atque absolvente. Ipse quoque Saherius cum quibus habere potuit ex nostro tentorio[f] [2] vel ex suo proprio, nam sociorum[g] pars maior iam in conflictum ierat, ut ceteris succursum prestaret, armatus urbem ingreditur. Iam vero inter vicorum angustias, prout hostium vel nostrorum maiora suppetebant per loca presidia, varia victoria adinvicem erat.

Cum tandem nostri in cimiterio quodam[3] hostium colligati atque in aciem instructi, superveniente domino Saherio, nam

---

[a] *anfractus* written in margin. There was perhaps something before it which has been clipped away in rebinding.

[b] The end of *adeo* has been clipped away in rebinding.

[c] An erasure of 4 millimetres follows *vix*.

[d] The end of *fere* clipped away in rebinding.

[e] The end of *iubentur* clipped away in rebinding.   [f] *temptorio.*   [g] *sotiorum.*

---

were discharged. The latter in this case were perhaps of the crossbow or stonebow type. Compare Rudolf Schneider, *Die Artillerie des Mittelalters* (Berlin, 1910), pp. 41, 47–50, and *passim*; G. Köhler, *Die Entwickelung des Kriegswesens und der Kriegführung in der Ritterzeit* (Breslau, 1889–90), III, Pt. 1, 141–55.

[1] The author's use of *urbs* and *suburbium* is difficult to understand. Apparently there was a section lying outside the city wall which he recognized as a part of the city and distinguishable from the suburb.

bardment of stones prevented a closer approach. And so a large part of the day was spent. But finally, just at sunset, our forces made their way through certain devious windings which were hardly passable even for unarmed men, and after a sharp engagement they seized a certain portion of the hill. When the enemy learned of this, they turned in flight, for they were a good distance from the stronghold of the upper city.

Meanwhile, the news of these events having reached the king's court, the lord Saher of Archelle was dispatched by the king and our constables to have us retire. For they said they had decided that next day the king and all the forces should make a general attack on the city, in order that there should be no occasion for greater losses to be suffered by a few. But when he reached us, almost all our men had gathered from the ships and were already so mixed up with the enemy in the city[1] that they could hardly be recognized except by the difference in their weapons. It was now almost nightfall. And when the lord Saher realized that we could not retire except to our very great disadvantage, he issued orders for all to hurry forward from the camps, as the bishop of Oporto blessed them and absolved them. And Saher himself with all the men he could get from our tent[2] and from his own (for the greater part of our associates had already entered the conflict) took arms and went into the city, in order that he might be at hand to succor the others. And now in the narrow defiles of the streets fickle victory leaned by turns to one side and to the other, according as our forces or those of the enemy were at hand in greater numbers in one place or another.

Finally, when our forces had been assembled in a certain cemetery[3] of the enemy and had been drawn up in battle array and the lord Saher of Archelle had come and taken com-

[2] The tent of Hervey de Glanvill is meant; cf. above, pp. 96–97, note 4.

[3] Castilho, *Lisboa antiga*, Pt. 2, II, 127, has identified this cemetery with the *Almocavár*, or Moorish burying ground, which was destroyed by order of King Manuel I at the end of the fifteenth century, but of which the name long survived thereafter. But in view of the location of the *Almocavár* so far to the northward, under the western slope of the Monte da Graça, it may be questioned whether this identification is correct. Compare below, p. 128, lines 14–18; *Guia de Portugal*, I, 267.

ceteri constabulariorum omnes aberant, omnem hostium impetum repulere. Inde magna eorum strages conficitur. Tum
demum in fugam versi sunt; nam a prima unde superius fuga,
cum se acrius imfestari non posse, pre vicorum quantitate, vel
nostrorum lassitudine comperuissent, leviter reparati fuerant.
Nunc tandem in fugam versi[a] predarum obiectione suarum,
cum multi nostrorum ad hanc iam intenderent, donec imfra
portas argumento subtili invenere viam. Milites tamen cum
archiferis et quibusdam iuvenibus expeditis, preda neglecta,
usque ad portas impressionem strenuissimam faciunt. Verum
enim prede intenti fedam aliter fugam fecissent. Sed nox interim conflictum dirimit, capto suburbio non sine evidenti
miraculo, quod quasi tria armatorum milia, XV. milia familiarum villam tot difficultatibus septam obtinerent. Milites vero
et quique electi iuvenes cum domino Saherio tota nocte armati
excubias pervigiles in medio montis quo erat eorum cimiterium
agunt, ne, relicto quod ceperamus, in crastino difficilior aditus
pateret. Quod et ita factum est tota nocte, horribili ex omni
parte conflagrante incendio.

Mane autem facto[1] circiter horam primam hostes exeunt, ut
nos ab urbe repellerent; supervenientibus ex omni parte regis
et nostrorum familiarium presidiis, iterum includuntur. Sicque
denique urbe obsidione inclusa, imfra suburbium sub muris
eorum hospitati sumus, non sine magna nostri eventus omnium ceterorum invidia. Hiis ex parte Flandrensium com-
pertis, muro urbis se includunt Mauri, relicto eis inexpugnato[b]
suburbio. Nostri interim, Normanni scilicet et Angli, excubias
per noctes singulas per quingentenos disposuere, ut, IX. re-
volutis noctibus, iterum prime vigilie initia fierent.[2] VIII. vero
batellos cum armatis contra urbem in flumine excubandos

---

[a] An erasure of 2.2 centimetres follows *versi*.   [b] *inexpugnati.*

[1] 2 July.

[2] This would indicate a force of 4,500 Anglo-Normans available for guard duty. The figure may perhaps be regarded as substantially correct.

mand (for none of the other constables were present), they repulsed every attack of the enemy and inflicted heavy losses upon them. Then the enemy finally turned in flight; for they had easily recovered from their first discomfiture above mentioned when they had discovered that we could not attack them more fiercely on account of the number of the streets or because of our weariness. And now at last having turned to flight, by the subtle argument of throwing away their goods, for many of our men were already turning to plunder, they managed to find a way back within the gates. Nevertheless, the knights and archers and certain light-armed youths, disregarding booty, pressed a strenuous onslaught right up to the gates. Indeed, except for this, those who were intent upon booty might have caused a disgraceful rout. But now night interrupted the conflict, when the suburb had been captured not without an evident miracle in that some three thousand armed men took a town of fifteen thousand families which was hedged about with so many obstacles. The knights and all the chosen youths with the lord Saher spent the whole night under arms on guard in the middle of the hill where the enemy cemetery was located, lest, if they should leave what they had taken, it would prove more difficult of access on the morrow. And so the whole night passed, while a dreadful fire was burning on all sides.

Next morning[1] about the first hour the enemy came out to drive us back from the city, but, the king's guard and our close associates coming up on all sides, they were once more shut in. And so, when the city had finally been hemmed in by the siege, we were lodged within the suburb beneath the wall, not without a feeling of considerable envy of our good fortune on the part of all the other besieging forces. When these events became known among the Flemings, the Moors abandoned the suburb on that side of the city to them without a contest and shut themselves up within the wall. Meanwhile our forces, that is, the Normans and the English, arranged for nightly guards of five hundred men in such a way that when nine nights had passed, the round would begin again with the first watch.[2] And they stationed eight small boats,

disposuere. Inventum est dehinc in nostra parte suburbii, in fossis in proclivo montis,[a] ad centum fere milia summarum[1] tritici et hordei[b] et milii et leguminum, subsidia scilicet maxime partis urbis. Nam imfra muros, loci quantitas et rerum familiarium copia rupisque solide [136v] durities, imfra vallem, aquarum copia fossas fieri prohibebant.

Interea Mauri per dies sepius irruptiones faciunt in nostros, nam contra nos tres portas habentes, duas in latere et unam contra mare,[2] facilem exeundi et redeundi licentiam habebant. Nobis vero congressus difficilis habebatur. Sed[c] non sine utrorumque detrimento[d] fiebat, sed eorum semper maiori.

Dum interim per dies et noctes excubaremus sub eorum muris, derisiones atque improperia multa nobis ingerebant, mille nos mortibus dignos iudicantes, quippe qui nostra fastidientes quasi vilia, aliena quasi pretiosa concupisceremus; nec aliam se nobis iniuriam fecisse commemorant, nisi quod nos, si quid optimi penes eos haberetur, possessione nostra dignum existimaremus, ipsosque indignos habendi iudicaremus; prolemque domi nascituram multiplicem nobis absentibus improperabant, nec ob id de obitu nostro cure uxoribus nostris fore, [sat]is[e] cum sibi domi spuria suppeteret progenies. Sed et si qui ex nobis superforent, miseros et inopes repatriandum promittebant, et subsannantes dentibus in nobis fremebant.

Convitiis insuper et verbis contumeliosis et probris beatam Mariam matrem Domini incessanter afficiebant, indignantes nobis, quod filium pauperis mulieris tanto quasi Deum veneraremur obsequio, ipsum dicentes Deum Deique filium, cum unum Deum solum a quo omnia que initium habent cepta sunt constet esse, nec aliquem coevum et divinitatis sue habere

---

[a] An erasure of 5 millimetres follows *montis*.   [b] *ordei*.

[c] An erasure of 4 millimetres follows *sed*, the reading of which is very doubtful.

[d] An erasure of 1.4 centimetres follows *detrimento*.

[e] The reading *satis* is doubtful, the beginning of the word having been clipped away in rebinding.

[1] The seam, or pack-animal load, was a measure of possibly as much as six or eight bushels.

[2] Evidently the three gates called Porta de Alfofa, Porta do Ferro, and Porta do Mar. See plan on opposite page; cf. Augusto Vieira da Silva, *A Cerca moura de Lisboa* (Lisbon, 1899: an off-print from *Revista de engenheria*), pp. 47–68.

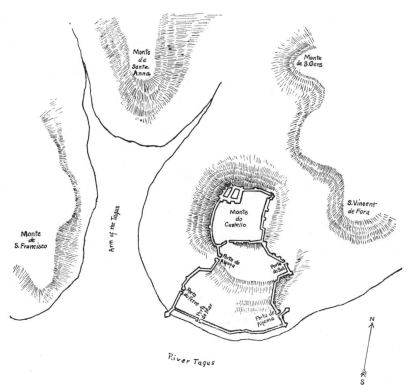

Plan of the Situation and Fortifications of Lisbon as they may have
been in 1147. Based mainly on Augusto Vieira da Silva, *A cerca moura
de lisboa*, Etampa I. The shore line may have altered considerably with
the tide, which at Lisbon normally varies between nine and twelve and
a half feet. The Arm of the Tagus has now been replaced by the central
portion of the city, which was built after the earthquake of 1755.

loaded with armed men, on guard against the city in the river.
Then almost a hundred thousand seams[1] of wheat and barley
and millet and pulse, provisions, that is to say, for the greatest
part of the city, were discovered in cellars in the side of the
hill. For within the walls, the scarcity of space and the vast
quantity of household effects and the hardness of the solid
rock and, in the valley, the abundance of water prevented
the construction of cellars.

Meanwhile from day to day the Moors made repeated sorties
against us, for, having three gates which opened upon us, two
on the side and one towards the sea,[2] they enjoyed convenient
egress and ingress, while it was difficult for us to attack. These
actions took place not without casualties on both sides, but
theirs were always the greater.

In the meantime, as we kept watch night and day beneath
their walls, they derided us and hurled many a taunt at us,
adjudging us worthy of a thousand deaths, as men who, for-
sooth, despising our own possessions as something vile, coveted
those of others as something precious; nor did they recall that
they had done us any injury, unless in this, that if they had
anything in their possession of the very highest quality, we
thought it ought to be ours and judged them unworthy to
have it. And they taunted us with numerous children about
to be born at home in our absence, and said that on this account our wives would not be concerned about our deaths,
since they would have bastard progeny enough. And they
undertook that if any of us should survive, we would return
to our home lands in poverty and misery; and they mocked
us and gnashed their teeth against us.

heckling.

Besides, they constantly attacked the blessed Mary, Mother
of the Lord, with coarse insults and abusive and shameful
words, declaring it unworthy of us that we should venerate
the son of a poor woman with as much reverence as if he were
God himself, and should call him both God and the Son of
God, although it was well known that there is one God only,
by whom all things which have a beginning were begun, and
that he has no one coeval with himself and a sharer in his

participem; ipsumque summe bonum atque perfectum, om-
niaque posse, et cum omnia possit, indignissimum fore et
inexpiandum tantam tamque excellentis divinitatis potentiam
humanis compagibus membrorumque liniamentis coartari, nec
id aliud [quam]ᵃ furiosum et saluti nostre contrarium credere
fore. Velᵇ hunc Marię filium prophetam inter optimos cur
non asser[eremus],ᶜ cum iniuriosum valde sit homini nomen
Dei usurpare?ᵈ Hec et hiis similia adversum nos calumpniantes
obtrectabant. Crucis insuper signum cum magna irrisione os-
tentare nostris; atque in illam expuentes, feditatis sue poste-
riora extergebant ex illa, sicque demum micturientesᵉ in illam
quasi obprobrium quoddam, crucem nostram nobis proiciunt.
Videbatur vero iterum Christus actualiter ab incredulis
blasphemari, falsa genuflexione salutari, malignantium sputis
rigari, vinculis affligi, fustibus illidi, crucis affigi opprobrio.ᶠ
Cuius ut decebat nos compassione in crucis adversarios acriores
fieremus.

Quod et factum est, divina eos obcecante iusticia. Quotiens
a nobis requisiti sunt, quotiens facultates et possessiones
eorum, solum ab urbe libere quo vellent secederent, eis con-
cesse sunt, aut integro iure sibi omnia remanere, solum urbis
munimentum nobis tradidissent, numquam tamen eorum obsti-
nationem nisi ultimo et pessimo dedecore finiri Deus noster
permisit. Previderat enim Deus maxime hiis temporibus
ultionem in crucis adversarios sub qualibuscumque homunciis
fieri. [137r] Dederat enim eos Deus, ut postmodum vidimus,
in passiones ignominię.¹

Interea ecclesie duę a Francis construuntur in sepulturam
defunctorum, una ab orientali parte a Colonensibus et Flandrensibus, ubi duo muti a nativitate, Deo adiuvante, officia
linguę susceperunt, altera ab Anglis et a Normannis ab occi-

ᵃ An erasure of 7 millimetres follows *aliud*. Apparently a correction was begun and
not completed. I follow Stubbs, *Itinerarium*, p. clxvi, in supplying *quam*, which the
sense seems to require.

ᵇ An erasure of 7 millimetres follows *vel*.

ᶜ The end of *assereremus* erased. Apparently a correction was begun and not completed.   ᵈ An erasure of 5 millimetres follows *usurpare*.

ᵉ *mingturientes*.   ᶠ *oprobrio*.

divinity; and that he is in the highest degree good and perfect and omnipotent, and that, because he is omnipotent, it would be most unworthy and inexpiable for so great a power, and a power of such supreme divinity, to be confined by human joints and features, and that to believe this would be nothing less than madness and contrary to our salvation. And why did we not say that this Son of Mary was a prophet among the greatest of the prophets, since it is very wrong for man to usurp the name of God? With these and similar calumnies they attacked us. Besides, they displayed the symbol of the cross before us with mockery; and spitting upon it and wiping the filth from their posteriors with it, and finally making water upon it as something vile, they threw it at us. And Christ was again seen actually blasphemed by unbelievers, saluted with mock genuflections, spat upon by wicked men, afflicted with chains, beaten with staves, and fastened to the opprobrious cross. Out of pity for which it was fitting that we should become more bitter against the enemies of the cross.

And this is just what happened, while divine justice made them blind. How often did we concede them their wealth and possessions, if only they would withdraw from the city and go whithersoever they wished, how often did we propose that everything should remain to them with their rights intact, if only they would surrender to us the fortifications of the city; yet our God never permitted their obstinacy to be ended except in the last and worst disgrace. For God had foreordained especially in these times that vengeance should be wrought upon the enemies of the cross through the most insignificant men. For God had given them up, as we afterwards perceived, unto vile affections.[1]

Meanwhile two churches were built by the Franks for the burial of the dead—one on the eastern side of the city by the men of Cologne and the Flemings, on a spot where two persons who were mute from their birth had with God's aid received their speech, the other on the western side by the English and

[1] Compare Romans 1: 26.

dentali parte.[1] Cum autem ibi per dies XV. sedissemus, machinas utrimque facere incepimus, Colonenses et Flandrenses suem, arietem, turrim ambulatoriam, nostri[a] turrim ambulatoriam nonaginta V. pedum altitudinis.

Omnibus ad hec agenda intentis, prodigiale quid a parte Flandrensium evenire contigit. Die namque dominica post expletionem misse sacerdos panem benedictum [vidit][b] sanguineum, quem dum cultello purgare iuberet, inventus est adeo cum sanguine permixtus, ut caro que numquam sine sanguine potest incidi. Divisus vero postea per frusta in huiusmodi specie etiam post urbis captionem multis diebus visus est.[2] Quidam vero hoc interpretantes aiebant gentem illam ferocem et indomitam, alieni cupidam, licet tunc sub specie peregrinationis et religionis, sitim sanguinis humani[c] nondum deposuisse.

Colonenses interim et Flandrenses V. fundis Balearicis[3] muros et hostium turres temptant concutere. Pactis tandem eorum machinis et ad murum deductis, vix arietem reduxere, ceteris igne et satis contumeliose consumptis. Turris vero nostra cum iam ad murum fere duceretur, sabloni inhesit

---

[a] *nostri* is preceded and followed by small erasures. It may have been written first without abbreviation, and then erased and replaced by the abbreviated form.

[b] A small erasure follows *benedictum*, and a verb is wanting to complete the sense. I have supplied *vidit*.   [c] *hummani.*

[1] The church of St. Vincent de Fora on the east and that of Santa Maria dos Mártires on the west. The latter (not to be confused with the present church of the Martyrs) was destroyed by the earthquake in 1755. Its site, on the Monte de S. Francisco, is now occupied by the Biblioteca Nacional. See the much fuller account in the *Indiculum fundationis monasterii beati Vincentii*, in *PMH, Scriptores*, I, 91; Castilho, *Lisboa antiga*, Pt. 2, II, 138-39.

[2] The language evidently indicates that the author was writing from Lisbon sometime after the conclusion of the siege. See above, pp. 38-39. The portent is more fully reported in *Indiculum fundationis monasterii beati Vincentii*, in *PMH, Scriptores*, I, 92: "Factum est autem ut populus ad certamen iturus, peractis missarum sollemniis, eulogiis uno pane benedicto cuperet premuniri. Ita enim cotidie consueverat. Cumque sacerdos vellet facere particulas quas singulis porrigeret, et iam uni ex panibus secandis culte immiteretur, res miranda, ecce seccati panis medietas cruentata reperitur sanguis desudans. Tunc sacerdos omnesque qui aderant in stuporem conversi sunt subitum . . ." The curious practice of a daily distribution of the *eulogia*, or *pain bénit*, as a protection in battle seems not to have been noticed by liturgical students. On the *eulogia* see *Catholic Encyclopedia* (New York, 1907-14), s.v. *Bread* and *Antidoron*; *Liturgia*, ed. R. Aigrain (Paris, 1931), pp. 715, 771.

the Normans.[1] And when we had been at the siege for a fortnight, we began on both sides to build engines—the men of Cologne and the Flemings constructing a sow, a ram, and a movable tower, and we a movable tower ninety-five feet in height.

While all were intent upon these enterprises, a portent appeared among the Flemings. For on a Sunday after the completion of mass, a priest observed that the blessed bread was bloody, and, when he directed that it be purged with a knife, it was found to be as permeated with blood as flesh which can never be cut without bleeding. And afterwards it was divided into fragments of the same bloody appearance, and it has now been seen for many days after the capture of the city.[2] And some, interpreting it, said that this fierce and indomitable people, covetous of the goods of others, although at the moment under the guise of a pilgrimage and religion, had not yet put away the thirst for human blood.

Meanwhile, the men of Cologne and the Flemings undertook to shatter the walls and the towers of the enemy with five Balearic mangonels.[3] But when at length their engines had been constructed and moved up to the wall, they barely succeeded in withdrawing the ram while the rest were burned, disgracefully enough. And our tower, when it had already been brought up almost to the wall, stuck fast in the sand and

[3] *Fundae Baleares*, as well as *instrumenta Balearia* and even *arcus Baleares*, are repeatedly mentioned by the chroniclers of the First Crusade. See *HC, Historiens occidentaux*, III, 221, 674, 691, 692; IV, 157, 253, 263, 324, 367, 471, 475, 602, 678. Is it possible that the name came into use through a misunderstanding of a passage in Isidore of Seville, *Etymologiae*, xiv, 6, 44: "In his primum insulis inventa est funda qua lapides emittuntur, unde et Baleares dictae; βάλλειν enim Graece mittere dicitur; unde et ballista, quasi missa, et fundibalum. Vergilius [*Georg.* i. 309]: *Balearis verbera fundae*"? In the Teutonic Source these engines are called mangonels: *Brief des Priesters Winand*, pp. 4, 5; Duodechin, in *MGH, Scriptores*, XVII, 27, 28; Arnulf, in *HF*, XIV, 326, 327. It is evident that they were projectile-throwing machines of the high-trajectory type. But as to the mode of propulsion, the authorities are disagreed. If the views of Rudolf Schneider, *Die Artillerie des Mittelalters*, *passim*, are sound, the propulsion can only have been supplied by a counterweight; Köhler, on the other hand, *Entwickelung des Kriegswesens*, III, Pt. 1, pp. 164–65, Pt. 3, pp. 536–37, is positive that the propulsion was in some way supplied by man power. Both authorities are agreed that no use was made of the torsion principle.

immobilis, a tribus eorum fundis irremissibiliter[a] per dies
noctesque concuss[a];[b] ubi non sine magno nostrorum labore
et detrimento in defendendo frustra, post dies quatuor com-
buritur[c] ab hostibus.[1] Inde nostri non parum consternati,
animis erectis vix imfra dies VIII. esse valebant. Sed cum
tandem per sex hebdomadas[d] urbem obsedissemus, comperto
quod eos fames aliquantulum perurgeret, [nostris][e] vero panis
et vini frugumque inestimabilis copia suppeteret, paululum
resumpsere animos. Naves terre deducunt, mala submittunt,
funalia domibus includunt, hyemandi signum. Colonenses vero
subterraneas fossas quinquies aggressi ut murum precipitarent,
totiens cassati sunt. Inde iterum nostri causa consternationis
habita, inter se multum murmurantes, quasi aliquid melius
alibi egissent, conqueruntur, cum post dies aliquot non parum
solaminis divina consulente misericordia, nobis evenire contigit.

Nam decem Mauri vespere sub muro ascendentes in scapham
contra castrum de Palmella navigantes exeunt. Qui a nostris
sub tanta festinatione prosequuti, ut scapham et omnia que in
ea portaverant desperati relinquerent. Imfra quam carte
plurimis transmisse lingua Caldea inscripte reperte sunt.
Exemplum unius, sicut per interpretem didici, huiusmodi
erat: [137v]

"Abbati Machumato, Eburensium regi,[2] calamitas Lyxbo-
nensium, regnum cum salute obtinere. Quante vero et mise-
rabiles atque inopinate nobis supervenerint clades, civitatis
nostre desolata vastitas non sine maximo nobilium sanguine,
luctus nobis, heu, heu, monimenta perpetui, protestantur. Iam
iam fere secunda lunatio preterit quoad Francorum classis, nos-

[a] irremisibiliter.

[b] The end of concussa is erased. Apparently a correction was begun and not completed.

[c] An erasure of 5 millimetres in the middle of this word, separating com from buritur.

[d] epdomadas.

[e] A blank space of 6 millimetres between perurgeret and vero, and something seems
wanting to complete the sense. I have supplied nostris. Stubbs supplied nobis.

[1] The burning of the tower may be dated about 6 or 7 August, since the author
seems to indicate that at the end of a week afterwards the siege had been in progress
for about six weeks, and since the general attack, in the course of which the Anglo-

was bombarded night and day without respite by three of
their mangonels until, after four days, when we had expended
great labor and suffered heavy losses in its vain defense, it
was burned by the enemy.[1] Wherefore our forces were not a
little demoralized, and they were hardly able to regain their
courage for a week. But finally, when we had been besieging
the city for six weeks and it had been learned that the enemy
were rather hard pressed by hunger, while an untold abundance of bread and wine and fruits was at hand for our forces,
they gradually plucked up their spirits. They drew the ships
up on dry land, lowered the masts, and put the cordage under
the hatches, as a sign that they were spending the winter.
But the men of Cologne five times began to dig mines for the
purpose of overturning the wall and were as many times over-
whelmed. Hence our forces again had cause for deep discouragement, and, murmuring much among themselves, they were
making such complaints as that they might have been better
employed elsewhere, when, after some days, there came to
us by the determination of divine mercy no small consolation.

For in the evening ten Moors entered a skiff beneath the
wall and rowed away in the direction of the castle of Palmela.
But our men pursued them so closely that they abandoned
the skiff in desperation, and everything they were carrying
in it. Letters were found in it, directed to several parties and
written in the Arabic language. An example of one, as I got
it from an interpreter, is as follows:

"To Abu Muhammad, king of Évora,[2] the unfortunate
people of Lisbon: may he maintain his kingdom in safety.
What great and terrible and unexpected disasters have come
upon us, the desolate ruin of our city and the great effusion
of noble blood—memorials, alas, of our everlasting grief—
proclaim. Already the second moon has almost passed since
the fleet of the Franks, which has been borne hither to our

Norman siege-tower became fast in the sand, is dated 3 August by Winand and Arnulf:
Brief des Priesters Winand, p. 4; *HF*, XIV, 326. Duodechin, however, dates the attack
15 August, *MGH*, *Scriptores*, XVII, 27.

[2] Abu Muhammad Sidrey ibn Wazir, lord of Évora and Beja. Compare Francisco

tris advecta finibus celi terreque marisque subsidiis, imfra muri artissimi ambitum inclusos coercuit.ᵃ Sed quid in hac miseriarum summa sperandum, perambiguum est, nisi solum auri beneficio expectare suppetias. Nobis una cooperantibus et urbem et patriam a barbaris liberatum per vos non ambigimus. Neque enim adeo sunt multi vel pugnaces; turris vero illorum et machine vi et armis a nobis combuste hec testantur. Sin aliter, caveat prudentia vestra; vos enim idem rerum et malorum exitus manet."

Relique vero hec eadem a parentibus et cognatis et amicis peccuniarumque debitoribus exorabant. Super hiis etiam Hallo, id est Deum, pro eis exorare, ut saltem supremosᵇ corporum ipsorum spiritus ab illo eternitatis receptaculo quo dilectus suus Machumatus vivit et gloriatur fraudari non sinat. Significaverunt etiam de panis et ciborum quantitate. His auditis nostri vehementer animis erecti per dies amplius hostes imfestare. Post paululum temporis cadaver cuiusdam submersi sub navibus nostris inventum est, brachio cuius carta huiusmodi alligata erat:

"Rex Eburensium Lyxbonensibus corporum libertatem. Iampridem datis induciis cum rege Portugalensium,[1] fidem refellere nequeo, ut eum scilicet vel suos bello perturbare velim. De cetero precavete. Salutem vestram peccuniis vestris redimite, ne sit perniecieiᶜ causa que salutis esse debuerat. Valete. Huic nostro nuntio aliquid impendite boni."[2]

Sic tandem omni suppetiarum spe cassataᵈ nostri vigilantius excubabant. A castro Suchtrio cum preda magna pars exercitus nostriᵉ rediit, nam loci natura a congressu castri vel obsidione [e]osᶠ prohibebat.

ᵃ *cohercuit.*   ᵇ *suppremos.*   ᶜ *pernitiei.*   ᵈ *cassatos.*   ᵉ *nostre.*
ᶠ A small erasure precedes *os.* Apparently a correction was begun and not completed.

Codera, *Decadencia y desparición de los Almoravides en España* (Saragosa, 1899), pp. 39–52, and references there cited.
[1] This truce seems not to be otherwise known. It was the policy of Affonso Henriques to enter into such agreements with ambitious Muslim chieftains, a policy which the

borders with the aid of heaven and earth and sea, has kept
us shut within the circuit of this close-drawn wall. And what
is to be hoped for amid this sum of woes is more than doubtful,
except only to look for succor by means of ransom. But with
our coöperation we doubt not that you will liberate the city
and the country from the barbarians. For they are not so very
numerous or warlike, as their tower and engines which we
have burned with force and arms bear witness. Otherwise,
let your prudence beware, for the same outcome of events
and evils awaits you."

And the other letters besought the same things from parents
and other relatives and friends, and from debtors; and besides, they besought them to pray for them to Allah, that is,
God, that, at the least, he would not permit them at the
moment of death to be cheated of that eternal retreat in which
his beloved Muhammad dwells in glory. They also gave information concerning their supply of bread and other foodstuffs.
When our men learned of these things, their spirits were
greatly encouraged to continue the attack against the enemy
for some days longer. After a short time the corpse of a man
who had been drowned was found beneath our ships; and on
an arm a letter was tied, of which the tenor was as follows:

"The king of Évora to the men of Lisbon, liberty of action.
Having long since entered into a truce with the king of the
Portuguese,[1] I cannot break faith and wage war upon him and
his people. For the rest, take heed in good time. Buy safety
with your money, lest that prove a cause of your hurt which
ought to be a cause of your well-being. Farewell. Give something worth while to this our messenger."[2]

a letter of bad tiding for the Muslims

So, finally, as the Moors' last hope of relief was destroyed,
our men kept watch the more vigilantly. A part of our army
returned from the castle of Cintra with a great quantity of
booty; for the nature of the site prevented them from attempt-
ing an assault upon the castle or a siege.

---

civil strife among the Muslims made very effective. Compare Herculano, *Historia de
Portugal*, II, 200–12, III, 53–54.

[2] Herculano, *op. cit.*, III, 30, has questioned the authenticity of this letter.

Dum hec aput nos geruntur rex omnem exercitum suorum dimisit, exceptis paucissimis militibus et domus sue procuratoribus, venditis victualibus suis vel transmissis aput Sanctam Hyreneam.[1] Solus episcopus Portugalensis semper usque ad urbis deditionem nobiscum remansit. Interim fame perurgente Mauros, de pauperibus prout quisque furtim poterat, nostris mancipatum se tradebat.[2] Sicque brevi actum est ut eorum acta et consilia parum [138r] admodum nostris[a] celari poterant.

Factum est item in una dierum ut quidam ex nostris Tagum aput Elmadam pisca[tum][b] transirent. Erat enim littoris illius harena piscatoribus habilior;[3] et venientes provintie illius Mauri plures occiderunt et quinque ex his Brittones captivos inde transtulere. Indignati igitur inde nostri, consilio ab omnibus utrimque[4] diffinito decretum est ut ducenti milites cum peditibus quingentis Elmadam depredatum mitterentur. Facta igitur hora transeundi, Colonenses et Flandrenses suos a transitu, invidia vel timore, vel qua causa nescio, a nostrorum societate subtraxere. Normanni igitur et Angli et qui nobiscum ex nostra parte manebant, omnium societate destituti, Saherium de Arcellis [et][c] militem tricesimum cum centum aut eo amplius peditibus expeditis ad prefinitum transmisere negotium. Qui vero, cesis bello amplius quingentis Mauris, cum captivis fere ducentis et capitibus amplius octoginta, non sine magna nostrorum leticia et hostium merore, eadem qua exierant die victores reversi sunt, uno solum ex nostris interempto. Capita vero hastilibus infixa quando a muris conspexissent Mauri, rogatum nostros obviam supplices,[d] ut capita cesa reciperent, exeunt. Que[e] accepta cum planctu et ululatu

---

[a] *nostris* written in margin.

[b] An erasure of 4 millimetres preceding and of one centimetre following *pisca*. I have followed Stubbs, *Itinerarium*, p. clxix, in reading *piscatum*.

[c] *et* is wanting. I have supplied it as being necessary to complete the sense.

[d] *suplices.*   [e] An erasure of 6 millimetres follows *Que.*

---

[1] Elsewhere the author calls it *castrum Scalaphium*, after the ancient Scalabis. Portuguese historians have found difficulty in explaining this passage. See Herculano, *Historia de Portugal*, III, 31–32; Castilho, *Lisboa antiga*, Pt. 2, II, 154.

[2] Compare *Brief des Priesters Winand*, p. 5; Duodechin, in *MGH, Scriptores*, XVII, 27; Arnulf, in *HF*, XIV, 326.   [3] This is still true today.

While we were carrying on the foregoing operations, the king dismissed all of his own forces except a small number of knights and the officers of his household, having either sold his provisions or sent them to Santarém.[1] Only the bishop of Oporto remained constantly with us until the surrender of the city. Meanwhile, the Moors being hard pressed by hunger, whenever any of their poor were able to do so secretly, they gave themselves up to our men.[2] And so it soon came about that the acts and plans of the enemy could be but little concealed from us.

Also it happened one day that some of our men crossed the Tagus to Almada to fish. For the sand on that shore was the more suitable for fishing.[3] And the Moors of that province came and killed a number of them, and carried five Bretons away captive. At this our men were very angry, and it was determined by the common counsel of all the forces in the two camps[4] that two hundred knights and five hundred foot soldiers should be sent to plunder Almada. But when the hour arrived for going over, because of jealousy or fear, or else from what cause I know not, the men of Cologne and the Flemings withdrew their contingents at the crossing from association with ours. Accordingly, the Normans and the English and those who were encamped with us on our side, although deprived of the support of all the others, sent Saher of Archelle with a thirtieth of the knights and more than a hundred foot soldiers to carry out the enterprise which had been determined upon. And having vanquished a force of more than five hundred Moors in battle, to our great joy and to the sorrow of the enemy they returned victorious, on the same day on which they had set out, with almost two hundred captives and more than eighty heads, although only one of our men had been killed. And when the heads had been impaled upon spears and the Moors beheld them from the walls, they came out to meet our men as suppliants and begged that they might have the heads which had been cut off. And having received them,

[4] The reference is to the two main bodies of the besiegers, the Anglo-Normans on the one side and the men of Cologne and the Flemings on the other.

multo imfra muros sustulere. Audita est autem per totam noctem vox doloris et eiulatio planctus miserabilis fere per omnes civitatis partes. Huius vero ausu facinoris preclari hostibus terrori maximo postmodum semper fuimus, Colonensibus et Flandrensibus et Portugalensibus honori. Libera transmeandi in Elmadam amodo via facta est.

Tum vero nostri potius intendentes operi, inter turrem et portam ferream[1] fossam subterraneam, ut murum precipitarent, fodere aggrediuntur. Qua comperta quoniam satis hostibus pervia, post urbem obsessam maxime nostrorum detrimento fuit, multis diebus in defensando frustra consumptis. Insuper due funde Balearice[2] a nostris eriguntur, una supra ripam fluminis a nautis trahebatur, altera contra portam ferream a militibus et eorum convictualibus. Hii omnes per centenos divisi, audito signo exeuntibus primis centenis, alii centeni subintrassent, ut inter decem horarum spatia V. milia lapidum iactarentur. Huiusmodi vero actio maxime fatigabat hostes. Iterum Normanni et Anglici et qui cum eis erant turrim ambulatoriam LXXXIII. pedum altitudinis [138v] incipiunt.[3] Colonenses iterum et Flandrenses ut murum precipitarent fossam contra murum editioris castri effodere incipiunt,[4] opus admirabile dictu habens aditus quinque, continuatum vero imfra XL. cubitorum latitudinis a fronte,[5] quod imfra mensem consummavere.

Interea fames et cadaverum fetor hostes, nam sepeliendi[a] locus imfra urbem deerat, miserabiliter angebant.[b] Sed et sub muris purgamenta que a navibus proiciebantur undis allata

[a] *sepeliendum.*   [b] *angebat.*

[1] Evidently the section of the western wall extending from the Porta do Ferro to the flanking tower which was located at the southwestern corner. See plan facing p. 130. Compare Castilho, *Lisboa antiga,* Pt. 2, II, 159.   [2] See above, p. 135, note 3.

[3] The Teutonic Source dates this enterprise between 8 September and the middle of October. It attributes its direction to a certain Pisan, *vir magnae industriae,* states that the expense of the construction was borne by the king, and seems to claim some part in the enterprise for the Flemish and German forces. *Brief des Priesters Winand,* p. 5; Duodechin, in *MGH, Scriptores,* XVII, 28; Arnulf, in *HF,* XIV, 326.

[4] A. Vieira da Silva, *A Cerca moura de Lisboa,* p. 43, and map II at end, locates this mine along the section of the eastern wall which extended upward from the present Limoeiro prison almost to the top of the Calçada de S. João da Praça—a situation which readily explains the inability of the besiegers to enter through the breach after

they bore them back within the walls with grief and wailing. And all that night the voice of sorrow and the miserable cry of lamentation were heard in almost every part of the city. And because of the daring of this brilliant exploit, we were ever afterwards the greatest terror to the enemy and held in honor by the men of Cologne, the Flemings, and the Portuguese. And the crossing to Almada was henceforth unobstructed.

Then our men, attending more strictly to the siege, began to dig a subterranean mine between the tower and the Porta do Ferro[1] in order that they might bring down the wall. When this had been discovered, for it was quite accessible to the enemy, it proved greatly to our detriment after the investment of the city, for many days were consumed in its vain defense. Besides, two Balearic mangonels[2] were set up by our forces—one on the river bank which was operated by seamen, the other in front of the Porta do Ferro, which was operated by the knights and their table companions. All these men having been divided into groups of one hundred, on a given signal the first hundred retired and another took their places, so that within the space of ten hours five thousand stones were hurled. And the enemy were greatly harassed by this action. Again the Normans and the English and those who were with them began the erection of a movable tower eighty-three feet in height.[3] Once more, with a view to bringing down the wall, the men of Cologne and the Flemings began to dig a mine beneath the wall of the stronghold higher up[4]—a mine which, marvelous to relate, had five entrances and extended inside to a depth of forty cubits from the front;[5] and they completed it within a month.

Meanwhile, hunger and the stench of corpses greatly tormented the enemy, for there was no burial space within the city. And for food they collected the refuse which was thrown out from our ships and borne up by the waves beneath their

the mining operation had caused the wall to collapse. See plan facing p. 130. Cf. *Guia de Portugal*, I, map opposite p. 270, also pp. 279–80.

[5] The earliest recorded example of mediaeval gallery mining, according to Köhler, *Entwickelung des Kriegswesens*, III, Pt. 1, 127.

comestum colligebant; unde ridiculum quoddam evenire contigit, ut quidam scilicet Flandrenses inter domorum ruinas
excubantes ficus comederent, et satiati partem in loco relinquerent. Quo a quattuor Mauris comperto quasi aves ad escam
clanculo pedetentim advenere. Quo comperto Flandrenses
huiusmodi reliquias sepius per loca ut eos inescarent, di-
spergebant. Tandem vero in locis consuetis retibus extensis
tres ex Mauris retibus involutos cepere, quod risui deinceps
maximo nobis fuit.

  Subfossato igitur muro impositaque ignis materia, nocte
eadem[1] sub gallicantu murus quasi cubitorum triginta[2] solotenus corruit. At vero Mauri qui murorum invigilabant excubiis
anxie clamare auditi sunt, ut iam finem laboribus diuturnis
imponerent ipsumque diem supremum et cum morte dividen-
dum fore, et hoc maximum fieri mortis solatium, si ipsam non
timentes semetipsos pro nostris mutuassent. Nam illuc ire
necessario unde redire non erat necessarium; nam ubique si vita
bene finisset non abbreviata diceretur: nam quantum debuis-
set, non quantum potuisset perdurasset, nec quam diu, sed
quam bene acta foret referret, bonam tantum clausulam
imposuissent. Omnes igitur Mauri circumquaque ad ruinam
muri defendendam[a] confluxere, repagula postium opponentés.
Exeuntes igitur Colonenses et Flandrenses ut experirentur
introitum repulsi sunt. Nam licet murus corruisset, loci natura
introitum solo prohibebat[b] aggere.[3] Sed cum eos cominus
obtinere[c] nequirent, impetu sagittarum prenimio eos eminus
affligebant, ut velut ericii[d] pilis hirsuti[e] immobiliter defendentes
ac si nil lesi paterentur, viderentur. Defensi sunt itaque ab eis

---

  [a] *defendendum.*   [b] *proibebat.*   [c] *optinere.*   [d] *yricii.*   [e] *yrsuti.*

  [1] 16 October. *Brief des Priesters Winand*, p. 6; Duodechin, in *MGH, Scriptores*, XVII,
28; Arnulf, in *HF*, XIV, 326.
  [2] Two hundred feet, according to the Teutonic Source. *Brief des Priesters Winand*,
p. 6; Duodechin, in *MGH, Scriptores*, XVII, 28; Arnulf, in *HF*, XIV, 326.
  [3] "Ad ruinam autem cum venissent mons aditu difficilis supereminebat." *Brief des
Priesters Winand*, p. 6; Arnulf, in *HF*, XIV, 326.

walls. A ridiculous incident occurred as a result of their hunger when some of the Flemings, while keeping guard among the ruins of houses, were eating figs and, having had enough, left some lying about unconsumed. When this was discovered by four of the Moors, they came up stealthily and cautiously like birds approaching food. And when the Flemings observed this, they frequently scattered refuse of this sort about in order that they might lure them on with bait. And, finally, having set snares in the accustomed places, they caught three of the Moors in them and thereby caused enormous merriment among us.

When the wall had been undermined and inflammable material had been placed within the mine and lighted, the same night[1] at cockcrow about thirty cubits[2] of the wall crumbled to the ground. Then the Moors who were guarding the wall were heard to cry out in their anguish that they might now make an end of their long labors and that this very day would be their last and that it would have to be divided with death, and that this would be their greatest consolation for death, if, without fearing it, they might exchange their lives for ours. For it was necessary to go yonder whence there was no need of returning; and, if a life were well ended, it would nowhere be said to have been cut short. For what mattered was not how long but how well a life had been lived; and a life would have lasted as long as it should, even though not as long as it naturally could, provided it closed in a fitting end. And so the Moors gathered from all sides for the defense of the breach in the wall, placing against it a barrier of beams. Accordingly, when the men of Cologne and the Flemings went out to attempt an entrance, they were repulsed. For, although the wall had collapsed, the nature of the situation [on the steep hillside] prevented an entry merely by the heap [of ruins].[3] But when they failed to overcome the defenders in a hand-to-hand encounter, they attacked them furiously from a distance with arrows, so that they looked like hedgehogs as, bristling with bolts, they stood immovably at the defense and endured as if unharmed. Thus the defense was maintained

et ab eorum congressu usque ad horam diei primam,[1] redeuntibus illis ad castra. [139r] Normanni vero atque Angli ut
sociorum vici suffragarent, armati veniunt, ut iam vulneratis
et lassatis hostibus introitum presumerent. Sed a Flandrensium
et Colonensium ducibus convitiis lacessiti, prohibiti[a] sunt,
rogantes nos ut per machinas nostras quoquomodo fieri posset
temptaremus aditum; nam hunc qui patebat aditum sibi non
nobis parasse aiebant. Sic autem per dies aliquot ab introitu
omnimodo repelluntur.

Tunc denique machina nostra compacta, vimineis undique
coriisque bovinis, ne igne vel saxorum impetu lederetur, im-
volvitur. Indictum super hec omnibus per naves ut vineas et
tuguria cancellata ex virgis facerent. Dominica itaque subsequenti[2] impositis in defensando necessariis, archyepiscopus, ut
ipso benedicente promoveretur, advocatur. Igitur post orationem et aspersionem aque benedicte, sacerdos quidam,[3]
sacrosanctam ligni dominici tenens in manibus particulam,
sermonem huiusmodi habuit:

"Eia! fratres, certamen in promptu est. Fervet opus; urget
adversarius.

"Nemo expavescat. Magnum enim fragilitatis humane
solatium, unumquemque angelum sibi delegatum custodem
habere sui; et ut huius custodie sanctissime moribus respondeatis, beati Pauli doctoris gentium sententia precedat,
qua ad Romanos dicitur: 'Reddite omnibus debita, cui honorem, honorem.'[4] Ad hoc enim mihi videtur respicere, honorem
debitum scilicet sic reddi, si quod debetur iusticie reddatur,
et nichil ex eius parte iniusticie concedatur. Similiter et veritati,
si que sua sunt ita reddantur, ut nichil ex eius partibus men-
dacio[b] relinquatur. Sapientie quoque et innocentie bonitatique,

---

[a] *proibiti.*   [b] *mendatio.*

[1] "Nihilominus autem nostri assiliebant, nec a pugna media nocte inchoata usque
ad diei horam nonam cessabant." *Brief des Priesters Winand*, p. 6; Arnulf, in *HF*,
XIV, 326.
[2] 19 October.
[3] The conjecture of Reinhold Pauli, in *MGH, Scriptores*, XXVII, 5, note 3, that this
priest was none other than the author himself seems probable; cf. above, p. 41.
[4] Romans 13: 7.

against the onslaught of the attackers until the first hour of the day,[1] when the latter retired to camp. The Normans and the English came under arms to take up the struggle in place of their associates, supposing that an entrance would be easy now that the enemy were wounded and exhausted. But they were prevented by the leaders of the Flemings and the men of Cologne, who assailed them with insults and demanded that we attempt an entrance in any way it might be accomplished with our own engines; for they said that they had prepared the breach which now stood open for themselves, not for us. And so for several days they were altogether repulsed from the breach.

At last our tower was completed and covered all around with collision mats of osiers and with oxhides in order that it might not be damaged by fire or by the impact of stones. Thereupon, an order was issued by proclamation throughout the fleet that all should make penthouses and mantlets of interwoven branches. And so, on the following Sunday,[2] when everything necessary for its defense had been put in position, the archbishop was sent for in order that the tower might be moved forward with his benediction. Accordingly, after a prayer and the sprinkling of holy water, a certain priest,[3] holding a bit of the sacred wood of the cross in his hands, preached the following sermon:

"Come, brothers, a struggle is at hand. The work grows hot; the enemy presses.

"Let no one be afraid. For it is a great comfort to human frailty that everyone has a guardian angel assigned to him; and, in order that you may respond in accordance with the character of this most holy guardianship, let the text of St. Paul, the teacher of the gentiles, point the way—the text in which he says to the Romans, 'Render to all their dues, honor to whom honor [is due].'[4] For this seems to me to mean that due honor is so rendered, if that which is due to righteousness is paid and no concession is made to unrighteousness. And likewise to truth, if that which belongs to it is so rendered that nothing is left to falsehood; and also to wisdom and inno-

ut nichil ex eorum bonis stultitię[a] vel calliditati vel malitie
permittamus. Quia quacumque occasione si ea que vera sunt
suppresseritis, non reddidistis honorem debitum iusticie et
veritati, sed dehonoravistis iusticiam et contumeliam veritati
fecistis; et cum Christus sit iusticia et sanctificatio et veritas,
si iusticiam conculcastis, eritis similes illis qui Christum cola-
phis ceciderunt et in faciem eius conspuerunt, et qui calamo
caput eius percutientes vertici eius spineam imposuere coro-
nam.[1] Et si ab angeli vestri custodia deviastis, reconciliari
studete Domino per penitentiam, et unde per inobedientiam
lapsi estis, illuc per mandatorum Dei obedientiam redire
satagite. Sed forsan dicetis ad hec, 'In quo mandata Dei
sprevimus?' Audite quid de vobis Machias propheta dixerit:
[139v] 'In eo quod admovistis ad altare panes pollutos et
escas ex rapina, et quod tales votivas vestras regi omnium
Deo obtulistis, quales si principibus vestris obtulissetis non
utique suscepte forent.'[2] Et in hiis omnibus Deum potius
irritastis quam placastis. Stultitie[b] atque insipientie ultime est,
ut homo Deum quoquomodo fallere existimet. 'Nam huius
mundi sapientia aput Deum stultitia[c] est.'[3]

"Sed quia dictum est, 'In malivolam animam non introibit
sapientia,'[4] auferte malitiam de medio vestri, quia nichil aliud
est male facere quam a disciplina deviare. Sapientiam illam,
fratres, querite que sursum est, non que super terram, sicut
docet apostolus.[5] Hanc autem soli mundicordes adipisci queunt.
Et ut in summe contemplatione sapientie, que utique animus
non est, nam est incommutabilis, aciem mentis figatis, necesse
se ipsum animus, qui commutabilis est, intueatur, et sibi ipse
animus quodammodo in mentem veniat, ut cognoscat se esse
non quod Deus est, sed tamen aliquid quod possit placere post
Deum. Melior est autem[d] animus cum pro Deo obliviscitur sui,

---

[a] *stulticię.*   [b] *Stulticie.*   [c] *stulticia.*   [d] *autem* written in margin.

[1] Compare Matt. 26: 67; 27: 29–30; Mark 14: 65; 15: 17–19.
[2] Compare Malachi 1: 7–8.   [3] I Corinthians 3: 19.   [4] Wisdom 1: 4.

cence and goodness, if all is so granted that we allow nothing of theirs to folly or craft or malice. For, if on any occasion whatsoever you have suppressed that which is true, you have not rendered due honor to righteousness and truth, but you have dishonored righteousness and insulted truth; and, since Christ is righteousness and holiness and truth, if you have trampled upon righteousness, you are like those who buffeted Christ, spat in his face, smote his head with a reed, and put a crown of thorns upon his head.[1] And, if you have deviated from the guidance of your angel, take care to be reconciled with the Lord through penance; and, through obedience to the commands of God, try to return to the place from which through disobedience you have fallen. But perhaps you will say, 'Wherein have we contemned the commands of God?' Hear what the prophet Malachi has said about you: 'In that ye have brought to the altar polluted bread and stolen food and that ye have made as your votive offerings to God, the king of all, things such that, if ye had offered them to your princes, they would surely not have received them.'[2] And in all these things you have angered God rather than appeased him. It is folly and perfect nonsense for a man to think of deceiving God in any manner. 'For the wisdom of this world is foolishness with God.'[3]

"But because it is said, 'Wisdom will not enter into a soul that deviseth evil,'[4] put away malice from among you, for to do evil is nothing but to depart from discipline. Brothers, as the apostle teaches, seek that wisdom which is above, not which is on the earth.[5] But only the pure in heart are able to attain it. And in order that you may fix the attention of the mind upon the contemplation of the highest wisdom, which, being immutable, is certainly not the understanding, it is necessary that the understanding, which is mutable, contemplate itself and that it in a certain manner enter into the mind, in order that it may recognize itself to be not what God is, but nevertheless something which, after God, is able to give satisfaction. But the understanding is better when it forgets

[5] Compare James 3: 15, 17.

et pre caritate incommutabilis Dei se ipsum penitus in comparatione nullius contempnit.

"Si autem sibi tamquam obvius placet ut ad perverse Deum imitandum sua potestate frui velit, tanto fit minor quanto se maiorem fieri cupit. Ad hoc est initium omnis peccati superbia,[1] et 'initium superbie hominis apostatare a Deo.'[2] Superbię autem diaboli accessit malivolentissima invidia, ut hanc homini persuaderet per quam se dampnatum sentiebat. Unde factum est ut pena hominem susciperet emendatoria potius quam interemptoria, ut cui se diabolus ad imitationem superbie prebuit, ei se Dominus ad humilitatis imitationem preberet.

"Assumpsit itaque Filius Dei hominem, et in illo humana perpessus est, ut sicut in carne et anima condempnatio fuerat, ita in carne et anima salus eterna fieret. Christus ergo pro Adam, qui factus est sub peccato, qui erat sine peccato introducitur, ut huius passione voluntaria qui invitus fuerat passus curaretur. Sed et inde isti omnium impurissimi nobis calumpniantur Mauri, cur Dei sapientia hominem aliter liberare non poterat, nisi susciperet hominem et nasceretur ex femina et omnia illa a peccatoribus pateretur. Poterat quidem omnino. Si aliter faceret, similiter eorum stultitie[a] displiceret. Si enim non appareret oculis peccatorum lumen eternum quod per oculos interiores videtur, mentibus inquinatis videri non posset. Nunc autem quia visibiliter nos commonere dignatur, ut invisibilia prepararet, [140r] displicet avaris quia non aureum corpus habuit. Displicet impudicis quod ex femina natus est.[b] Displicet superbis quod contumelias patienter tulit. Timidis quia mortuus est; et ut vitia sua videantur defendere, dicunt non in homine sed in Dei Filio sibi hoc displicere. Filius vero Dei, ut catholica credit et veneratur ecclesia, hominem as-

[a] *stulticie.*   [b] *femina natus est* written in margin.

[1] Compare Ecclus. 10: 15.   [2] Ecclus. 10: 14.

itself before God, and, for the love of the immutable God, esteems itself as nothing in comparison with him.

"But if it should, so to say, easily be pleasing that it desire to exercise its power perversely to imitate God, it diminishes itself to just the extent that it wishes to enhance itself. At this point enters pride, the beginning of all sin;[1] and 'the beginning of man's pride is to apostatize from God.'[2] And to the pride of the Devil was added most spiteful envy, in order that he might tempt man to that through which he perceived himself to have been damned. Wherefore it has happened that corrective rather than destructive punishment has been so allotted to man that to whomsoever the Devil has offered himself for the imitation of his pride, the Lord has offered himself for the imitation of his humility.

"And so the Son of God became man and in that capacity bore with patience human sufferings, in order that, as he had suffered condemnation in the flesh and spirit, so there should be eternal salvation in the flesh and spirit. Therefore, in place of Adam, who became a sinner, Christ, who was without sin, is brought in, in order that by his voluntary sacrifice, he might be saved who had suffered unwillingly. But in this connection those most vile of all people, the Moors, taunt us with the question why God in his wisdom could not have delivered man except by becoming a man and being born of woman and suffering all those things at the hands of sinners. Of course he could have done so. But, if he had done otherwise [than he did do], he would displease them in their folly just the same. For, if the eternal light which is seen through the inner eye appears not to the eyes of sinners, it could not be perceived by the minds of the defiled. But now because, in order to prepare for things invisible, he deigns to forewarn us visibly, he offends the avaricious because he had not a body of gold; he offends the shameless because he was born of woman; he offends the proud because he patiently endured insults; the timid because he died. And in order that they may appear to defend their vices, they say that these things offend them not in a man but in the Son of God. But the Son of God, according to the belief

sumpsit, ut in eo humana pateretur. Hec est hominum medicina tanta que quanta sit cogitari non potest. O medicinam omnibus consulentem, tumentia comprimentem, tabescentia reficientem, superflua resecantem, necessaria custodientem, perdita reparantem, depravata corrigentem! Que ergo superbia sanabitur, si humilitate Filii Dei non sanatur? Que avaritia, si Filii Dei paupertate non sanatur? Que iracundia, si Filii Dei patientia non sanatur? Que impietas, que caritate Filii Dei non sanatur? Postremo que timiditas sanari potest, si resurrectione eius non sanetur?

"Et vos, fratres karissimi, Christum sequuti, exules spontanei, qui pauperiem voluntariam suscepistis, audite et intelligite, quia inchoantibus promittitur sed perseverantibus premium donatur. Sed et hic perseverare nequit, qui adhuc a bone actionis initio neggligens vel ignorans oberrat. Ignorans, si penitendo resipiscat vel recognoscat, cum lacrimis et gemitu oret cum propheta dicens, 'Delicta iuventutis meę et ignorantias meas ne memineris,'[1] postea ut adicere mereatur cum apostolo, 'Misericordiam consequutus sum quia ignorans feci.'[2] Neggligentes cum omni diligentia 'dignos fructus penitentię'[3] agant, ut qui se illicita aliquando perpetrasse meminerit, illicitis abstinere consuescat. Si enim vultis, fratres, peccata vestra dimittere Deum, exorate ut eius gratia vos preveniat ut desiderium vestrum in bonis suis consummare dignetur. Summo ergo opere in initio conversionis vestre cavendum est, ne vel ea quę reliquistis adhuc in mentis affectu vestre cohereant, quia nimirum in futuro punietur in opere quod hic male conscia delitescet in mente.

"'Nolite,' fratres, 'nolite sperare in iniquitate, et rapinas nolite concupiscere';[4] sed 'sperate in Domino, et dabit vobis

---

[1] Psalms (Vulgate) 24: 7; (English) 25: 7.   [2] I Timothy 1: 13.
[3] Matt. 3: 8; Luke 3: 8.   [4] Psalms (Vulgate) 61: 11; (English) 62: 10.

and worship of the universal church, became man in order that as such he might endure human sufferings. This is a medicine for men of such strength that its potency passeth understanding. Oh, medicine that healeth all sickness, reducing swellings, restoring corruptions, cutting away the superfluous, preserving the necessary, repairing losses, correcting distortions! What pride shall be cured, if it be not cured by the humility of the Son of God? What avarice, if it be not cured by the poverty of the Son of God? What proneness to anger, if it be not cured by the patience of the Son of God? What impiety is there which is not cured by the love of the Son of God? Lastly, what fear can be cured, if it may not be cured by his resurrection?

"And you, most dearly beloved brethren, who have followed Christ as voluntary exiles and have willingly accepted poverty, hear and understand that the prize is promised to those who start but is given to those who persevere. Yet he cannot persevere who still loiters at the beginning of a worthy enterprise in ignorance and neglect. Let the ignorant, if through repentance he comes to his senses and recognizes his fault, pray with tears and groans, and say with the prophet, 'Remember not the sins of my youth nor my ignorances,'[1] in order that afterwards he may deserve to add with the apostle, 'I obtained mercy because I did it ignorantly.'[2] Let the neglectful with all diligence bring forth 'fruits meet for repentance,'[3] in order that he who remembers that he once acted unlawfully may become accustomed to abstaining from unlawful acts. For, brothers, if you wish God to forgive your sins, pray that his grace may so anticipate you that he may deem your desire worthy of consummation in his blessings. Therefore, at the beginning of your conversion the greatest care must be exercised lest your affections still cling to those very things which you have given up; for there will surely some day be outer punishment for what now lies concealed in a guilty conscience.

"Brothers, 'trust not in oppression, and become not vain in robbery';[4] but 'trust in the Lord, and he shall give thee

petitiones cordis vestri.'[1] Reconciliamini iterum Deo, et reinduite Christum, ut sitis filii eius immaculati. Mementote [140v] mirabilium Domini que operatus est in vobis, cum iam novo penitentie abluti baptismate de terra vestra et de cognatione egrederemini, quomodo per aquam nimiam et tempestatum procellas vos illesos transvexerit, hucque insuper advecti, quo impetu Spiritus ducentis suburbium hoc in quo manemus invasimus, quomodo non sine evidenti miraculo captum est fere absque nostrorum sanguine. Exhibete[a] ergo vos iterum ad hoc negotium, quales huc advenistis, et secure promitto vobis hostium vestrorum potentias frangere. Non enim ego sed Dominus, qui digne petentibus semper annuit et favet, confitentibusque numquam veniam negare consuevit.

"Non resistent adversum vos, quia nimirum quos fidei ignorantie error dehonestat, hos proculdubio ex difficultate actionis cruciatus affligat. Nam ignorantiam cecitas sequitur, difficultatem vero mentis angustia cum molestia corporis comitari solet. Nolite, fratres, nolite timere; nolite expavescere; contristari fugite; stupefieri vilipendite. Si vos Deus noster ab huius urbis introitu tam longi laboris dispendio excluserit, iccirco profecto in vobis hoc operatus est, ut assiduitas laboris continui patientiam in vobis solidaret, eademque solidata perseverantie probatiores redderet. Expergiscimini aliquando, fratres, et capescite arma. Non enim vobis cum Gigantibus pugnandum vel cum Laphitis, fures enim et latrones inermes et timidi sunt, quos etiam tot ineptiis stipatos inordinata ipsorum et confusa multitudo prepediet.

"Ecce, fratres, ecce lignum crucis dominice. Flectentes genua proni in terram decubate; rea tundite pectora, Domini prestolantes auxilium. Veniet enim, veniet. Videbitis auxilium Domini super vos. Adorate Dominum Christum, qui in hoc

[a] *Exibete.*

[1] Psalms (Vulgate) 36: 3, 4; (English) 37: 3, 4.

the desires of thine heart.'[1] Be reconciled again with God, and put on Christ once more in order that you may be his immaculate sons. Remember the marvelous work of the Lord which he has wrought in you, when, after you had been cleansed by the new baptism of repentance, you were going forth from your country and kinsmen, how he has brought you unharmed over the vast waters and through violent storms, and how he has also brought you hither, where through the inspiration of the [Holy] Spirit we have invaded this suburb in which we still remain, and how, not without an evident miracle, it has been taken almost without bloodshed on the part of any of our men. Therefore, show yourselves once more in this undertaking such men as you were when you arrived here, and I confidently promise you that you will shatter the power of your enemies. For it is not I but the Lord, who always grants and shows favor to those who make a worthy request, and who is accustomed never to deny forgiveness to those who make confession.

"The enemy will not stand against you because those whom the error of ignorance of the faith degrades, torment will surely strike with a difficulty of action. For blindness follows ignorance, and a difficult action is usually accompanied by anguish of mind and distress of body. Brothers, be not afraid; shun discouragement; despise terror. If our God has prevented you from entering this city after so long and costly an effort, assuredly he has done this in order that continuous labor might strengthen your patience, and that the same, being strengthened, might make you the better tested of perseverance. Now, brothers, at last arouse yourselves and grasp your arms, for not with the Giants or the Lapithae must you fight, for your enemies are thieves and robbers, helpless and afraid, who, crowded as they are by a clutter of trash, will be hampered by their confused and disordered multitude.

"Behold, brothers, behold the wood of the cross of the Lord. Bend your knees and lie prone upon the ground. Strike your guilty breasts, while you await the aid of the Lord. For it will come, it will come. You shall perceive the help of the Lord

salutifere crucis ligno manus expandit et pedes in vestram
salutem et gloriam. In hoc vexillo, solum non hesitetis, vin-
cetis.[1] Quia si quem hoc insignitum mori contigerit, sibi
vitam[a] tolli non credimus, sed in melius mutari non ambigimus.
Hic ergo vivere gloria est, et mori lucrum.[2]

"Ego vero ipse, fratres, in tribulationibus et laboribus
vestris particeps premiorumque vestrorum socius[b] sicut vobis
spondeo [141r] mihi fieri opto. Deo opitulante in hac machina,
huius ligni sacrosancti custos et comes inseparabilis, vita
comite vobiscum manebo. Certus quia nec fames neque gladius
neque tribulatio neque angustia nos a Christo separabit.[3] Et
profecto securi de victoria hostes invadite, quibus victorie
premia sunt gloria sempiterna. Paulus vero Iudeorum ad-

[a] *vita.*   [b] *sotius.*

[1] The close association in the speaker's mind between the sacred relic which he was
holding in his hands and the emblem of the cross with which crusaders were signed and
which was displayed on the banner under which the operations at Lisbon were being
conducted (see below, p. 174, lines 16–17, 20–21) is natural. Hence the use of the word
vexillum.

The use of the cross-banner (*vexillum crucis*) had undoubtedly become general well
before the Second Crusade. The *sanctissimae et dominicae crucis vexillum* is mentioned
by Fulcher of Chartres (*Historia Hierosolymitana*, ed. H. Hagenmeyer, Heidelberg,
1913, p. 650) in connection with events of the year 1122; and numerous banners bearing crosses were represented in the crusade window which was executed for the abbey
of Saint-Denis at the command of Abbot Suger about 1144. See Bernard de Mont-
faucon, *Les Monumens de la monarchie françoise* (Paris, 1729–33), I, Plates L–LIV;
cf. C. W. David, *Robert Curthose, Duke of Normandy* (Cambridge, Mass., 1920),
Appendix G and the references there cited.

But the words of the speaker also seem to imply some acquaintance with the vision
of the cross of light in the heavens with its accompanying inscription (now familiar
to western ears in the form: IN HOC SIGNO VINCES) which, according to Eusebius (*Vita
Constantini*, i, 28), confirmed the acceptance of Christianity by Constantine the Great
before his victory over Maxentius in Italy in the year 312; and there may well have
been an association in the speaker's mind between the use of the cross-banner as an
emblem of war by crusaders and its parallel use by Constantine. See N. H. Baynes,
"Constantine the Great and the Christian Church," in British Academy, *Proceedings*,
XV (1929), 345–48 and notes 20–36 on pp. 394–406; cf. Andreas Alföldi, "The Helmet
of Constantine with the Christian Monogram," in *Journal of Roman Studies*, XXII
(1932), Pt. 1, pp. 9–23. This vision, associated not with the triumph over Maxentius
but with a great victory of Constantine over barbarians on the banks of the Danube,
was widely spread throughout the East and the West in connection with the popular
legend of the invention of the cross by Constantine's mother, Helena, which seems
first to have taken shape in Syria, perhaps early in the fifth century, and which found

above you. Adore Christ, the Lord, who on this wood of the saving cross spread out his hands and feet for your salvation and glory. Under this ensign, if only you falter not, you shall conquer.[1] Because, if it should happen that anyone signed with this cross should die, we do not believe that life has been taken from him, for we have no doubt that he is changed into something better. Here, therefore, to live is glory and to die is gain.[2]

"Brothers, I myself, a participant in your trials and labors and a sharer in your rewards, desire that it may be done to me even as I promise that it shall be done to you. With God's aid, I, the guardian and inseparable companion of this sacred wood, will remain with you in this engine while life shall last. I am persuaded that neither famine nor the sword nor tribulation nor distress shall separate us from Christ.[3] And being actually certain of victory, fall upon the enemy, the rewards of victory over whom are eternal glory. Indeed, Paul, advocate

---

its way to England, perhaps by way of Ireland, in time to serve as the source of Cynewulf's *Elene* in the last half of the eighth century or early in the ninth. See *The Old English Elene, Phoenix, and Physiologus* (ed. A. S. Cook, New Haven, etc., 1919), pp. xiv–xv, and the references there cited. But so far at least as western historical texts are concerned, another version of Constantine's conversion held the field at the beginning of the crusading period, and the vision of the cross in the heavens with its now famous inscription would seem to have been unknown or ignored. See C. B. Coleman, *Constantine the Great and Christianity* (New York, 1914), pp. 77–81, 135–41; for the East see Philostorgius-Photius: Philostorgius, *Kirchengeschichte* (ed. Joseph Bidez, Leipzig, 1913), p. 7.

The adoption of the cross at the Council of Clermont (1095) as the sacred sign of crusaders had an entirely independent origin, being due to Pope Urban II, who appears to have derived his inspiration from two parallel texts of the Gospels, viz. Matthew 10: 38 and Luke 14: 27. See the passages from the chroniclers of the First Crusade collected by Hagenmeyer in his edition of Fulcher of Chartres, *Historia Hierosolymitana*, p. 141, note 12. However, by the time of the Second Crusade a knowledge of the vision of Constantine was being recovered by historical writers in the West. Otto, bishop of Freising, in his *Chronica sive historia de duabus civitatibus* (ed. A. Hofmeister, Hanover and Leipzig, 1912), p. 184, quotes the account of it directly (with the inscription in a corrupt Greek form: ΘΟΘΥѠ ΝΥΚΑ) from Rufinus, who, in translating the *Historia ecclesiastica* of Eusebius, added matter from the *Vita Constantini*, the original source. A brief reference in Henry of Huntingdon, *Historia Anglorum* (ed. Thomas Arnold, London, 1879), p. 30, can leave little doubt that he too knew of the vision from Rufinus.

[2] Compare Philippians 1: 21.   [3] Compare Romans 8: 35, 38–39.

vocatus, et magister noster qui ex gentibus ad fidem venimus, pro vobis etiam orare audet ultra quam fas est pro fratribus suis secundum carnem. (Vestris precibus iuvantibus, opto ut simile aliquid pro vobis audeam dicere.) Nam ultra mandatum Dei[a] nititur qui proximos non sicut se sed plusquam se diligit. Denique etiam se abiecto nos pro se induci orat ad Christum. O singularem mentis magnificentiam! O celestem spiritus calorem, extra pietatem, ut ita dicam, pro pietate, fieri cupit, dum anathema optat a Christo[1] tantum ut isti salvi fiant.

"Deus pacis et dilectionis, qui facit utraque unum et nos invicem tradidit nobis; qui elevat de terra inopem et de stercore erigit pauperem;[2] qui 'elegit David servum suum et sustulit eum de gregibus ovium,'[3] cum esset iunior in filiis Iesse; qui dat verbum evangelizantibus virtute multa, ad perfectionem predicationis sue et exhibitionem operis sui, tenens manus nostras in voluntate sua nos dirigat, et cum gloria nos assumat; ipse regentes regat, ut possimus[b] gregem eius cum disciplina, et non in vasis pastoris imperiti.[4] Ipse virtutem et fortitudinem populo suo prestet; ipseque sibi mundum et candidum gregem atque in omnibus immaculatum ac supernis ovilibus dignum exhibeat, ubi est habitatio letantium, in splendoribus sanctorum, ut in templo eius omnes dicamus gloriam, grex et pastores, Iesu Christo Domino nostro, cui est gloria in secula seculorum. Amen."

Ad hanc vocem ceciderunt omnes proni cum gemitu et lacrimis in facies suas. Iterumque ad iussum sacerdotis omnes erecti, venerabili crucis dominice signo in nomine Patris et Filii et Spiritus Sancti consignati sunt.

Sicque demum cum magna voce Dei postulantes auxilium, quasi cubitis XV. machinam contra murum appropinquavere.

---

[a] *mandatum Dei* repeated by an evident error.

[b] The reading of the manuscript is certain. Stubbs (*Itinerarium*, p. clxxiv) amended by substituting *pascamus* for *possimus;* but this seems to create as many difficulties as it removes. Perhaps some infinitive such as *regere* has been inadvertently omitted.

[1] Compare Romans 9: 3.   [3] Compare Psalms (Vulgate) 112: 7; (English) 113: 7.
[2] Psalms (Vulgate) 77: 70; (English) 78: 70.   [4] Compare Zechariah 11: 15.

of the Jews and teacher of us who have come to the faith from the gentiles, dares to pray for you even beyond that which is lawful for him to do for his own brethren according to the flesh. (With your prayers I wish that I may venture to say something similar on your behalf.) For he strives beyond that which the command of God requires, in that he loves his neighbors not as himself but more than himself. And finally, he prays that, himself being rejected, we before him may be led to Christ. Oh singular magnanimity! Oh heavenly ardor of the spirit! Beyond piety, so to say, for the sake of piety, he wishes it so to be done, while he wishes himself accursed from Christ,[1] only that these shall be saved.

"May the God of peace and love, who maketh one out of two and delivereth us mutually one to another; who raiseth up the poor out of the dust and lifteth the needy out of the dunghill;[2] who 'chose David his servant and took him from the sheepfolds,'[3] although he was the younger of the sons of Jesse; who giveth his word with mighty power to those who proclaim the gospel unto the perfection of his preaching and the display of his works—holding us by the hand, may he direct us in accordance with his will and receive us with glory; may he so control us who lead that we may rule over his flock with discipline and not with the instruments of a foolish shepherd.[4] May he supply courage and strength to his people. And may he exhibit the flock clean and white and spotless in all respects and worthy of the heavenly fold, wherein is the abode of those who rejoice in the splendor of the saints; so that in his temple we all, both the flock and the shepherds, may say, Glory to our Lord, Jesus Christ, to whom be glory for ever and ever. Amen."

At this word all fell down upon their faces with groans and tears. And again at the command of the priest all stood up and were signed with the revered sign of the cross of the Lord in the name of the Father, the Son, and the Holy Spirit.

And so, at last, with a loud voice calling on God for aid, they moved the engine forward some fifteen cubits towards the wall. On this occasion one of our men was struck and

Ibi quidam nostrorum a muris percussus iactu funde [141v] interiit. Iterum in crastino[1] contra turrim que est in angulo civitatis contra fluvium[2] machina deducitur. Ad quam autem hostes omnia sue defensionis presidia comportaverant. Quo comperto, eorum premeditata facile cassantur. Nam nostri machinam contra fluvium ad dextram declinantes, turrim quasi cubitis viginti preterierunt iuxta murum fere ad Portam Ferream que turrim[a] respicit.[3] Ibique baliste[4] et archiferi nostri a turri predicta hostes fugaverunt, non valentes impetum sagittarum ferre; nam a parte posteriori[b] que urbem respicit turris patebat. Hostibus autem a turri et a muro machine vicino nostre turbatis, nocte superveniente paululum quievimus, redeuntibus omnibus ad castra, relictis in eius custodia ex nostris centum militibus et ex Gallecianis C., cum archiferis et balistis et iuvenibus aliquot expeditis. Prima igitur noctis vigilia maris alluvio machinam circumfluens exeundi vel commeandi nostris prohibeb[at][c] viam. Comperto autem a Mauris quod nos maris refluvium seclusisset, in duas cohortes per portam predictam machinam pedetenus invasere. Ceteri autem super muros, incredibilis multitudinis, admota lignorum materia cum pice et lino et oleo et omnimodis ignium fomentis, machine nostre iniciunt. Alii vero super nos saxorum intolerabilem proiciebant grandinem. Habebatur autem sub alis machine, inter ipsam et murum, tugurium vimineum quod vulgo cattus Waliscus dicitur, in quo septem de provintia Gipeswicensi commanebant iuvenes, qui illud semper post machinam conduxerant. Sub hoc autem cum hiis qui imfra erant quidam nostrorum frustatim ignium materias quantum poterant concidebant. Ceteri vero, effossis sub machina scro-

[a] The scribe may have written *murum* and then altered it to *turrim*.

[b] *posteriori* is preceded by a small erasure. Apparently the scribe wrote *que* and then removed it.

[c] *proibeb*, which is followed by an erasure of 4 millimetres. Evidently a correction was begun and not completed.

[1] 20 October.

[2] On this tower at the southwestern corner of the wall of the city, see Vieira da Silva, *A Cerca moura de Lisboa*, pp. 29, 58–60. See plan facing p. 130.

[3] It seems impossible to form a clear idea of this maneuvre and of the position to which the siege-tower was brought. Possibly *dextram* was written for *sinistram*.

killed by the shot of a sling from the wall. Again next day[1] the engine was moved up towards the tower of the city which stands at the corner towards the river;[2] to which also the enemy had brought the full garrison for its defense. When this was discovered, their plans were easily defeated; for our men, turning the engine to the right towards the river, passed the tower at a distance of about twenty cubits and brought it near the wall almost at the Porta do Ferro which overlooks the tower.[3] And then our crossbowmen[4] and archers drove the enemy in flight from the aforesaid tower, for they could not withstand the attack of our arrows; for the tower was open on the rear which overlooks the city. When the enemy had been driven in confusion from the tower and from the wall near our engine, and when night was coming on, we quieted down by degrees and retired to camp, leaving the engine in the keeping of a hundred of our knights and a hundred Gallegans, together with a number of archers and crossbowmen and light-armed youths. Then during the first watch of the night the incoming tide flowed around our engine and cut our forces off from communication with it. When the Moors observed that the rising tide had cut us off, they issued in two companies through the aforesaid gate and attacked our machine. And the others upon the wall, an incredible multitude, brought up articles of wood, together with pitch and flax and oil and every kind of inflammable matter, and hurled them at our engine. And still others discharged an intolerable hail of stones upon us. But there was beneath the wings of our engine, between it and the wall, a penthouse of plaited osiers, which is commonly called a Welsh cat, in which were seven youths from the district of Ipswich who kept it constantly in position behind the engine. And under this some of our men, with the assistance of those who were inside the engine, beat out the burning matter piece by piece as best they could. And others dug trenches underneath the

[4] The word *baliste* here, as well as in line 15 below, evidently designates men rather than weapons.

bibus in eisque manentes, globos ignium distrahebant.[a] Alii
in superioribus tabulatis per foramina coria desuper tensa
irrigabant; in quibus caudarum scope forinsecus in ordine
dependentes totam irrigabant machinam. Ceteri vero instructi
in aciem a porta progressis viriliter restiterunt. Defensa est
itaque ea nocte labore ad[142r]mirabili, paucis ex nostris, Deo
protegente, admodum lesis, Maurorum vero parte maxima cominus eminusque cesa.

Mane autem facto,[1] machina nostra maris alluvione iterum
secluditur. Convenientes iterum Mauri, alii per portam in
nostros proruunt, quo congressu rector de galeata regis percussus interiit, alii a muris saxorum turbine nostros concu-
tiunt, admotis super hec fundis Balearicis.[2] Supermurales
vero scaphas incentivis ignium repletas machine nostre VIII.
solum pedibus a muro distanti iniciunt, ut dictu difficillimum
sit quantis laboribus sudoribusque, verberibus ac plagis innumeris maximam diei partem protraxerint omni sociorum
auxilio destituti. Ibi vero artifex noster,[3] saxo crure lesus,
omni nos sui spe solatii destituit. Galletiani quoque cum se
mari circumdatos conspexissent, vel vulnerati vel vulneratis
similes, quidam armis proiectis, quidam armati, turpiter
legentes vadum consuluere fuge, exceptis solum sex ex eorum
numero. Tum demum refluente mari, hostes lassati[b] conflictum dimittunt, omni bona spe in perpetuum destituti. Milites
vero nostri et qui in machine custodia fuerant electi exeuntes,
alios vice eorum suffraganeos[4] prius introduxerunt, cum illam

---

[a] *distraebant.*
[b] An erasure of 1.6 centimetres follows *lassati.*

[1] 21 October.
[2] See above, p. 135, note 3.
[3] Perhaps the Pisan engineer who is referred to in the Teutonic Source. See above,
p. 142, note 3.
[4] Perhaps some of the German and Flemish forces from the other side of the city.
Compare *Brief des Priesters Winand*, pp. 6–7: "Interim milites regis qui ab arce turris
pugnabant, mangnellis Sarracenorum territi, minus viriliter pugnabant, usque adeo
quod Sarraceni exeuntes turrim concremassent, si quidam de nostris qui casu ad ipsos
venerant non obstitissent. Huius periculi fama cum ad nostras pervolaret aures, meli-
ores nostrae partis exercitus ad defendendam turrim (ne nostra spes in ea adnullare-

engine and, lying in them, drew away the balls of fire. Still others in the upper stories poured water through holes upon the hides which were suspended from above so that the tails hanging in order on the outside irrigated the whole engine. And still others, drawn up in fighting formation, manfully resisted those who had come out from the gate. So the engine was defended through that night by a prodigious effort, very few of our men being wounded, thanks to the protection of God, but the greater part of the Moors being cut to pieces in hand-to-hand or distant combat.

Next morning[1] our engine was again cut off by the tide. And again the Moors returned to the attack, some rushing upon us through the gate—in which encounter the commander of the king's galley was struck and killed—others bombarding our forces from the wall with a hail of stones, for Balearic mangonels[2] had been brought up for the purpose. And they threw down skiffs filled with burning matter from the walls upon our engine, which was only eight feet from the wall, so that it would be most difficult to describe with what labor and sweat, with what blows and numberless wounds, our men held out through the greater part of the day, while they were deprived of all assistance from their comrades. And there our engineer,[3] cruelly wounded by a stone, deprived us of all hope of his consolation. The Gallegans also, with the exception of only six of their number, when they saw themselves surrounded by the sea, either being wounded or like men wounded, disgracefully selected a ford and took counsel of flight, some throwing away their arms, others with their arms upon them. But finally the sea receded and the enemy gave up the contest in exhaustion, being deprived forever of all real hope. Then our knights and the others who had been picked to guard the engine, having previously introduced others of their supporters[4] in their places, retired after they had defended the

---

tur) transmisimus. Videntes autem Sarraceni Lotharingos tanto fervore in arcem turris ascendentes, tanta formidine territi sunt, ut arma summitterent et dextras in signum pacis sibi dari peterent." The statement of Arnulf (*HF*, XIV, 327) is much the same, except that to the Lotharingians he adds the Flemings.

duobus diebus et nocte una,[1] numquam armis depositis, agonia
fere intolerabili defendissent.

Hora autem quasi[a] decima, mari retrahente, nostri in harena
conveniunt ut machinam muro pedibus solum quattuor adi-
cerent, ut sic facilius pontem[2] elicerent. Ad hanc igitur muri
defensionem omnes circumquaque Mauri conveniunt. Sed cum
pontem quasi duorum cubitorum emissum viderent, et iam
pene fieri nobis introeuntibus, ut nec vita reliqui victis foret,
voce magna conclamantes, nobis videntibus arma deponunt,
manus submittunt, inducias vel usque mane supliciter postulantes. Advocato itaque Frinando Captivo ex parte regis,
Herveo de Glanvilla ex nostris partibus, date sunt inducie,
acceptis inde obsidibus quinque, ne machinas nostras [142v]
noctu impedirent vel sibi aliquid interim nostri detrimento
repararent;[3] noctuque insuper deliberandum, ut in crastino
civitatem nobis traderent, si sic aput eos deliberatum foret.
Sin aliter, armis experiri cetera. Frinandus vero Captivus et
Herveus de Glanvilla cum iam fere esset noctis vigilia prima,
acceptis obsidibus, eos regi tradunt, quod fere maximum dis-
cordię seminarium fuerat, quod non nostris eos tradidissent;
nam existimabant proditionem[b] per hos a rege, nam moris sui
erat velle fieri, Frinandum Captivum et Herveum de Glanvilla
in hoc succensentes.

Summo igitur mane,[4] convocatis Colonensibus et Flandrensibus, constabularii nostri una cum senioribus castra regis
adeunt, auditum quid veteratores illi sibi deliberassent. In-
terrogati, urbem regi tradendam, aurum et argentum ceteras-

---

[a] *qua* corrected by the addition of *si* in margin.   [b] *prodicionem.*

[1] 20–21 October.

[2] The drawbridge at the top of the movable tower, to be let down upon the wall.

[3] 21 October. The Teutonic Source gives this as the date when the victory was con-
summated, although the city was not actually entered until 24 October. *Brief des
Priesters Winand*, p. 7; Duodechin, in *MGH, Scriptores*, XVII, 28; Arnulf, in *HF*, XIV,
327.

[4] 22 October.

engine in an almost unbearable contest for two days and a night[1] without ever putting down their arms.

About the tenth hour, the sea receding, our forces assembled on the sand in order that they might move the engine up to a distance of but four feet from the wall, so that they might the more easily put out the bridge.[2] Whereupon the Moors gathered from all sides for the defense of the wall at the point which was threatened. But when they beheld the bridge extending about two cubits, and perceived that our entrance was about to bring it to pass that not even life would be spared to the vanquished, they cried out with a loud voice and put down their arms as we looked on, and extended their hands as suppliants and demanded a truce, if only until morning. And so Fernando Captivo was summoned on behalf of the king and Hervey de Glanvill on our behalf; and a truce was granted, and five hostages were received as a guarantee that they would not place obstacles in the way of our engines during the night or make any repairs to their advantage and our detriment.[3] Moreover, they were to decide during the night to surrender the city to us on the morrow, if that should be the result of their deliberations; otherwise the issue would be left to the arbitrament of arms. And Fernando Captivo and Hervey de Glanvill, when it was already almost the first watch of the night, having received the hostages, delivered them to the king—an act which proved to be almost the very worst nursery of discord, for the reason that the hostages had not been handed over to our forces. For they thought that they were being betrayed by the king through the leaders since it was in accordance with his character to desire such a thing to happen. And they were inflamed with anger against Fernando Captivo and Hervey de Glanvill on this account.

Early next morning,[4] therefore, when the men of Cologne and the Flemings had been summoned, our constables together with the older men went to the king's camp to hear what decision those crafty fellows had arrived at for themselves. When questioned they said that they were in favor of handing the city over to the king and delivering the gold and silver

que omnes civium facultates in manibus nostris dandum
favent. Ad hec responsuri nostri exeunt.

Fremit igitur et tabescit hostis antiquus, iure pristino nunc
demum spoliandus. Vasa iniquitatis sue in omnes et per omnes
excitat. Cuius adeo malitię virus invaluit, ut vix aut nullatenus
alter alteri assensum per diem prebuerit, invicem discindentes.
Nam cum iam fere ad introitum portarum ventum, nisi sue
propiciationis dexteram Deus noster opposuisset, concordia
lesa foret. Ea namque bonitatis sue clementia ab initio societatis nostre semper erga nos usus est, ut cum multis et in-
tractabilibus discidiorum causis etiam duces nostri modera-
minis sui gubernacula desperati relinquerent, tum denique
Spiritus Sancti inspirans favonius, quasi quodam solis meri-
diani vibraculo caliginose nubis intemperiem reverberans,
concordię recurrentis gratiorem nexum conficeret.

Cum igitur in consilio nostre responsionis essemus, naute
nostri cum sibi similibus fatuis, conspiratione facta per quen-
dam sacerdotem Bristowensem sacrilegum, in harena convenere. (Erat autem hic moribus pessimis, ut postmodum eo
latrociniis deprehenso cognovimus.) [143r] Qui ab humili sermone paululum incitari ut ad vociferationem usque pertrans-
irent incepere; indignum ferentes tot et tantos domi militieque
preclaros ditioni senatuique paucorum subiacere, quibus potius
super hiis negotiis consulto opus non fore sed impetu. Quippe
qui preveniente Spiritu huc advecti quicquid agerent eius
impetu optime fieri. Nam penes primates[a] suos neque consilium
neque ceptum usquam nisi frustra fuit. Nam illis absentibus
suburbium captum est, hiisdem nescientibus Elmada subacta;

---

[a] *Nam penes primates* written over an erasure of 2.5 centimetres. The spreading of
the ink has made the first word all but illegible.

and all the other property of the citizens into our hands. Our men went out to decide upon their reply to this.

Then the Old Enemy, now finally about to be despoiled of his former rights, growled and was consumed with rage. He roiled the vials of his wickedness against all and through all; and the poison of his malice so far prevailed that amid repeated dissensions not one, or hardly one, agreed with another throughout the day. Indeed, when we were now almost at the entrance of the gates, concord would have been broken had not our God interposed the right hand of his propitiation. But from the beginning of our association he always exercised the clemency of his goodness towards us, so that when from many and uncontrollable causes of discord even our leaders in desperation lost control of their tempers, then at last the breath of the Holy Spirit, as it were, repelling the chill of a misty cloud by a certain gleam of the noonday sun, reëstablished the grateful bond of a returning concord.

Accordingly, while we were in council as to our reply, our seamen, together with other fatuous fellows of their own kind, assembled on the sand; for a conspiracy had been started [among them] by a certain renegade priest of Bristol. (He was of the very worst morals, as we afterwards learned when he was arrested among thieves.) And they began by degrees to be so excited by his humble speech that they ended in an uproar, bearing it as an indignity that so many men, and men so famous both at home and abroad, should be subject to the authority and rule of a few leaders, with respect to whom they declared that what was needed in this enterprise was not consultation but inspiration. Indeed, whatever had been done under the inspiration of the [Holy] Spirit by those who had been brought here under its guidance had been done for the best, whereas under the chiefs there was never a plan or an undertaking but ended in failure. While they were absent the suburb had been taken; without their knowledge Almada was reduced; and, if they had been guided by this inspiration as they should have been, the mutineers asserted that the city

si hoc ut deceret veherentur impetu, iampridem urbem rece-
pisse vel aliquid lucri maius egisse aiebant.

Sed quid de huiusmodi iniuriosis dicemus, nisi vim quandam
malis moribus insitam naturaliter, ut paucorum scelus multitudinis innocentiam devenustet, cum e diverso bonorum rari-
tas flagitia multorum excusare nequeat, si velit? Sed quis non
exacerbescat cum virtutum sinceritatem vitiorum crimina-
tione sordidari videat, cum[a] quid velint, quidve nolint, nec in
bonis quid placeat, nec in malis quid displiceat, discernentes
nesciant? Si humilem viderint, abiectum vocant. Si erectum,
superbire censent. Si minus instructum, propter imperitiam
irridendum credunt. Si aliquatenus doctum, propter scientiam
dicunt inflatum. Si severum, horrent tamquam crudelem. Si
indulgentem, facilitate culpant. Si simplicem, ut brutum de-
spiciunt. Si acrem, vitant ut callidum. Si diligentem, super-
sticiosum decernunt. Si remissum, negligentem iudicant. Si
sollertem, cupidum. Si quietum, ignavum pronuntiant. Si abs-
temium, avarum predicant. Si prandendo pascatur,[b] edacem
damnant. Si pascendo ieiunantem, vanum loquuntur; liberum,
pro improbo condempnant. Verecundum, pro rustico. Rigidos
ab austeritate caros non habent. Blandi aput eos communione
vilescunt. Ac si utrolibet genere vivatur, semper tamen bona-
rum partium mores, pungentibus maledicorum linguis, bicipi-
tibus hamis inuncabuntur.

Huius igitur tumultus eruptio in Herveum de Glanvilla
delata est, qui non sibi sed regi [143v] obsides tradidisset,
simulque quosdam ex ipsis, quasi degeneres, expertes urbis
peccuniarum abiudicasset. De quibus amplius quadrigentis ex
castris proruentes circumquaque armati perscrutantur, licet
eum absentem noverint, voce magna clamantes, "Tollatur
impius, puniatur proditor." Hoc itaque comperto cum castris

---

[a] *cum* written in margin.   [b] An erasure of 2.2 centimetres follows *pascatur*.

would long since have been taken or something else accomplished of even greater profit.

But how shall we describe such insults except as a certain violence naturally implanted in bad character, as a result of which the guilt of the few disfigures the innocence of the many, although, on the other hand, the fewness of the good cannot excuse the disgraceful acts of the many, even if it would? Who would not become indignant at seeing the sincerity of virtue soiled by the accusation of vice, when those who criticize know not what they want or do not want, or what is satisfactory in good things or unsatisfactory in evil? If they see anyone humble, they call him abject; if proud, they judge him haughty; if but little instructed, they think him to be ridiculed for his inexperience; if at all learned, they say he is puffed up on account of his knowledge; if severe, they shudder at such cruelty; if indulgent, they blame his slackness; if simple, they despise him as a stupid; if keen, they avoid him as crafty; if diligent, they think him overscrupulous; if easygoing, they adjudge him neglectful; if shrewd, covetous; if quiet, they pronounce him lazy; if abstemious, they declare him miserly; if in eating he indulges himself, they damn him for a glutton; if given to fasting, they call him vain; if frank, they condemn him for an impudent; if shy, for a rustic. The rigorous they do not like because of their austerity; the mild lose respect among them from association. Whichever way of life be led, the character of the good will always be caught on one point or the other of a two-pronged hook, for the tongues of slanderers are sharp.

Now this tumultuous outbreak was directed against Hervey de Glanvill, because he had delivered the hostages to the king rather than to themselves, and also because he had adjudged certain of them who had been guilty of some base offense to have no share in the riches of the city. More than four hundred of them rushed out from camp under arms and made a wide search for him, though they knew him to be absent, while they yelled, "Away with the wretch, let the traitor be punished." When news of this was received while we were in the

interessemus regis, a quibusdam senioribus nostrorum obviam itum est compescendum eorum vehementie initia. Hiis retroactis, ad ea que superius responsuri convenimus.

Obsides vero comperto quod inter se nostri contentiose egissent, orationis prime verba retractantes dissimulant. Regi vero et suis omnia nobis superius promissa vel predicta velle facere et tenere aiebant: nostris, nec pro morte quicquam; nam impuros, imfidos, impios, crudeles, qui nec dominis suis etiam parcere nossent. Que res nostros maximo pudore suffudit. Iterum cum rege in concilio ventum est; maxima diei parte sic consumpta, acquieverunt[a] tandem in hoc obsides, ut si eorum alcaiz una cum genero suo omnibus facultatibus suis libere potietur, concivesque cuncti cibariis suis, fore uti civitas traderetur nobis. Sin autem, armis experiri cetera.

Normanni quoque et Angli quibus bellorum casus gravissimo oneri fuerat, longa fatigati obsidione, concedi oportere aiebant, honestumque nec peccuniam vel cibaria honori[b] urbis capescende preponendum. Colonenses vero et Flandrenses quibus semper habendi innata cupiditas, longi itineris dispendia suorumque interitum multumque itineris superesse commemorantes, nil reliqui fieri posse hostibus decernebant. In hoc tandem luctamine adducti, ut omnes facultates sue et cibaria soli alcaie donarentur, sola eius Arabica iumentina excepta, quam ut sibi aliquo extorqueret argumento comes de Aerescot concupierat. In hoc demum eorum fixa sententia stetit, nostris quam indigne ferentibus. Nocte dirimente concilium, obsides in sententia sua perseverant, Francis ad utrumlibet se habentibus, pacem vel bellum scilicet.

[a] *aqquieverunt.*
[b] Apparently *horiori*, which seems to make no sense.

king's camp, some of our elders went over to repress this out-
burst of violence. Upon their return we met in council to make
reply to the proposals above mentioned.

But the hostages, having learned that our forces were involved in a controversy among themselves, retracted the
words of their first entreaty and resorted to dissimulation.
So far as the king and his men were concerned, they said that
they were willing to respect and to perform all the commit-
ments which they had made; but for our forces they would
not for their lives do anything, since these were base, faithless,
disloyal, and cruel men, who did not even recognize an obligation to spare their own lords—a turn of events which covered
our men with the greatest shame. Once more a council was
held with the king, and when most of the day had thus been
spent, the hostages at last consented to this, that if the alcayde
and his son-in-law should freely receive all their property and
all the citizens should receive their food, the city would be
surrendered to us in full possession, but that otherwise the
issue should be left to the arbitrament of arms.

The Normans and the English, for whom the vicissitudes
of wars had been a heavy burden, and who were fatigued by
the long siege, said that the concessions ought to be granted
and upright conduct, not property or foodstuffs, preferred
to the honor of taking the city. But the men of Cologne and
the Flemings, in whom there is ever an innate covetousness
of possessing, calling to mind the expenses of their long journey
and the death of their men and that a long voyage yet lay
before them, were determined that nothing could be left to
the enemy. In this debate they were finally induced to concede that the alcayde alone should be granted food and all
his property, with the single exception of his Arabian mare
which the count of Aerschot so coveted that he extorted her
for himself by some argument. At this point they finally stood
their ground immovably, while our men bore it with much
indignation. As night put an end to the council, the hostages
still persisted in their position while the Franks were divided
between two policies, namely, peace and war.

In crastino[1] autem urbis aditum ferro experiendum decreverunt, reversis omnibus ad castra. Cum interim Colonenses et Flandrenses indignati quod rex obsidibus, ut videbatur, favisset, ex castris armati proruunt, ut obsides a castris regis vindicandum in eos violenter eriperent, tumultus atque armorum strepitus fit undique. [144r] Nos vero, cum in meditullio inter regis et eorum castra adhuc colloquentes expectaremus, que parabantur regi nuntiamus. Christianus vero dux Flandrensium et comes de Aerescot, eorum tumultu comperto, vix etiam armati eorum inceptum compescunt. Dein conciliatum pro suis sedato tumultu regem adeunt, protestantes huius actionis immunes se fore. Acce[p]ta itaque ab eis securitate, tandem animo recepto, iubet suos arma deponere, obsidionem relicturum in crastinum se multum asserens; sed et honestatem urbi capescende non postposuisse, imo pro nichilo omnia ducere, si ea caruisset, aiebat; verumptamen hiis affectum iniuriis, hominibus impuris, audacissimis, quodlibet ausuris ultra associari[a] nolle. Recepto vix tandem animo, ut quid in crastino vellet deliberaret, acquievit.[b] Deliberatum est itaque in crastino ut omnes utrimque duces nostri pro se et suis fidelitatem regi tenendam facerent, dum in terra sua morarentur.

Hiis ita utrimque firmatis, sicut pridie poposcerunt Mauri concessum est de urbe tradenda.[2] Decretum est itaque inter nos ut centum XL. armatorum ex nostris partibus et centum

[a] assotiari.   [b] aqquievit.

[1] 23 October.

[2] "Unde factum est ut alchaida princeps eorum hoc pacto nobiscum conveniret, ut noster exercitus omnem supellectilem eorum cum auro et argento acciperet, rex autem civitatem cum nudis Sarracenis et tota terra obtineret": Arnulf, in *HF*, XIV, 327; *Brief des Priesters Winand*, p. 7. "Quod et factum est, et pactum inter nos et eos ita firmatum est, ut nobis omnem supellectilem, tam in auro quam in argento, vestibus et equis, mulis, regi civitatem redderent; ipsi vero, si pactum inter nos non infringerent, cum integritate membrorum depositis armis abirent": Duodechin, in *MGH, Scriptores*, XVII, 28. Compare the words of Helmold quoted above, p. 112, note 1.

But on the morrow[1] when all had returned to camp, they
decided that an attempt should be made to enter the city at
the point of the sword. Meanwhile, the men of Cologne and
the Flemings, waxing indignant because the king, as it seemed,
was favoring the hostages, rushed out of their camps under
arms in order that they might seize the hostages with violence
from the king's camp and take vengeance upon them. And
there was tumult and clashing of arms all around. But since
we were still engaged in conversation and awaiting the turn
of events in the middle ground between the king's camp and
theirs, we reported to the king what was about to happen.
But when Christian, leader of the Flemings, and the count
of Aerschot learned of the outbreak of their forces, they
promptly put a stop to it, although they were hardly armed.
Then, when the tumult had been quieted, they went to con-
ciliate the king on behalf of their forces, protesting that they
themselves were innocent of this action. Accordingly, when
he had taken security from them and had at last recovered
his temper, he ordered that their forces should put away their
arms, declaring roundly that he would postpone the siege
until the morrow; and he said that he would not put honor
second even to the taking of the city, that, on the contrary,
he would account all things for naught if it should be wanting;
indeed, that disgraced by these outrages, he was unwilling
any longer to associate with abandoned men—the most insolent desperadoes who would do anything. Finally, having
with difficulty recovered his equanimity, he agreed to consider what he wished to be done upon the morrow. And
so it was decided next day that our leaders from both divisions for themselves and for their men should swear fealty
to the king, to be kept so long as they remained in his country.

When these matters had thus been settled on both sides,
the terms of the surrender of the city on which the Moors
had insisted on the previous day were conceded.[2] Accordingly,
it was decided among ourselves that one hundred and forty
armed men from our forces and one hundred and sixty from

LX. ex Colonensibus et Flandrensibus civitatem pre omnibus ingrederentur, atque munimentum superioris castri in pace tenerent, ut in ipso hostes peccunias et facultates suas omnes iuramento probatas coram nostris deferrent, et hiis ita coadunatis, urbem postea a nostris perscrutari, si quid amplius allati penes aliquos inventum[a] in cuius penatibus fuerit, dominum ipsius capite plectendum, et hoc modo omnes spoliatos extra urbem in pace dimittendos. Aperta itaque porta et ad hoc delectis data intrandi copia, Colonenses et Flandrenses argumentum fallendi callidum excogitantes, ut sui honoris causa preintrarent, a nostris impetrarunt. Accepta itaque huiusmodi licentia et preintrandi occasione, amplius ducentis ex eis cum denominatis supra subintrant, exceptis aliis quos iam per muri ruinam que ex eorum patebat partibus intromiserant, nullo nostrorum nisi denominatis presumente aditum. Precedente itaque archiepiscopo et coepiscopis cum dominice crucis vexillo,[1] duces nostri una cum rege [144v] et qui ad hec fuerant delecti subintrant.[2]

O quanta omnium leticia! O quanta omnium specialis gloria! O quanta pre gaudio et pietate lacrimarum affluentia, cum ad laudem et honorem Dei et sanctissime virginis Marię crucis salutifere vexillum in summa arce positum subacte in signum urbis ab omnibus videretur, precinente archyepiscopo et episcopis cum clero et omnibus, non sine lacrimis, admirabili iubilo *Te Deum laudamus* cum *Asperges me*[3] et orationibus devotis! Rex interim muros editioris castri pedes circuit.

---

[a] *inventum* is followed by *f* and an erasure of 7 millimetres. Apparently *fuerit*, which belongs after *in cuius penatibus*, was first written, and then not entirely erased.

[1] See above, p. 156, note 1.   [2] 24 October.

[3] The antiphon (from Psalms [Vulgate] 50: 9) intoned during the ceremony of aspersion with holy water, a rite of purification prescribed by the church for various occasions, such as the consecration and dedication of churches, the reconciliation of churches whose consecrated character has for any reason been lost, etc. See *Liturgia*, pp. 144–50, 157–59, 751–52, and *passim*. The more general aspersion here referred to seems to be unknown to ordinary liturgical practice.

the men of Cologne and the Flemings should enter the city before all the others, and without violence occupy the stronghold of the upper castle, in order that within the same the enemy might bring their money and possessions, acknowledged under oath, before our men, and that, after these things had all been collected, the city might be searched by our forces—if anything more should be found in anybody's possession, the owner of the house in which it should be discovered was to be made to suffer for it with his head—and that in this manner the whole population, after it had been despoiled, should be released outside the walls. And so, the gate having been opened and an opportunity of entering obtained for those who had been chosen for the purpose, the men of Cologne and the Flemings, contriving deception by a clever argument, obtained the consent of our men that they should go in first for the sake of their honor. And when they had thus obtained permission and an opportunity of entering first, more than two hundred of them slipped in along with those who had been designated, as above mentioned, besides others whom they had already introduced through the breach in the wall which stood open on their side. But none of our forces presumed to enter, except those who had been designated. And so, the archbishop and his fellow bishops leading the way with a banner bearing the sign of the cross,[1] our leaders, together with the king and those who had been chosen for the purpose, made their entry.[2]

Oh, what rejoicing there was on the part of all! Oh, what especial pride on the part of all! Oh, what a flow of tears of joy and piety, when, to the praise and honor of God and of the most holy Virgin Mary, the ensign of the salvation-bearing cross was beheld by all placed upon the highest tower in token of the subjection of the city, while the archbishop and the bishops together with the clergy and all the people, not without tears, intoned with a wonderful jubilation the *Te Deum laudamus* together with the *Asperges me*[3] and devout prayers! The king, meanwhile, made the circuit of the walls of the upper castle on foot.

Colonenses igitur et Flandrenses, visis in urbe tot adminiculis cupiditatis, nullam iurisiurandi vel fidei religionem observant. Hinc illinc discurrunt; predas agunt; fores effringunt; penetralia cuiusque domus rimantur; cives proturbant, et contra ius et fas contumeliis afficiunt; vasa vestesque dissipant; in virgines contumeliose agunt; fas et nefas equipendunt; furtim omnia distrahunt^a quę fieri omnibus communia debuerant. Episcopum vero civitatis antiquissimum,[1] preciso iugulo, contra ius et fas occidunt. Ipsumque civitatis alcaiz, asportatis omnibus a domo sua, capiunt. Iumentinam suam, de qua superius, ipse comes de Aerescot propriis manibus arripuit, eamque requisitus a rege et ab omnibus nostris in tanta obstinatione retinuit, ut diceret ipse alcaiz, quod iumentina sua sanguinem micturiens^b pullum perdidisset, actionis obscene callide imprimens vitium. Normanni vero atque Angli, quibus fides et religio maximo constabat, contemplantes quid huiusmodi portenderet actio, in loco denominato quieti sedebant, malentes observare manus ab omni rapina quam fidei et societatis coniuratæ^c statuta violare, que res comitem de Aerescot et Christianum et eorum primarios maximo pudore suffudit, quorum iam evidenter iureiurando postposito nostris non permixta patebat cupiditas. Sed tandem in se reversi, precibus obnixis aput nostros impetraverunt, ut reliquas urbis partes nostri pariter cum suis pacifice ad partes adunarent, ut sic denique post portiones acceptas omnium, [145r] iniurias et subreptiones in pace discuti*ant*^d emendatum parati quod male presumpsissent.

---

^a *distraunt.*   ^b *migturiens.*   ^c See above, p. 47.

^d Reading doubtful; *discutiunt* may have been written first; then partly erased to change to *discutiant,* and the correction never completed.

Thereupon the men of Cologne and the Flemings, when they saw so many temptations to greed in the city, observed not the bond of their oath or plighted faith. They rushed about hither and thither; they pillaged; they broke open doors; they tore open the innermost parts of every house; they drove out the citizens and treated them with insults, against right and justice; they scattered utensils and clothing; they insulted maidens; they made wrong equal with right; they secretly snatched away all those things which ought to have been made the common property of all the forces. They even slew the aged bishop of the city,[1] against all right and decency, by cutting his throat. They seized the alcayde himself and carried everything out of his house. And his mare above mentioned, the count of Aerschot seized with his own hands, and at the demand of the king and of all our men that he give her up, he held on to her so obstinately that, because with an emission of blood she had lost her foal, the alcayde himself spoke out and branded the abominable action as disgusting. But the Normans and the English, for whom good faith and scruples of conscience were matters of the highest import, remained quietly at the posts to which they had been assigned, while they wondered what such an event might portend, preferring to keep their hands from all rapine rather than violate their engagements and the ordinances of the oath-bound association—an episode which covered the count of Aerschot and Christian and their principal followers with shame, since through the disregarding of their oath their unmixed greed now stood openly revealed to us. But finally having come to their senses, they obtained from us by insistent prayers that our men upon the same footing with theirs should peacefully bring together the remainder of the booty of the city with the portions already collected, in order that thus at last after shares had been apportioned to all, they might nullify the insults and the thefts in peace by being prepared to give satisfaction for what they had wrongfully taken in advance.

[1] The Mozarabic bishop. See above, pp. 114–15 and note 2.

Despoliatis igitur in urbe hostibus, a primo sabati mane[1] per tres portas usque ad quartam feriam subsequentem indesinenter exeuntes visi sunt tanta[a] gentium multitudo ac si tota in ea Hyspania confluxisset. Compertum est deinceps magne admirationis miraculum, quod ante[b] urbis captionem per dies quindecim hostium cibaria fetore intolerabili ingustabilia sibi facta que postmodum nobis et ipsis grata acceptaque gustavimus. Spoliata igitur civitate, inventa sunt in fossis ad modum VIII. M. summarum[2] tritici et hordei,[c] olei autem ad modum XII. M. sextariorum.[3] De ritu et eorum religione que supra diximus oculis postmodum vidimus. Nam in eorum templo,[d] quod VII. columpnarum ordinibus cum tot cumulis[e] in altum consurgit, mortuorum cadavera ferme ducenta, exceptis languidis amplius octingentis, cum omni squalore et feditate sua in eo manentibus inventa sunt.

Capta vero urbe cum eam XVII. hebdomadibus[f] obsedissemus,[4] Suctrienses, data munitione sui castri, regi se dedere. Castrum vero de Palmella a custodibus relictum, a rege vacuum suscipitur. Receptis igitur circumquaque munitionibus civitati pertinentibus, magnificatum est Francorum nomen per universas Hyspanie partes, irruitque timor super Mauros quibus verbum huius actionis divulgabatur.

Electus est subinde ad sedem pontificatus ex nostris Gislebertus Hastingensis,[5] rege, archyepiscopo, coepiscopis, clericis,

---

[a] *visi sunt tanta* written in different ink over an erasure of 4 centimetres.

[b] An erasure of 5 millimetres follows *ante*.   [c] *ordei*.   [d] *templum*.

[e] Stubbs, *Itinerarium*, Glossary, p. 454, and Hamilton, *PMH, Scriptores*, I, 405, have both read *cumalis*, but there is no doubt that *cumulis* is the correct reading.

[f] *epdomadibus*.

[1] 25 October.   [2] See above, p. 130, note 1.

[3] A *sextarius*, or sextar, was a measure of uncertain volume, perhaps containing between a pint and a quart.

[4] From Saturday, 28 June, when the fleet arrived at Lisbon, to Friday, 24 October, when the entry into the city occurred, was a day less than seventeen weeks. Stubbs, *Itinerarium*, p. clxxx, erroneously reads *XVI* for *XVII*.

[5] Bishop of Lisbon until his death which, according to Rodrigo da Cunha (*Historia ecclesiastica da igreja de Lisboa*, Lisbon, 1690, Pt. 2, fol. 73r), took place on 27 April, 1166. His election is noted and his talents are praised in the *Indiculum fundationis monasterii beati Vincentii*, in *PMH, Scriptores*, I, 92. He is named as one of the witnesses of an early grant by King Affonso to the monastery of St. Vincent de Fora, *ibid.*, p. 93.

Accordingly, when the enemy within the city had been despoiled, from early Saturday morning[1] until the following Wednesday so great a multitude of people was seen steadily filing out through three gates that it seemed as if all Spain had flowed together into it. Then we learned of a very wonderful miracle, namely, that for a fortnight before the capture of the city the victuals of the enemy became inedible on account of an intolerable stench, although afterwards they tasted agreeable and acceptable both to us and to them. And when the city had been ransacked, we found in the cellars as much as eight thousand seams[2] of wheat and barley, and twelve thousand sextars[3] of oil. Concerning their religion and their use, the things which we have said above we afterwards observed with our own eyes. For in their temple, which rises aloft on seven rows of columns surmounted by as many arches, we found almost two hundred corpses, besides more than eight hundred sick persons who were staying there in all their filth and squalor.

When the city had been taken after we had besieged it for seventeen weeks,[4] the inhabitants of Cintra surrendered the stronghold of their castle and gave themselves up to the king. And the castle of Palmela, after it had been evacuated by its garrison, was occupied by the king while empty. And so, the strongholds appurtenant to the city in the surrounding country having been taken, the name of the Franks was magnified throughout all parts of Spain, and terror seized upon the Moors among whom tidings of this action were made known.

Then Gilbert of Hastings[5] was chosen from among our

According to Cunha (*op. cit.*, Pt. 2, fol. 69v) he was consecrated bishop by John, archbishop of Braga. Brandão (Brito, *Monarchia Lusytana*, Pt. 3, p. 238) gives, from the Livro da Sé de Braga, the text of his acknowledgment of subjection to the church of Braga and, from the same source, a record of the presence of his representative, Eldebredus, archdeacon of Lisbon, at a council held by the archbishop at Braga in 1148. He contested the ecclesiastical rights which the king had granted to the Templars at Santarém after its capture from the Moors in the spring of 1147, as is indicated by a note appended at the end of the king's charter, dated April, 1147, in favor of the Templars: Marquis d'Albon, *Cartulaire général de l'ordre du Temple*, No. 439. His suc-

laicis omnibus electioni eius assensum prebentibus. Die vero
qua omnium memoria sanctorum celebratur,[1] ad laudem et
honorem nominis Christi et sanctissime eius genitricis purifica-
tum est templum ab archiepiscopo et coepiscopis quattuor[2] et
reparatur inibi sedes episcopatus, cum hiis castris et vicis
subscriptis: trans Tagum, castro Alcacer, castro de Palmella,
Elmada provintia; citra Tagum, castro Suchtrio, castro Scala-
phio, castro Lora. Sunt autem termini eius ab Alcacer castro
usque ad castrum Lora, et a mari occidentali usque[a] civitatem
Eburensem.

Subsequuta est deinceps tanta Maurorum lues ut per
here[145v]mi vastitates, per vineas et per vicos et plateas
domorumque ruinas innumera cadaverum milia feris avibusque
iacerent exposita, exanguibusque similes vivi super terram gra-
direntur, signumque crucis supliciter amplectentes deoscula-
rentur, beatamque Dei matrem Mariam bonam predicarent,
ut ad omnes actus vel sermones etiam in extremis agentes
Mariam bonam, bonam Mariam intermiscerent, miserabiliter-
que reclamarent.[3] Et quid aliud nobis hec intuentibus videri
potest, nisi illud Ysaye vaticinium impletum in nobis cum

[a] An erasure of 2 centimetres follows *usque*.

---

cess in the contest is recorded in the *pax et convenientia* which was arranged between
him and the Templars by the king in February, 1159: Brandão, *op. cit.*, Pt. 3, p. 226.
By a charter of donation, made with the assent of the king and queen, and dated
1 January, 1150, he established houses and prebends for thirty-one canons. Cunha,
op. cit., Pt. 2, fol. 71r–72r. The witness list at the end of this charter is remarkable for
the foreign names which it contains, the most certain being Gilbert of Kent (*Gilbertus
de Chent*). Bishop Gilbert was back in England in 1150 seeking recruits for a fresh
struggle against the Moors: "Gilbertus episcopus Olisiponis, praedicans in Angliam,
plurimos sollicitavit in Hyspaniam proficisci, Ispalim obsessuros et expugnaturos:"
John of Hexham, *Historia*, in Simeon of Durham, *Opera omnia* (ed. Thomas Arnold,
London, 1882–85), II, 324. He is said to have introduced into his cathedral the breviary
and missal of Salisbury. They were continued in use there until displaced by the
Roman liturgy in 1536: Cunha, *op. cit.*, Pt. 2, fol. 72v; José Pereira de Santa Anna,
Chronica dos Carmelitas . . . nestes reynos de Portugal, Algarves, e seus dominios (Lisbon, 1745–51), II, 33, 82–83; idem, *Dissertaçao apologetica, historica, liturgica, dogmatica,
e politica* (Lisbon, 1751), pp. 56–57; J. B. de Castro, *Mappa de Portugal* (Lisbon, 1762–
63), III, 102. Pereira de Santa Anna infers that the use of Salisbury prevailed throughout the diocese of Lisbon.

forces to be bishop, and the king, the archbishop, his fellow bishops, the clergy, and the laity all gave their assent to his election. And on the day on which the memory of All Saints is celebrated,[1] to the glory and honor of the name of Christ and of his most holy Mother, the temple was purified by the archbishop and his four fellow bishops,[2] and the episcopal see was restored therein, with jurisdiction over the following castles and villages: beyond Tagus, the castle of Alcácer do Sal, the castle of Palmela, the province of Almada; on this side of Tagus, the castle of Cintra, the castle of Santarém, the castle of Leiria. And its limits extend from Alcácer to Leiria, and from the western sea to the city of Évora.

Then there followed such a pestilence among the Moors that throughout the desert wastes, in vineyards, in villages, and squares, and among ruins of houses unnumbered thousands of corpses lay exposed to birds and beasts; and living men resembling bloodless beings went about the earth, and, grasping the symbol of the cross, they kissed it as suppliants and declared that Mary the Mother of God was good, so that in all their acts and speeches, even when already *in extremis*, they interspersed the words *Maria bona, bona Maria*, and cried out pitiably.[3] And what else could occur to us as we wondered at these things than that the prophecy of Isaiah was happily being fulfilled in us in which it is said, "And the bridle

---

[1] 1 November. This is the latest date mentioned by this author, who gives no indication as to the sequel. According to Duodechin, after the winter had been passed in Lisbon the crusaders continued on their way to Jerusalem: "His ita feliciter gestis, nostri in eadem civitate usque ad Kalendas Februarii hiemaverunt; exinde per varia discrimina navigantes, sicut devoverant, ad dominicum sepulchrum pervenerunt" *MGH, Scriptores*, XVII, 28. That the king's bid for colonists met with some success is indicated by Helmold: "Factaque est illic cristicolarum colonia usque in presentem diem." *Cronica Slavorum*, p. 118. The northerners evidently remained for some time dominant in the monastery of St. Vincent de Fora at Lisbon. *Indiculum fundationis monasterii beati Vincentii*, in *PMH, Scriptores*, I, 93.

[2] John, archbishop of Braga, and presumably Peter, bishop of Oporto; Menendus, bishop of Lamego; Odorius, bishop of Viseu; and Gilbert of Hastings, bishop of Lisbon.

[3] Evidently Mozarabs, as Herculano has said. Their bishop had been murdered during the sack of the city. See above, pp. 114–15 and note 2, pp. 176, 177.

gaudio, quo dicitur, "Et frenum erroris quod erat in maxillis populorum versum est in canticum facte solemnitatis"?[1]

Recolentes igitur nos tales fuisse gratias agamus Creatori, quod a servitio creature colla mentis excussimus. Nam dum freno erroris maxillas constricti laudem confessionis Deo dare nesciebamus; ergo dum confessionis laudem Deo reddimus in sanctificata solempnitate gaudemus. Respondeamus ergo moribus tante misericordie Redemptoris nostri, et quia lucem cognovimus, pravorum operum tenebras declinemus, predicantes magnalia Dei que operari dignatus est in nobis. Tradidit enim Deus noster crucis adversarios in manibus nostris. Severissima namque super eos ultio divina adeo incubuit, ut dum urbem destructam castrumque eversum, agros depopulatos, terram[a] in solitudinem redactam, nullum in agris incolam, luctus gemitusque eorum conspicimus, vicis eorum et eventus malorum misereri libeat, condolerique et compati eorum infirmitatibus, et quod nondum finem habeant flagella celestis iusticie, certe quia nec inter nos Christianos etiam correcte sunt inter flagella actionis culpe. Dolendum et gaudendum est. Nam cum perversos quosque Deus omnipotens percutit, pereuntium miserie condolendum et iusticie iudicis congaudendum. Ergo nostrum quisque semetipsum districte diiudicans, divina consideret iudicia, non solum ad vindictam malorum sed ad eruditionem bonorum facta, donis quosdam reficiens, alios flagellis erudiens. Non autem in iustificationibus nostris hostes prostravimus, sed in miseratione Dei multa.[b] Mentem ergo nostram donorum abundantia non elevet, nec nos habere quod alteri deest iactemus, nec hostium miseriam gloriam nostram existimemus, quos forsan miseria trahet ad gloriam, nos autem elatio ad miseriam; quos enim vult Deus indurat, et

---

[a] *eorum* written after *terram*, and then erased.

[b] The sentence *Non autem . . . Dei multa* is written before *donis quosdam reficiens alios flagellis erudiens*. The correct order is indicated by a superscribed *.b.* before *Non autem* and a superscribed *.a.* before *donis*. A peculiar sign resembling T is placed after *erudiens* to mark the end of the transposed text. This misplacement of the text perhaps accounts for the bad grammar of *reficiens* and *erudiens*, which, it seems, must agree with *iudicia*.

[1] Compare Isaiah 30: 28, 29.

of error that was in the jaws of the people was turned into the song of a solemnity that was kept" ?[1]

Recalling then that we too have been such [namely, sinners] let us give thanks to the Creator that we have released our spiritual necks from servitude to the creature. For while the jaws were constrained by the bridle of error, we knew not how to render the praise of confession to God. Therefore, when we render the praise of confession to God, we do rejoice in a holy solemnity. Therefore, let us respond in our morals to such mercy on the part of our Redeemer, and, because we have known the light, let us turn away from the darkness of evil deeds and proclaim the mighty works which he has deigned to work through us. For our God has delivered the enemies of the cross into our hands. And divine vengeance has pressed upon them with such severity that, as we see the city in ruins and the castle overthrown, the fields depopulated, the land reduced to solitude, with no inhabitant in the fields, and as we behold their mourning and lamentations, we are inclined to feel pity for them in their vicissitudes and evil fortunes and to suffer with them on account of their infirmities and to feel sorry that the lashings of divine justice are not yet at an end; and particularly are we moved to sorrow because not even among us Christians have sins been corrected amid the scourgings of this action. There is a necessity for both sorrow and rejoicing. For when the omnipotent God strikes down sinners, whoever they be, one must grieve for the sufferings of the perishing yet rejoice at the justice of the judge. Therefore, let each one of us, strictly judging himself, reflect that divine judgments are rendered not only for the punishment of the wicked but for the instruction of the good, encouraging some with gifts, correcting others with scourges. Not in our own righteousness have we overthrown the enemy, but through the great compassion of God. Accordingly, let not the abundance of his gifts arouse our pride, and let us not boast that we have what another lacks, nor esteem as our glory the misery of the enemy—whom perchance affliction will draw to glory, but elation, us to affliction. For God hardeneth whom he will,

quos vult ad [146r] misericordiam provehit;[1] ut in Iob dicitur,
"Ipso concedente pacem quis est qui condempnet? ex quo
absconderit vultum suum quis est qui contempletur eum?"[2]
Nemo ergo discutiat cur stantibus nobis Christianis gentilitas
hec in infirmitate succubuerit. Nemo discutiat cur alius venus-
tetur ex dono, alter affligatur ex merito. Si enim miretur quis
nos Christianos venustatos, "ipso concedente pacem quis est
qui condempnet?" Si hostes consumptos obstupescit vel
afflictos, "ex quo absconderit vultum suum, quis contempletur
eum?" Itaque consilium summe et occulte virtutis sit satis-
factio aperte rationis. Unde in evangelio Dominus cum de
huiusmodi causa loqueretur, ait, "Confiteor tibi, Domine
Pater celi et terre, quia abscondisti [hec] a sapientibus et pru-
dentibus et revelasti ea parvulis."[3] Atque mox tamquam ratio-
nem, quandam absconsionis ac revelationis adiungens, ait,
"Ita, Pater, quoniam sic[a] placitum fuit ante te."[4] Quibus
nimirum verbis exempla humilitatis accipimus, ne temere
superna consilia discutiamus de aliorum electione et aliorum
depressione. Videntes ergo sed non intelligentes divine animadversionis iudicium hostibus inculcatum, conscientie nostre
immunditiam atque impuritatem consideremus, et cum timore
et angustia spiritus dicamus Deo, "Parce iam, Domine, parce
operi manuum tuarum. Quiescant, Domine, opera ire tue.
'Cesset iam manus tua, sufficit,'[5] Domine. Iam vero iam satis
est, quod hucusque adversus hos pro nobis decertasti. Sed
convertatur potius si fieri potest luctus eorum in gaudium,
'ut cognoscant te solum Deum vivum et verum, et quem
misisti Iesum Christum,'[6] filium tuum, qui vivis et regnas per
omnia secula seculorum. Amen."

---

[a] *Ita, Pater, quoniam sic* written over an erasure of 2 centimetres.

[1] Compare Romans 9: 18.   [2] Job 34: 29.

and on whom he will he hath mercy.[1] As it is said in Job, "When he giveth quietness, who then can make trouble? and when he hideth his face, who then can behold him?"[2] Therefore, let no one discuss why with us Christians standing erect these pagans have fallen down in sickness. Let no one discuss why one is made comely by divine grace while another is afflicted according to his deserts. For if anyone wonder that we Christians have been made comely, "When he giveth quietness, who then can make trouble?" If he confounds the enemy, wasted and afflicted, "When he hideth his face, who then can behold him?" And so let the counsel of the most high and hidden virtue be the satisfaction of open reason. In the Gospel, when a subject of this sort was under discussion, the Lord said, "I thank thee, O Father, Lord of heaven and earth, that thou didst hide these things from the wise and understanding, and didst reveal them unto babes."[3] And presently, adding a certain explanation of the hiding and revealing, he said, "Yea Father, for so it was well-pleasing in thy sight."[4] From which words, assuredly, we receive examples of humility, to the end that we should not rashly discuss the divine counsels concerning the election of some and the damnation of others. Observing, therefore, but not understanding, the judgment of divine chastisement imposed upon the enemy, let us consider the uncleanness and impurity of our own consciences, and with fear and anguish of spirit let us say unto God, "Spare now Lord, spare the work of thine hands. Lord, let the works of thy wrath be still. Lord, 'it is enough, stay now thine hand.'[5] It is indeed enough that thou hast fought for us thus far against them. But rather, if it be possible, let their sorrow be turned into joy, 'in order that they may know thee, the only living and true God, and Jesus Christ, whom thou hast sent,'[6] even thy Son, who liveth and reigneth for ever and ever. Amen."

[3] Matt. 11: 25.   [4] Matt. 11: 26.   [5] I Chronicles 21: 15.   [6] John 17: 3.

Glossary

OF UNUSUAL MEDIAEVAL WORDS OR OF COMMON WORDS
APPEARING IN UNUSUAL FORMS OR USED IN UNUSUAL
SENSES

ALCAIZ, abl. ALCAIE, 94, 170, 176—an alcayde, or commander of a fortress
among the Moors in Portugal and Spain

AREA, AE, 118—an arena, perhaps an error for HARENA; cf. Sen. *Ep.* xxii. 1

AURUM, I, 94—a tax, or taxes in general

BALISTA, AE, 124, 160—a crossbow (or stonebow), or a missile shot from
the same; also a crossbowman. See above, p. 125, note 3, p. 161, note 4.

BUSTALIUM, II, 96—a gravestone

CALDEUS (for CHALDAEUS), in the phrase LINGUA CALDEA, 136—Arabic, or
the language of the Moors in Portugal and Spain

CATTUS, I, 160—a cat or penthouse for the protection of besiegers from
missiles

CIRCO, ERE, 174—to go around, to make a circuit of

CONDOLEOR, ERI (deponent form, for CONDOLEO), 182—to suffer with, to
feel pity for

CONVICTUALIS, IS, 142—a table companion

CONVICTUS, US, 56—employ

CUMULUS, I, 178—probably an arch; Stubbs (*Itinerarium*, p. 454) defined
it as a cupola

FUNDA BALEARICA, 134, 142—a Balearic mangonel, a projectile-throwing
machine of the high-trajectory type. See above, p. 135, note 3

GALEATA, AE, 162—a galley

GARCIONES FUNDIFERI, 124—troops armed with slings

HALLO, 138—Allah, the god of the Muslims

IDOLATRIA, AE (MS YDOLATRIA, for IDOLOLATRIA), 64—idolatry

INEXPIO, ARE, in the gerundive form INEXPIANDUS, 132—inexpiable.

INVIVO, ERE, 78—to live during a period of time (?); perhaps an error for
VIVO

IUMENTINA, AE, 170, 176—a mare

MUTUO, ARE, 144—to exchange

PANNUSCULUS, I (for PANNICULUS), 104—a rag

PAULULUM, 136, 160, 166—gradually

PEDATICA, AE, 112—a toll or custom, levied on ships and goods

POMUM CITREUM (MS CETRIUM), 92—a citron (*citrus medica*); cf. the obsolete
English pomecedre and pome-citron

PRENIMIUS, 144—very intensive

SENATUS, US, 166—authority or rule

SUPERMURALIS, 162—upon a wall

SUS, IS, 134—a siege-machine called a sow

TUGURIUM, II, 146, 160—a penthouse or mantlet made of interwoven branches

TYSIS, IS (for PHTHISIS), 92—consumption

VENIO, IRE, 106—to become; apparently equivalent to DEVENIO

VIBRACULUM, I, 166—a flash or ray or beam or gleam (used of sunlight breaking through clouds)

WORMA, AE, 66—scarlet cloth (?); see above, p. 66, note 2

Selected Bibliography

The sources listed below constitute the key narratives and letters concerned with the Conquest of Lisbon. For a more detailed bibliography on all aspects of the Second Crusade, see Alan Murray's work in: Martin Hoch and Jonathan Phillips, eds., *The Second Crusade: Scope and Consequences* (Manchester: Manchester University Press, 2001).

Bernard of Clairvaux. "De consideratione ad Eugenium papam." In Jean Leclercq and Henri Rochais, eds., *Opera*. 8 vols. Rome: Editiones Cisterciences, 1957–77.3:379–493. Translated in: Anderson, John and Elizabeth Kennan. *Five Books on Consideration: Advice to a Pope*, Cistercian Fathers Series, no. 37. Kalamazoo: Cistercian Publications, 1976.

———. "Epistolae." In Jean Leclercq and Henri Rochais, eds., *Opera*, 8 vols. Rome: Editiones Cisterciences, 1957–77. Vol. 7–8. Translated in: James, Bruno Scott. *The Letters of St. Bernard of Clairvaux*, new edition. Stroud: Alan Sutton, 1998.

David, Charles Wendell. *De expugnatione Lyxbonensi*. New York: Columbia University Press, 1936.

Edgington, Susan. "The Lisbon Letter of the Second Crusade." *Historical Research* 69 (1996): 336–39. Translated in: Edgington, Susan. "Albert of Aachen, Saint Bernard, and the Second Crusade." In Martin Hoch and Jonathan Phillips, eds., *The Second Crusade: Scope and Consequences*. Manchester: Manchester University Press, 2001.

Eugenius III. "Der Text der Kreuzzugsbulle Eugers III." In Paul Rassow, ed., *Neus Archiv der Gesellschaft für ältere deutsche Geschichtskunde* 45 (1924): 302–5. Translated in: Riley-Smith, Louise and Jonathan. *The Crusades, Idea and Reality: 1095–1274*, 57–9. London: Arnold, 1981.

———. "Epistolae et Privilegia." In Jean Migne, ed., *Patrologia Latina*, 217 vols. Paris: Garnier Fratres, 1844–64. Vol. 180.

Guibert of Nogent. "Dei gesta per Francos." In Robert Huygens, ed. *Corpus Christianorum Continuatio Medievalis*. Turnhout: Brepols, 1996. Vol. 127A. Translated in: Levine, Robert. *The Deeds of God Through the Franks*. Woodbridge: Boydell, 1997.

Helmold of Bosau. *The Chronicle of the Slavs.* Francis Tschan, trans. New York: Columbia University Press, 1935.

Henry, Archdeacon of Huntingdon. In Diana Greenway, ed. and trans., *Historia Anglorum.* Oxford: Oxford University Press, 1996.

Hiestand, Rudolf. *Papsturkunden für Kirchen im Heiligen Lande.* Göttingen: Varderhoeck and Ruprecht, 1985).

Odo of Deuil. *De profectione Ludovici VII in orientem* (The Journey of Louis VII to the East). Virginia G. Berry, ed. and trans. New York: Columbia University Press, 1948.

Otto of Freising. *Gesta Friderici I Imperatoris.* Bernhard von Simpson, ed. Hannover: Hahn, 1912. Translated as: Otto of Freising. *The Deeds of Frederick Barbarossa.* Charles Mierow, trans. New York: Columbia University Press, 1953.

SECONDARY MATERIALS

The best analysis of the contemporary sources, scope, and aims of the Second Crusade remains the magisterial article by Giles Constable, "The Second Crusade as Seen by Contemporaries," *Traditio* 9 (1953): 213–79. For a detailed but dated narrative outline, see: Virginia Berry, "The Second Crusade," in Kenneth Setton, ed., *A History of the Crusades*, 6 vols. (Madison: University of Wisconsin Press, 1969–89), 1:463–512. For a briefer but more up-to-date account, see: Jean Richard, *The Crusades c.1071–c.1291* (Cambridge: Cambridge University Press, 1999), 153–69.

Secondary works relating to the Conquest of Lisbon include:

Bennett, Matthew. "Military Aspects of the Capture of Lisbon, 1147." In Martin Hoch and Jonathan Phillips, eds., *The Second Crusade: Scope and Consequences.* Manchester: Manchester University Press, 2001.

Constable, Giles, "A Note on the Route of the Anglo-Flemish Crusaders of 1147." *Speculum* 28 (1953): 525–26.

Hehl, Ernst-Dieter. *Kirche und Krieg im 12. Jahrhundert: Studien zu kanonischem Recht und politischer Wirklichkeit.* Stuttgart: Hiersemann, 1980.

Livermore, Harold. "The 'Conquest of Lisbon' and Its Author." *Portuguese Studies* 6 (1990): 1–16.

Phillips, Jonathan. "Saint Bernard of Clairvaux, the Low Countries, and the Lisbon Letter of the Second Crusade." *Journal of Ecclesiastical History* 48 (1997): 485–97.

———. "Ideas of Crusade and Holy War in *De expugnatione Lyxbonensi* (The Conquest of Lisbon). In Robert Swanson, ed. *Holy Land, Holy*

Lands, and Christian History. Studies in Church History. Vol. 36. Woodbridge: Boydell, 2000. 123–41.

Rogers, Randall. *Latin Siege Warfare in the Twelfth Century*. Oxford: Clarendon Press, 1992.

Other studies relevant to the crusading background of the Conquest of Lisbon include:

Barber, Malcolm. *The New Knighthood: A History of the Order of the Temple*. Cambridge: Cambridge University Press, 1994.

Bull, Marcus. *Knightly Piety and the Lay Response to the First Crusade: The Limousin and Gascony c.970–c.1130*. Oxford: Clarendon Press, 1993.

Epstein, Stephen. *Genoa and the Genoese, 958–1528*. Chapel Hill: University of North Carolina Press, 1996.

Gervers, Michael. *The Second Crusade and the Cistercians*. New York: St. Martin's Press, 1992.

Kedar, Benjamin. *Crusade and Mission: European Approaches Toward the Muslims*. Princeton: Princeton University Press, 1984.

Phillips, Jonathan. *Defenders of the Holy Land: Relations Between the Latin East and the West, 1119–87*. Oxford: Clarendon Press, 1996.

———. "Papacy, Empire, and the Second Crusade." In Martin Hoch and Jonathan Phillips, eds., *The Second Crusade: Scope and Consequences*. Manchester: Manchester University Press, 2001.

Russell, Frederick. *The Just War in the Middle Ages*. Cambridge: Cambridge University Press, 1975.

Riley-Smith, Jonathan. *The First Crusade and the Idea of Crusading*. London: Athlone, 1986.

Many excellent works on the history of the Iberian peninsula have appeared in recent years. For collections of primary sources in translation, see: Olivia Constable, *Medieval Iberia: Readings from Christian, Muslim, and Jewish Sources* (Philadelphia: University of Pennsylvania Press, 1997); Richard Fletcher and Simon Barton, eds., *The World of El Cid* (Manchester: Manchester University Press, 2000).

The following secondary references are either general textbooks or concentrate on a specific aspect of the Second Crusade in Iberia:

Barton, Simon. "A Forgotten Crusade: Alfonso VII of León-Castile and the Campaign for Jaén (1148)." *Historical Research* 73 (2000).

Jaspert, Nikolas. "*Capta est Dertosa, clavis Christianorum*: Tortosa and the Crusades." In Martin Hoch and Jonathan Phillips, eds., *The Second*

Crusade: Scope and Consequences. Manchester: Manchester University Press, 2001.

Kennedy, Hugh. *Muslim Spain and Portugal: A Political History of al-Andalus*. London: Longman, 1996.

Livermore, Harold. *A New History of Portugal*, second edition. Cambridge: Cambridge University Press, 1976.

Reilly, Bernard. *The Contest of Christian and Muslim Spain, 1031–1157*. Oxford: Blackwell, 1992.

———. *The Kingdom of León-Castilla Under King Alfonso VII, 1126–57*. Philadelphia: University of Pennsylvania Press, 1998.

Williams, John. "The Making of a Crusade: The Genoese Anti-Muslim Attacks in Spain, 1146–8." *Journal of Medieval History* 23 (1997): 29–53.

Index

Mediaeval names of persons are arranged alphabetically under the English form of the Christian name, mediaeval place names alphabetically under the modern form. Bibliographical citations are, with rare exceptions, to the first or main reference only.